D1295870

Mind and Emotion

Other Wiley Books by the Author

J. M. Mandler and G. Mandler, editors,
Thinking: From Association to Gestalt,
Perspectives in Psychology Series, 1964.

G. Mandler and W. Kessen
The Language of Psychology, 1959.

MIND AND EMOTION

George Mandler

University of California at San Diego

John Wiley & Sons, Inc.

New York London Sydney Toronto

Library of Congress Cataloging in Publication Data:

Mandler, George.
    Mind and emotion.

    Bibliography: p.
    Includes indexes.
    1. Cognition. 2. Emotions. 3. Human information processing. I. Title.
BF311.M23   153.4   75-15727
ISBN 0-471-56690-X
ISBN 0-471-56691-8 pbk.

Printed in the United States of America

10 9 8 7 6 5 4 3 2 1

for Peter and Michael

George Mandler received his Ph.D. from Yale University in 1953. He is presently Professor of Psychology and Director, Center for Human Information Processing at the University of California, San Diego. A former Chairman of the Psychology Department at UCSD, Professor Mandler was previously affiliated with Harvard University (1953–60) and the University of Toronto (1960–65). Since 1971, he has been Editor of the *Psychological Review*. Professor Mandler was a Guggenheim Fellow, 1971–72; was a Fellow at the Center for Advanced Study in the Behavioral Sciences, 1959–60; is a member of the Society of Experimental Psychologists; and is on the Board of Trustees, Association for the Advancement of Psychology. His previous publications include (with W. Kessen) THE LANGUAGE OF PSYCHOLOGY (Wiley, 1959) and (with J. M. Mandler) THINKING: FROM ASSOCIATION TO GESTALT (Wiley, 1964).

Preface

This book represents a conceptual integration of modern mentalism and current knowledge about emotional experience and behavior. In a very special sense it also represents personal integration. For about 20 years I have maintained two major, but separate, empirical, and theoretical interests in psychology. One arose out of an early concern with human learning, a subsequent disillusion with the theoretical poverty of functionalist and associationist approaches to verbal learning and memory, and my developing strong commitment to a cognitive, or rather a mentalistic, view of the human information-processing system. The other interest, running parallel with the first, sometimes changing places with it in taking precedence in my immediate preoccupations, was an interest in human emotion, first and primarily concentrated on anxiety. During the past decade my involvement with "cognitive" matters effectively restricted my concern with "emotional" topics to some commentary on theoretical matters. However, it was this very restriction to the broad view, rather than an immediate concern with empirical matters, and the primary node of thinking cognitively in psychology that prepared the ground for the combining of my cognitive and emotional interests. There was no particular point in time when I became aware of the need to fit my views of emotional phenomena within cognitive boundaries, but the first ideas about this book developed when it became clear that any consistent view of man from the point of view of information processing must find a place for phenomena other than purely cognitive ones.

In the spring of 1971 I taught a senior course on emotion for the first time and was surprised that no book was available to serve as a general but advanced introduction to the topic. My increasing interest in the relation of mind and emotion, the apparent place for a book on emotion, and the prospects of a sabbatical year and a Guggenheim Fellowship settled the matter. A first draft was completed toward the end of my sabbatical year in Oxford. Its primary effect was to show me the lacunae in the text and my knowledge that demanded extensive additional work before a second draft could be completed. However, the pressures and depressions of the academic and postsabbatical world delayed that accomplishment for another two years.

This book will provide an introduction to the topic of emotion for the student of psychology, suggest one possible integration of emotional and cognitive phenomena, and also present a reasonable defense of a modern psychology of the mind. I will be more explicit in the body of the book about my use of the terms "mind" and "mentalism." Briefly, they refer to the view of man as an integrated complex of transformational, interpretive, and structural mechanisms.

All input is subjected to some transformations—all output is the result of structural mechanisms. In my personal history this conception started with an early enchantment with *Gestalt* concepts, an enchantment that was tempered—and temporarily abandoned—by the weight and substance of Hullian promises and prospects. I have abundantly documented elsewhere my disenchantment with the theoretical poverty of stimulus-response, associationistic concepts. However, my concern with functional input-output consistencies has left its mark in my respect for B. F. Skinner's vigorous opposition to S-R psychology. His functional definitions of stimuli and responses were, I always thought, in the traditions of a cognitive rather than a physicalistic psychology. Being able to read psychology in this fashion, I still respond to demands for the specification of controlling events. However, my major concerns have been with an attempt to specify cognitive mechanisms that generate experiences and actions and with an analysis of a functioning mental system. Prior reinforcement histories, vague appeals to stimulus-response contiguities, and the search for specific "causes" are neither adequate nor unequivocal. The search for mechanisms has characterized much of recent psychology, which might properly be called *mechanismic* psychology, in contrast to the pejorative and often misunderstood adjective—*mechanistic*.

My commitment to an information-processing analysis is not much more than a commitment to a flowchart psychology, a search for processes and mechanisms, some of which may be operative only on some small aspect of human action and experience, but the relation among which makes possible limited theorizing and attempts at integration that do not pretend to megalotheoretical views of psychology.

In no sense do I present a theory of emotion, much less of the mind. What I hope to do in respect to the former is to specify what the important psychological variables are or might be that affect or control a certain class of human action and experience. Much too little is known about any of these variables to specify their unequivocal operation. My description of the mental system must be even more general. That, however, is as it should be—the specification of the complete mental apparatus can never be complete and, at the present time, cannot be more than a *façon de parler*. As such, I present it as no more than an essay about one psychologist's view of the mind. However, even as an approach to a mental language, it suggests specific ways of looking at the mental apparatus that is more than verbal and that suggests certain theoretical and empirical outcomes. I can only hope that these suggestions will be useful in the future.

I want to speak of mind *and* emotion in the strongest sense of the copula. Only an understanding of mental mechanisms in general will make it possible to understand any of the subsystems of human thought and action. A theory of semantic networks, for example, must also eventually tell us how innocuous events are translated into functional releasers of autonomic activity; otherwise, it is—at least—incomplete.

Finally, the book illustrates my increasing unhappiness with the illusions and inadequacies of some current philosophical work that pretends to provide its readers with explanations of human action, thought, and emotion.

Oxford, April 1972   George Mandler
La Jolla, June 1975

Acknowledgments

My debts—both personal and institutional—cannot be enumerated. The Guggenheim Foundation, coupled with the freedom of a sabbatical from the University of California, made it possible for me to embark on a new venture that was grant- and position-independent. The hospitality of Professor L. Weiskrantz and the Department of Experimental Psychology at Oxford created both the isolation and colleaguial support that I find essential for my work. The forebearance of students and colleagues at various universities in Great Britain, Scandinavia, and Germany, where I first presented some of these ideas, was admirable and highly useful.

My major debt is to Jean Mandler, whose wisdom and patience reacted to and interacted with my flights of fancy, who helped me across lacunae of sterility, held reality up to my fantasies of mental life, understood me often before I did, and helped discard what I would have been foolish to maintain. I also want to express my continuing indebtedness to William Kessen, a true intellectual friend and boundless adviser and critic.

I want to acknowledge the help of many other friends and colleagues who commented on my manuscript at various stages of development, particularly to C. R. Gallistel, A. Graesser II, U. Neisser, and D. A. Norman. Many others from whom I have learned and borrowed will, hopefully, be identifiable in the body of the book. My gratitude to them is not diminished by their names not appearing here.

My work on this book was supported, in addition to the grant from the Guggenheim Foundation, by grants from the University of California and the National Institute of Mental Health to the Center for Human Information Processing.

I am very grateful to Anita Fitzgerald, Arlene Jacobs, and Megan Kenyon who helped in the preparation of the manuscript at various stages.

Acknowledgment is made for parts of the book that have previously appeared elsewhere. Parts of the material on pp. 176-188 appeared under the heading "Anxiety" in D. L. Sills (ed.) *The international encyclopedia of the social sciences.* Vol. I. Copyright © 1968 by Crowell, Collier and Macmillan. The section on pp. 190-199 is reprinted with some changes by permission of the American Psychological Association and my coauthor, W. Kessen. Various other sections of Chapter VIII are used, as noted there, by permission of Holt, Rinehart and Winston, Inc., and D. L. Watson. Parts of Chapter III appeared previously in slightly changed form in R. Solso (ed.) *Information Processing and cognition: The Loyola symposium.* Hillsdale, N.J.: Lawrence Erlbaum

Associates, 1975. Parts of Chapter VII appeared previously in different form in D. Levine (ed.) *Nebraska symposium on motivation: 1964.* Lincoln, Neb.: University of Nebraska Press, 1964.

G. M.

CONTENTS

Chapter I
A Psychological Analysis

Psychology and Common Experience[1]

More than any other field of knowledge, psychology has been both the beneficiary and the prisoner of man's most fascinating proclivity— to explain the world around us, to understand what surrounds us, to make up stories (i.e., myths, religions, folktales, and sciences) that explain and make comprehensible the evidence of our senses, stories that, in turn, shape that very evidence. Over the centuries the men and women who made up the most convincing stories were elevated to a special position in the life of the mind; first they were the prophets, then the philosophers and, finally, the scientists. One built on the other, first painfully clearing away the accumulated rubble of ordinary discourse, somewhere breaking through to a new way of looking at the world, a way that was somehow alien to the common language and the folk beliefs, a method or structure that in the truest sense of the word "did not make sense." The growth was slow and often misunderstood, as when Galileo first realized that mathematics was the language of science but never really used it. It took Newton, not only to reach the new high ground of mathematical analysis, but also to realize that rejection of a concept by common sense and common understanding was not relevant to the building of a system. When he postulated "attraction" in the *Principia*, he was told by his natural philosopher colleagues that this concept was a dead end, but his answer is the important one, that it might not seem reasonable but, when he used it in a systematic sense in his axiomatic system, it did explain the data.

The pressure on psychology to "make sense," to be consistent with "common knowledge," is infinitely stronger. It may have become even more difficult with the advent of ordinary language philosophy, which

[1]Some sections of this chapter have previously appeared in Mandler (1975a).

1

was aware of some of the rubble in the ordinary language that produced confusion and pseudoproblems but often insisted, in unnecessary addition, that underneath the rubble—but within common sense and the ordinary language—lay the kernels of understanding human motives and actions. Unfortunately, Freud's basic insights were clouded by his system and his language; otherwise, philosophers would not continue to look for the explanations of human actions in reasons and intentions and in the structure of the surface language. Freud's insight was that there are forces that act like wishes, desires, reasons, and intentions but that are not available to inspection, awareness, and reason. Quite rightly that formulation did not "make sense" because a wish or an intention is, by definition, part of the aware, sensing organism. If Freud had only changed the language and showed that these forces, by some other name, had the same *consequences* as some of our conscious wishes, desires, and intentions, much of the misunderstanding of the misnamed and misrepresented unconscious might not have further muddied the waters of an objective psychology of the past 50 years. Consider, in contrast, the many-faceted "unconscious" processes and mechanisms that crowd our present theories of sensation, perception, cognition, learning, and syntax without drawing the slightest concern about their "scientific" status.

Psychology's present business then is still to clear away rubble, to take with it the insights of the everyday world, without its myths and fictions. The call for a psychological Newton is misplaced because it may be too early or unnecessary. It may be too early because too much learning is still to be done, and it may be unnecessary because psychology can build on the other sciences, not by becoming like physics (which resulted in one unfortunate turn in the road), biology, or astronomy, but because the accumulation and interpenetration of Newtonian, Mendelian, and other methods and structures may be enough now to build a psychology that will be its own master.

In the same sense it seems useful not to fall into the trap of trying to explain what "emotion" *is;* that would be to follow the error of trying to explicate the common language. Nor can we yet aim for a deterministic, mathematical theory. But we can, by analyzing the system of forces and processes that make up the human organism, suggest how certain behaviors, feelings, and experiences might be produced. We cannot specify all or most of these forces or their specific structures, but we can indicate some of the subsystems that process information and show that the outcome of these forces and processes produces behaviors and experiences that, appealing to common experience, we might consider akin to what we call emotion. Thus we might start not with the aim of *explaining* emotion but, instead, with describing a system that has as its product some of the observations that have been called "emotion" in the common language. However, this outcome, if successful, would be only gravy for the main dish. The system would still be viable if it makes psychological sense and explains certain human actions—that is all such an endeavor may reach for. If it also appeals to some parts of common sense and restructures it in a meaningful way, all the better. But the eventual aim is psychological theory, not an analysis of human experience expressed in phenomenal, existential, or ordinary language.

The Intent of Mentalism

What I intend to present is a psychological rather than a physiological or phenomenological view of human action and experience. As will be abundantly obvious in the following pages, by a psychological theory I mean essentially a mentalistic theory in a psychologist's sense of mentalism and mind, a psychological or mentalistic theory that ascribes certain theoretical fictions to the human organism. I shall use terms such as "structures" and "organizations" as the constituents of this mentalistic theory. But the term "mind" is used deliberately in order to specify exactly what a contemporary psychologist means when he calls himself a mentalist. I wish to imply no more and no less than the theoretical system that structures readiness, attention, and search for environmental inputs, transforms these inputs as a result of complex processing mechanisms that include self-correcting and self-instructing systems, and then structures its output to the environment in line with its interpretation of environmental and systematic requirements. It is in this sense that I wish to use the word "mental" and to call the theoretical system ascribed to the organism the *Mind*.

A mentalistic psychology also makes certain claims that set it apart from some historical antecedents of the past 50 years. It is both in the theoretical structure and in the language that describes the behavior of the organism that a mentalistic psychology breaks with the behavioristic tradition. The major contribution, perhaps the only contribution, that the behaviorist revolution has made to the development of contemporary psychology has been its insistence on the observable as the final output and testing ground of psychological theories. The rejection of introspective language either to describe theoretical entities or as the final givens of the system marked an important turning point toward an objective psychology. (See Mandler, 1967b, for a discussion of similar issues in the area of verbal behavior.) A modern mentalistic psychology is concerned with the unequivocal prediction of observable events, but it does not insist on a physicalistic interpretation of its observational terms or its theoretical concepts. As has been argued at length before, for example, by Mandler and Kessen (1959), there is nothing in principle that precludes terms such as "schizophrenic" or "helpless" or "happy" to be used as observational terms in the psychological language. The conditions for their use are the same conditions as those for the use of so-called physicalistic terms, although it is true that they have taken longer to develop the kinds of invariance in usage that physicalistic terms enjoy.

Another aspect of the behaviorist development has been its insistence on operational definitions of its terms. Again, it has been pointed out before (Mandler and Kessen, 1959) that operationism was, in the first instance, developed for an area that enjoyed unequivocal well-articulated theories (specifically, physics), and a blatant operationism is, in the second instance, not particularly useful theoretically. The old saw that "intelligence is what the intelligence tests measure" is an admission of theoretical impotence, not a royal road to empiricist purity. The complexity of the human organism and the intricacy of the processes and operations that need to be inferred in order to make theoretical sense of its reaction to and operation on the environment require a highly articulated theoretical system, most of which is not subject either to inspection or to operational definition. The quality and utility of a theoretical system is, in the long run, found in its unequivocal use to make, even very few, predictions about observable events.

Not a Physiological Analysis

With this general characterization of our use of the term "mentalistic" we can quickly justify the avoidance of physiological concepts and theories. The use of physiological theories about the structure and the function of the human brain is an important part of contemporary psychology. However, there is no logical or empirical requirement that a psychological theory must, at this point, show a correspondence with or even make contact with neurophysiological theories. It can well be argued, and I shall return to this issue shortly when discussing the mind-body problem, that physiological theories are concerned with developing the same complex structure of theoretical processes, although in the language of neurophysiology, that the psychologist invokes for his explanatory system. Inquiries about the relationship between these two systems are both important and interesting but neither necessary nor mandatory for the psychologist who is developing his own theoretical structure. It is in this sense of cultivating our own garden instead of copying the neighbors' efforts that I would opt for a psychological theory that is independent, although in the long run not ignorant, of physiological hypotheses.

Similarly, a psychological theory should heed, but need not uncritically accept a comparative, evolutionary view of behavior. The difficulty of defining or even bordering the vast sprawling conglomerate of human behavior and feeling that is subsumed under the emotions is, surely, in part a function of its heritage, its evolutionary antecedents. The prewired, instinctual reactions to threat, sexuality, and pain, which have created flight, fight, and sexual action systems, are influenced partly by the autonomic nervous system and partly determined by releasing stimuli. However, the primitive reactions of our evolutionary forebears have given way to a highly refined and extensive repertory of behavior, feeling, and thought. Every now and then the archaic emotional reactions, seen so clearly in lower animals, shine through the intricate web of emotional behavior. This dim parentage has seduced some modern writers to write about and explain emotions in terms of these prehistoric antecedents. However, that attempt is as valid and as futile as trying to explain Rembrandt in terms of the development of the opposing thumb.

The contrast of psychological and physiological structures has been oversimplified for purposes of illustration. In fact, both psychologists and physiologists are currently working with mixed structures. Whenever we find that a particular physiological structure is adequate and useful for a mental system, using criteria that are not at all clear at the present time, we will incorporate these physiological structures in our mental system. Conversely, physiologists frequently appeal to psychological systems in order to clarify what are, for the time being, only hypothesized physical processes. One of the nicest and most productive examples of a judicious mixture of physical and mental systems has been Hebb's (1949) use of physiological and psychological data.

Finally, a variety of psychological and physiological findings can be found that are compatible with any one of the several philosophical "solutions" to the mind-body problem (e.g., Smart, 1970). However, the choice of any one of these positions, on logical, extraempirical grounds, needlessly preempts the openness of future psychological and physiological theory and research (Gray, 1971a).

Not a Philosophical Analysis

If a psychological theory is not necessarily physiological it is certainly not philosophical in method or intent. The distinction is between the philosophical (often phenomenological and intuitive) system that tries to make sense of man talking about himself— including his feelings and purposes—and a psychological system that creates a language and a theory to explain man—including the thoughts and actions that are philosophy's starting point.

It is futile to try to arrive at a psychologically meaningful statement about cause-effect relationships in human thought and behavior merely by a reflective analysis of experience or the ordinary language. The ordinary or common language is shot through with folk wisdom and folk psychology. Such an influence is most dangerous when least obvious. It is easy to reject the contradictions of "Absence makes the heart grow fonder" and "Out of sight out of mind" as the worldly useful and scientifically useless results of folk psychology, but it is more difficult to understand that extensive analyses of ordinary language talk about emotion, feeling, and thinking are built on similar but much less obvious foundations. Ordinary language often is an ill- or well-informed commentary on psychological processes that are not available for inspection or introspection to the thinking and behaving organism. Just as the development of language may, in part, be the development of commentary and gloss on preexisting cognitions and meanings (cf. Macnamara, 1972) so may the common language in the adult still comment rather than explain. Such commentary includes the reasons and feelings the common language adduces for "explaining" an actor's action as well as the phenomenological reports that, again regardless of protestations from philosophers of another stripe, must be couched in ordinary language in order to be available for analysis. To the extent that philosophy aspires to no technical language of its own, these analyses are necessary and appropriate, but we cannot speak English (or any other common language) if we wish to discover the determinants of human thought and action, nor can we speak technical psychology if we wish to be poetic.

The ordinary language is, from one point of view, an extremely sensitive and highly differentiated commentary on persons and their actions, including the thoughts and behavior of the speaker. There is no reason why such a language should not be sensitive and useful, just as there is no reason why such a language and its structure should have any explanatory power or causal import. The ordinary language talking about people and their behavior is, of course, no different than the ordinary language talking about physical events or biological events. However, nobody claims that a proper way to do physics is to use the ordinary language description of physical events, although physics did start with such statements and rapidly diverged from them. Similarly, psychology did start with the discourse of the ordinary language about people and behavior but quickly discovered that ordinary discourse was not adequate to describe the causes and demonstrable antecedents of behavior and experience. The ordinary language continues to talk about physical events in a nonphysical language. For example, we can talk about our golf game, which deals primarily with the interaction of physical forces and their consequences, in a language (a common language) that has very little to do with physics.

A proper evaluation of and sensitivity to the nuances of phenomenal experience and the ordinary language have become the province of the philosopher. However, it is not reasonable for philosophers to claim that they are dealing with something else, that is, psychology or the elaboration of causal chains that lead to behavior and experience. The proper understanding of the ordinary language as a subjective theory of human action is a philosophical enterprise; an evaluation of the origins of that language, its antecedents, and referents is a psychological one.

I do not intend to preempt the concerns of philosophers in their understanding of human discourse and their theoretical attempts to structure that discourse. I do claim that philosophers frequently are engaged in two probably incompatible tasks: first, the discussion in ordinary and philosophical language of problems of perception, morality, knowledge and, second, the use of the structure of that language and discourse to make statements about the causes and conditions of human thought and behavior. The latter psychological enterprise needs methods of verification and scientific theories; the former takes the ordinary and philosophical language as given and tries to find out what the structure of that system is. Thus a philosophical system about knowledge, a system in which people talk about what they believe they know and how they believe they know things, has no logical or psychological one-to-one correlation with the theoretical-empirical attempt to build a psychological theory that explains how the human individual acquires knowledge, perceives the world, engages in ethical endeavors, *and* talks about it (cf. Piaget, 1971). Thus philosophy is an enterprise that reconstructs a system, usually in the ordinary language but frequently in a special philosophical language that is not concerned with a theoretical structure, which deals with the variables that explain and control human thought and behavior and human talk about such thought and behavior. In a sense, then, the philosophical enterprise is an examination of the commentary on human thought and behavior developed within ordinary language over the centuries. This is clearly different from a scientific enterprise, which develops theories, tests them experimentally or observationally, rejects them and erects new ones in the usual give and take of empirical theory and research.

I have no quarrels with the attempt to understand the glosses and comments on thought and behavior developed by the ordinary language. But that language, and thereby any system that tries to structure it reasonably and comprehensibly, is not subject to the usual test and retest of scientific theories. It frequently tends, as Piaget (1971) has pointed out, to maintain intuitively obvious but factually false notions about its object. Most philosophers view their activities in that light, and this argument applies primarily to those who have implicitly or explicitly suggested that their analyses give us an insight into the causes and structures of human thought and action. It is one thing to try to understand what the ordinary language intends to convey by statements about intentions. It is a different matter when one implies that such an analysis will reveal some fundamental psychological effects of "intentions" on actions. Similarly, an analysis of the concept of mind, as it is used in the ordinary language, provides interesting insights into confusions that abound in that language (e.g., Ryle, 1949), but it is an entirely different matter when we assume that such an analysis provides any fundamental insights into the relationship between psychological (mental) theories and physiological ones.

None of this denies the importance of some initial insights into possible mental structures and causal sequences that may arise out of the ordinary language—psychology, as all other sciences, uses the ordinary language as a starting point and, as it develops, leaves that ordinary language behind at an increasing pace.

Emotion and the Common Language

One important pitfall that ordinary language and thought imposes on us is the belief in the reality of its concepts and terms. If the obvious is taken for granted (which, unfortunately, is not always the case in philosophy), that explanations generated by a recently evolved featherless biped cannot but be models of the world, convenient fictions that help our limited understanding; then the tendency to take folk theories as ultimate truths must lead to holding on to distinctions and concepts that are not and cannot in principle be ultimate descriptions of the structure of reality. To take folk concepts too seriously is to confer on man—at least historical man—a godlike status. If God created man, the argument goes, then man might have godlike insights, particularly if the "insights" have been around for a few hundred years. If, however, Man created god, then he can arrogate unto himself the same characteristics of insight into ultimate truth with which he has imbued Him. Such a position implies a degree of pretentiousness about the status of this sometimes pitiful little animal that I cannot share. It also hinders the development of the kind of game playing that I find so attractive in science—the erection and destruction of hypotheses with a claim to better and better approximations of reality, but never a claim to ultimate truth. To claim that such a truth is available by a proper examination of our phenomenal selves or by the proper analysis of language is, at least, a hindrance and, at worst, a wall that keeps us from playing man's most productive game—science.

Because men and women have talked about their thoughts and emotions, both discretely and discreetly, we may assume that there may be lawful relations among events, variables, thoughts, and behaviors, but the folk psychology these thoughts express neither seeks nor cares for an unequivocal explanation. It does provide the most important starting points for science: the initial hypotheses and the description of the most general consistencies. But we must go beyond common experience instead of trying to imagine that because some men and women sometimes can talk about specific emotions, can make distinctions among discrete emotions, can individually and anecdotally assert some rational theory or some irrational defense that these are therefore the necessary and sufficient building blocks of a science. Our language must be painfully built *out of* the layers of myths and pretensions and insights that make up common parlance and consciousness.

Philosophers and psychologists who have looked to ordinary language as the royal road to developing a satisfactory scientific language (both syntactically and semantically) often fail to apply a fundamental distinction in the primary *function* of these two languages. Common language serves—in the first instance—as communication and, as such, it is appropriately redundant, vague, overinclusive, and ambiguous. A common language that would be nonredundant, precise, and unambiguous would require much more cognitive effort on the part of both speaker and listener than the organism usually has available. Scientific language, on the other hand, is a vehicle for description and explanation. If *it* were redundant, vague, and overinclusive, it would fail exactly on the requirements of precise definition and unequivocal explanation.

Consider the adequacy of distinguishing between heavy and light packages, loud and soft noises, and angry and joyful feelings for most communicative purposes. But the heavy-light and the loud-soft distinction are totally inadequate for scientific purposes. Why, then, should we expect angry-joyful to be adequate?

Consider the following additional difficulties if we were to permit the common language to be our guide to the emotional states and terms that a psychological theory of emotion should be able to explain. First, there is little disagreement that such a theory should account for states that are commonly termed anxiety, joy, fear, euphoria, and probably even love and disgust. But is lust an emotion—or is sexual feeling to be handled separately? Are we to be required to explain feelings of pride? Of accomplishment? Of empathy? Of dislike? Or, even worse, are we to construct national theories of emotion so that a German theory may account for *Lust* and *Unlust,* for *Gemütlichkeit,* or *ängstlich* (which does not strictly mean anxious); or a French theory for feelings of *ambience.* What are the boundaries of a theory of emotion, what terms in the ordinary language are the relevant referents to be explained? And worse, is there even a German requirement for such a theory, since that language has no true equivalent for the English term emotion?

A typical argument to such protestations of confusion consists of an appeal to consensual (intuitive?) judgment. After all, it is said, we all know what we are talking about when we talk about emotions, and these counterexamples are either irrelevant or esoteric. I do not believe that a serious theory of anything should depend on extensive intuitive judgment, nor do I think that the counterexamples are exotic—they are necessary and useful aspects of our flexible and redundant common language.

If none of these reasons is an adequate justification for believing in the inevitable and necessary existence of a theory of emotions *per se,* we must look elsewhere for a proper goal of the theoretical and empirical study of emotion. None of the metapsychological arguments, whether based on innate *a priori* ideas or feelings, on inevitable evolutionary remnants of mating and fighting behavior, or on phenomenal or linguistic givens argues logically that the reality that we wish to model is best approached by a single, unified theory of emotion.

The Mind-Body Problem—An Inconvenient Fiction

It is interesting that preoccupations with the mind-body problem occur primarily in philosophical and metapsychological writings; it has rarely bothered the working psychologist when he is trying to develop his theories and research. However, some bow in the direction of the problem seems to be required of every writer on metapsychological problems.

My position is relatively simple. We are developing a psychological (i.e., mental) theory of a circumscribed set of human behavior and experience. No claim is made that the theoretical structures to be developed have any necessary correlate in the physical substratum or, specifically, in the brain. There is no doubt that we are talking about a physical system, the human organism. But we are talking about concepts and theories that do not claim a reduction to a physical basis. Thus the position is that it is possible to build a psychological system that makes no claims or disclaimers about its relation to the physical structure of the organism. The question about the relationship between this structure and a physical (i.e., is, neurological or neurophysiological) structure in the broadest sense is left entirely open. You may speculate, as I do, that some physiological correlates of the structures to be developed here may someday be found. However, at the present time it is not necessary to specify what these relationships are or even might be. The mind-body problem will become a problem not because it can be spoken and discussed, but because adequate theories of mental structures and physical structures exist that require correlation. By adequate I mean either physiological or mentalistic theories that are, in fact, unequivocal, prescriptive theories instead of the·speculations of nineteenth- or even twentieth-century philosophers and metapsychologists.

Much of the difficulty that has been generated by the mind-body distinction stems from the failure to consider the relationship between well-developed mental and physical theories. Typically, mind and body are discussed in terms of ordinary language definitions of one or the other. Since these descriptions are so far from well-developed theoretical systems that they are a different category of quasisystematic statements, it is doubtful whether the problems of mind and body as developed by philosophers are directly relevant to the scientific distinction between mental and physical systems.

Once it is agreed that the scientific mind-body problem concerns the relationship between two sets of theories, the enterprise becomes theoretical and empirical, not metaphysical (see Mandler and Kessen, 1959; and Mandler, 1969, for earlier discussions of this issue). If, however, we restrict our discussion of the mind-body problem to the often vague and frequently contradictory speculations of ordinary language then, as centuries of philosophical literature have shown, the morass is unavoidable and bottomless.

For example, we could, in the ordinary language sense, ask how it is that physical systems can have "feelings." Such questions assume that we know the exact nature of the physical system and, more important, the structure of a mental system that produces "feelings." Usually, however, the question is phrased as if "feelings" are the basic characteristics of the mental system instead of one of its outputs. The assertion of a feeling is a complex outcome of the kind of mental system that will be espoused here. Not only is the experience of a feeling an output, but its expression, through a language system, is the result of complex mental structures that intervene between its occurrence in consciousness and the output in the language system. More simply, then, a question of the relation of feelings to physical systems turns out to be at least premature if we agree that feelings, however defined, are the outputs of a complex mental system, and that the "physical" observations are outputs from a similarly complex physiological system. But then the question about the relation (the correspondences) between physical systems and feelings requires that we know what the physical theory and the mental theory are about, that these should be unequivocal in their prediction, and specified in great detail as to their structure. Until these goals are achieved, scientific questions about the mind-body problem are premature and irrelevant.

Retrospect and Prospect

The following chapters are written in the developing tradition of modern cognitive psychology, primarily the theoretical developments that have taken place since the mid 1950s. Cognition refers to the complex series of events and translations that are ascribed to the fully functioning human being. These events start with the transformations of environmental input that invariably generate functional mental events. Following these transformations, complex structures that are acquired and innate relate the transformed information to past experiences, to outcomes, and to future expectations. At the output side, both preestablished action structures and newly integrated behavioral structures receive the transformed output from the mental system and act on the environment. The consequences of such actions feed back into the system and change it, producing a continuing process of adapting and changing structures that relate environmental input to behavioral output.

The tradition of modern cognitive psychology has been marked by two characteristics that set it apart from its predecessors. First, it has adopted the theoretically neutral but systematically useful device of the flowchart. By considering the various subsystems within the mental organization as essentially independent entities connected by theoretically specifiable relationships, it has opened up theoretical psychology to a pluralism that is in sharp contrast to the monolithic theories of the 1930s and 1940s. Thus, within the flowchart model, we may work within a particular system of, for example, visual perception or auditory processing or memory or attention, without necessarily involving any assumptions or theoretical changes in any other parts of the system. This approach, together with general advantages of control system theories, has made it possible for psychologists, as has been the case in the other sciences for many years, to work on minitheories instead of on the megalotheories of earlier years. Thus we are relieved of the necessity of tackling the impossible and illogical task of constructing a "theory" of psychology or learning or behavior. Specialists in various areas may work on theories of attention, short-term memory, long-term memory, visual perception or, as in the present case, the interaction between physiological arousal and cognitive analysis. The second change in modern cognitive psychology has been in the recognition that cognition and conscious thought are two different concepts. This view has liberated cognitive psychology to deal with cognitive variables that are neither in consciousness nor intuitively obvious. Thus, while the cognitive psychologists of the early part of the twentieth century were still largely indebted to introspective, philosophical approaches, their modern descendants are primarily theorists, often independent of the introspections of their human subjects but still attentive and sensitive enough to attend to these events when they become theoretically and empirically useful and fruitful.

It is difficult to credit any one group of individuals with the growth of this approach in contemporary psychology. The influence of information theory, although waning in its specific application to psychological phenomena, has done much to encourage the current conceptual approaches to psychological phenomena. Probably the most important single volume that has furthered the early development of the approach of viewing the human as an information processing system was Miller, Galanter, and Pribram's book (1960). While relatively little specific empirical work has developed out of their presentation, they made the information-processing approach and other aspects of modern cognitive psychology both respectable and palatable. Their rejection of associationism and of some of the debilitating strictures of orthodox behaviorism was an important step toward the proliferation of cognitive and information processing models. In the later stages of this development an important step was Neisser's *Cognitive Psychology* (1967), which pulled together much of the current state of the art in human information processing. But these are only milestones and fail to give credit to the many psychologists both in the United States and elsewhere who have helped to develop a new spirit of theory and adventure in a field that was in danger of becoming tired and moribund.

One of the most impressive recent attempts to use contemporary concepts for old and persisting problems is Bowlby's monumental work on *Attachment and Loss* (1969, 1973). Much can be learned from Bowlby's intense knowledge of psychoanalytic theory and his brilliant syntheses of psychoanalytic notions with mechanisms of control systems and modern ethological concepts. I shall have occasion, throughout this book, to refer to the relevance of his ideas to the present endeavors. However, these references are inadequate to appreciate adequately a most important recent development in the theory of human personality and development.

In the context of an information-processing model it is necessary to place the field of emotion within the larger context of a conception of the human mind. Therefore the following two chapters are a general overview of human mental organization and consciousness. This presentation will stress the aspects of the system that are of particular interest to the problem at hand, but it will necessarily spill over into related areas. Chapter 4 shows how a particular subsystem that may be responsible for much of the behavior called emotional fits into the general system described in Chapters 2 and 3, and how this subsystem operates and produces its unique outputs. After this general view of emotional experience and behavior, Chapter 5 reviews theories and evidence on emotion, with special reference to the theories that are cognate to the system presented here. Chapter 6 deals specifically with the conditions of arousal (i. e., the physiological aspects of emotion) and addresses both theoretical and empirical aspects of the arousal system. Chapter 7 deals with the interruption of thought and action and its particular relevance to problems of emotion. In the last two chapters I shall present some specific applications of the theoretical notions presented here. Chapter 8 is a compilation of some previous considerations of the problem of anxiety and their relation to a cognitive model of emotion. Finally, in Chapter 9, a variety of topics ranging from individual differences in emotional experience and behavior, to sexual emotion, to psychotherapy and some peculiarities of the emotional system will be treated.

Chapter II
Mind–A System and Its Functions

Mind as a System

In this chapter I shall outline a general view of processing systems that may best represent the variety of actions, thoughts, experiences, and feelings and the organizations, transformations, plans, and programs that characterize the human organism. The intent is not to present a "theory" of mankind or a general theory of human psychology. The analysis of the human system to be presented is programmatic rather than theoretical, structural rather than specific. The development of system analyses—in the broad sense—has misled many readers of such attempts to mistake a programmatic picture of the system for a theoretical position. A theory for all of *psychology* is, in principle, as impossible as the endeavor toward such a theory is misled. It is no more possible to develop a general psychological theory than it is to develop a general chemical theory or a general biological theory or a general astronomic theory. Psychologists have learned that minitheories provide the best approach toward an understanding of the system as a whole. What is subsequently required is to show how transfers of information take place between one such subsystem or minitheory and others.

In that sense theories of perception, learning, sensation, psychopathology, attitude formation, and so forth need not be deducible from a general theory of learning or perception or whatever. Instead, these subsystems and minitheories can exist in their own right, and it is not even encumbent on the theorist to show how his minitheory of acoustic information processing, for example, is parallel to or tied in with a theory of speech production. Such an outcome is highly desirable, but it is not necessary, and the last 30 years in the history of psychology have shown the utility of this approach.

In order to develop properly the subsystem that we are interested in, one that may be related to the congeries of behaviors and experiences that are labeled emotion, some indication of the programmatic outline of the whole system is useful.

The character of the general information-processing system is not only important, but its label seems to be of some consequence, particularly to psychologists who, sometimes extraneous to their activities, tend to be jealous of their ideological identities. From my point of view the system represents what the psychologists mean by Mind. It is the system of organizations and structures ascribed to an individual that processes inputs (including inputs from its own actions and experiences) and provides output to the various subsystems and the world. The intricacies of that system suggest something as complex as is implied by the surplus meaning of the term mind. In the interface between psychology and neurophysiology the *Mind* system could be equivalent to the neurological mechanisms that are ascribed to the brain and its elaborations. Thus, if we wanted to do neurophysiology, we would say that the psychologists' *Mind* is capable of processes that should find their parallel in neurological, physiological mechanisms. Since it is likely that any mechanism manufactured by the psychologist is capable of being represented by some known neurological mechanisms, there are no physiological constraints on the kind of processing mechanisms and structures that we wish to put into the system. Similarly, the psychologist who, perhaps for reasons of childhood trauma, is opposed to any terms that contain words like "mind" or "mental" may find comfort in the fact that the *Mind* system, as viewed here, is also the system that contains the complete past history of the individual; it contains structures that operate as a result of that past history and, of course, as a result of prewired, innate, genetic structures. Finally, it is unlikely the system is the same mental system that is referred to by the philosopher, since the mentalism of the contemporary philosopher is frequently a system of processes that is available to inspection. The system that we wish to use is not available to inspection; it is a theoretical fiction that contains all the theoretical structures that have been developed by psychologists to explain observable and experienced events. Thus the system contains generative grammars, neural counters, the unconscious, and all other theoretical fictions that have been useful to psychologists. Whether it also contains the "true" structure of the mental apparatus is, of course, both unknown at present and subject to investigation and elaboration.

So far I have indicated only a general metapsychological position for the use of the concept *Mind* but, since it encompasses all the systems involved in psychological functioning, for present purposes, some restriction to less inclusive subsystems becomes necessary. I shall refer to the *cognitive-interpretive* system to summarize many of the functions of primary interest to the analysis of emotion and mind. Its name indicates that the system is cognitive in that it engages in complex processing or "thinking"; it is interpretive in that it takes input and transforms it into functional units.

In addition to the cognitive-interpretive system I shall be concerned in particular with structures that organize and structure action, arousal, and consciousness. I shall discuss consciousness and arousal in later chapters; the structure of action will be discussed later in this chapter.

The cognitive-interpretive system is involved at all stages of processing. Not only does it receive input from the environment and distributes that input as functional signals to other systems, but it also takes output from arousal and action systems and, as part of this feedback, may change the functional signal, or generate perceptions of actions and arousals. The perception of arousal is particularly important in the further development of the "emotional" subsystems with which I shall deal later.

The Structure of Mind

Organization and Structure

Before discussing the relations among structures and organizations, some definitional housecleaning is in order. Cognitive psychologists have been talking about structures, organizations, systems, and schemas for some decades, and the skeptical observer frequently sees little advantage accruing in these terms over such old-fashioned uses as stimuli, responses, or even unobserved mediating events couched in stimulus-response terms.

The advantage is, in the first instance, one of allusion. When talking about organizations and structures, I intend them to carry along such notions as complexity and relatedness. For example, physical events measured in physical terms such as amplitude and frequency of soundwaves are transformed by structures into the functional units that are acted on by the organism. People do not hear amplitude, they hear loudness—and complex transformations are needed to go from amplitude to the experience of reported loudness. If there were in fact a one-to-one relationship between physical measurement and human experience or response, we should gladly forego any such complex notions as structures—or theories. The relation between a "physical" Giant Panda and one's cognitive interpretive experience of it is immensely more complex. But how I see, hear, feel, like, or examine that particular large patch of black and white is fashioned by my genetic constitution and my past experience represented in cognitive structures.

Structures are organized. Organization is defined by stable relationships among elements. These elements may be sensations, perceptions, phonemes, words, action sequences, behaviors, syntactic units, or the elements themselves organized into groupings, categories, and concepts. Organized sets of relations form structures that, in turn, determine what is perceivable, sayable, or doable. The cognitive structures determine what is selected from the environment—events that cannot be organized in a structure cannot, in the first instance, be perceived. Actions that are not organized are at best chaotic (i.e., ineffectual).

The origin of cognitive structures may be experiential or genetic or, more likely, the results of an interaction of the two. They have, among other functions, the role of organizing past experience. In that function they integrate present events with the representation and generation of past history. Garner (1974) makes a heuristic distinction between intrinsic and extrinsic structures. He says that intrinsic structure "is inherent in the stimulus itself," while extrinsic structure "occurs when the stimulus denotes or signifies something other than itself." While the distinction has heuristic value, it does not easily survive more intensive analysis. Any property of the stimulus must perforce be analyzed and processed by the organism. Thus intrinsic structure would not be perceived if the organism does not have certain appropriate structures that make the analysis of these properties possible. Color is not perceivable by a color-blind organism. But the general dimension of Garner's distinction is useful, since it arranges structures from those that permit little or no individual variabilities to those that show great variability and idiosyncracies among individuals.

Finally, and to stay with Garner, we also equate meaning with structure. Thus a set of events on which we cannot impose any relations is meaningless. Meaning is not some sum of meanings of individual elements but, instead, "the structure itself is meaningful" (Garner, 1962).

At the action side, similar arguments need to be invoked. I generally prefer to use the term action to behavior. The latter term may be applied to individual observable movements of organisms, but these are rare. The term action, on the other hand, is used to imply and assert the organization of behavior. Action is organized and, in our scheme of things, is theoretically dependent on the invocation of action structures. And, to come full circle, we maintain, with Piaget, that actions may themselves be represented internally and may be the antecedent conditions for structures or schemas that organize the world.

Mental Structure—Conscious and Unconscious

The minimal requirements of mental structure that we need for later descriptions of the emotional subsystem are: inputs from environmental events; a system of structures that interprets such events and performs the complex transformations on input that is known to be characteristic of human beings; two output systems, one of them an action system and the other one a physiological arousal system; and a provision for feedback, in the one case to provide for the perception of arousal, in the other for the monitoring of action. Since some of these functions are conscious, the notion of consciousness will be developed more fully in the next chapter. For now, the function of consciousness is best left underdefined. One of the difficulties that psychologists often face is the demand to define new theoretical notions precisely and uniquely. This has been partly due to the mistaken identification with operationism, which was designed for well-developed and highly specific sciences. During the early stages of developing theoretical systems, it is often useful not to define any particular construct too precisely but, instead, to rely on its development as well as an appeal to plausibility to define its operations. This is what I do with the notion of consciousness.

Two important aspects of consciousness must be noted in this representation. First, it is a state that is not available to inspection by the observer; specifically it is not available to inspection by the scientist dealing wih the system. As such, it is a theoretical entity, the content of which can only be inferred but never directly inspected by the observer. Second, the various transformational structures must have access to all aspects of external observable action *as well as* to internal experience (observable only by the subject).

I have previously suggested that mind includes all the theoretical, inferential, unobservable events that are ascribed to the human mental system. It includes all the theoretical notions on how external events are transformed by appropriate structures and then executed in observable action and arousal systems. Included within that body of theory are the transducers that operate on energy inputs (the sense organs), the hypothetical neural events that transform these analysed and transduced inputs, and all the major systems that provide transformational mechanisms prior to output. These systems include the perceptual and sensory systems and their transformations, output systems that may very often be self-starting and, generally, all the working hypotheses and rules about relations between input and output, among structures, among outputs, and even among inputs. In short Mind is a summary of all the inferences we have made about the structures that mediate between input and output, about relationships among those structures, as well as the history of those structures, whether they be preprogrammed or built up as a part of the life history of the individual.

I restrict myself here to two output systems, although they are clearly evocative rather than precise. For our purposes we need a physiological arousal system and an action system that includes a language processor and producer. One of the functions of the language system is to provide some imprecise observable external expression of the contents of consciousness.

The major purpose of this general schema is to present a way of looking at mental organization. This particular system represents what at least one psychologist would like to see as necessary and desirable features of a diagram of human mental organization. It has some evocative use in that, without being a theory, it has certain consequences about the relationship between inputs and outputs, between action and consciousness that may be useful in future discussions. One of its advantages is that it makes it possible to understand the sense in which some psychologists and philosophers have talked about mentalism: by referring to that part of the mental organization that is coextensive with consciousness and partly accessible through the language output. However, that part of the mental organization is obviously only a very small cross section, constrained by the vast number of organizations and structures that are not represented in consciousness and constrained as well by some of the hypotheses that may exist in consciousness but that are not, in fact, representations of actual transformations or structures.

The cognitive-interpretive system is an organized system of structures that operates on the the input from the external world. These organizations and structures interpret the world—broadly defined and including any and all perceptible events whether they take place inside or outside the skin of the actor. The system provides the effective, interpreted cues for action, arousal and, most important, interpretations and characterizations of the surround. The system is, by definition, different from individual to individual in its content and effects, but it is, in principle, identical from individual to individual when we are concerned with the form of its structures, with the way in which they may be modified, and with the structures that are prewired (i.e., existing at birth or developing during the process of maturation). The system processes inputs from the sense organs, but it is also self-generating in that it contains programs and transformations that, under given circumstances, will seek information and add information when such is lacking from the external world.

Since the operation of the cognitive-interpretive system is theoretical (i.e., fictional), its contents and functions are inferred from input-output relations. It is only after it has had some perceptual or behavioral consequence that the system is observable—by its effects. In that sense it is equivalent to Freud's notion of the unconscious that "in its innermost nature . . . is as much unknown to us as the reality of the external world, and . . . is as incompletely presented by the data of consciousness as is the external world by the communications of our sense organs" (1938).

Thus mind, in our sense, is as little available to inspection by introspection as Freud's unconscious is. Self-awareness reflects the conscious consequences of mental operations; introspection deals with the conscious *results* of the cognitive-interpretive system. Neither nineteenth-century psychologists nor twentieth-century philosophers can reasonably claim any insight into these structures of the mind, which are as inaccessible to the individual as are the operations of the neurons and molecules that presumably underlie its operations. Worse than that, since the cognitive-interpretive system does have self-referential instructions as, for example, to be self-consistent or "rational," its outputs may reveal not the operations of its structures alone but the operations of structures that, in effect, conceal the work of other components. Thus phenomenology and introspection are just as much output of the mind to be explained by its unknown, and therefore constructed, organizations as are other actions, percepts, emotions, and feelings.

The Structure of a Cognitive-Interpretive System

The world external to man is structured, and the human mind puts structure on that world. It is the nature of the human enterprise, including the scientific enterprise, that these structures can never be completely disentangled. The scientist, of course, tries to determine what the structure of the world is, but *qua* scientist and human, he can only do that within the limit of the structures contained within his own mental organization. That mental organization, that particular structure of the mind, is constrained in three ways, by the evolutionary history of the species, by the historical and social constraints that operate on a particular culture or class, and by the specific life experiences of the individual.

The activities of the psychologist as a scientist in trying to arrive at reasonable theoretical constructions of the human mind have often been seen by many philosophers and psychologists to be somehow different and differently constrained than the activity of other scientists. There is no logical justification for that assertion. Presumably, the theoretical structures that we can build up about an observed set of events (in this case the actions and experiences of other human beings) are no more constrained by the mental structure of the observer than are the observations of physical, biological, or astronomic events. There is no doubt that the limitations of human mental organization constrain what we can experience and what we can think about (anything else would elevate man into the place of a god). However, there is nothing in that constraint to say that the kinds of theories we can make up about mental structures are peculiarly influenced by our own mental structures *any more* so than our theories about the structure of the atom. To say that only part of the "real" world is knowable is, of course, empty, since, by definition, we do not know what is not knowable. Whereas this limitation should be recognized, we can and do enlarge our knowledge of the world. Some of the methodological and technological extensions of man have made both structures and events of the world knowable that were unthought of prior to these advances. We need only think about the extensions of the electromagnetic spectrum beyond the visible limits or the contributions of the microscope or the discovery of subatomic particles or the operation of unconscious structures.

The notion that mental structure is influenced by the evolutionary history of the species is a truism at this point in scientific history. Consider the special characteristics of the sensory apparatus and the analytical systems that support it; we need not even go into complex behavioral structures that ethologists have by now so well established. The notion that mental processes are subject to historical and social constraints is less popular in the recent positivistic history of Western science, but the evidence is fairly conclusive that sociohistorical processes influence at least the distribution of various kinds of thought processes (e.g., Luria, 1971). Finally, even with the current return of nativism in opposition to the behavioristic tradition, there is little doubt that many of the mental structures operating in everyday life are a function of the particular cultural, social, and individual experience of the individual and the group. Even the most ardent defender of a nativist position on language will admit to the importance of individual experiences in developing the structures that are specific to a particular language. In the area of less complex action systems and the structures that underlie the business of daily living, individual experience and cultural influence on that experience become of great importance.

How far have we come in specifying the kinds of structures that are capable of storing the knowledge we have of the world in which we live? It is obvious that in order to know what something means we need to know what its relationship is to other events and propositions that form part of our past experience. These knowledges and relations must be represented by some sort of structural system.

The Structure of Memory Networks

The most important advances toward the development of a first approximation of a knowledge-storing system of mental structures occurred during the past 10 years. Since we are dealing with the placing of an event in terms of past experiences, it deals with the structure of long-term memory. In this area a number of theoretical developments tend to point in common directions. It is therefore useful to consider some of the network theories of long-term memory. Fortunately, Norman (1973) has summarized the current state of the art.

While Norman's presentation focuses on one particular memory model (Rumelhart, Lindsay, and Norman, 1972), most of the general points he makes and that will be abstracted here are applicable to other current models as well (e.g., Quillian, 1968; Collins and Quillian, 1972; Kintsch, 1972; and others). These networks represent our knowledge of the world and the relational concepts that structure this knowledge. Basically, the central notion is the concept of a node in a graphical representation; these nodes represent concepts and, in a graph, may be presented in some directed relation one to the other. For example, nodes *a* and *b* are in a particular relation such that *a* stands in relation *r* to *b*, but this does not imply that *b* stands in the relation *r* to *a* unless so specified. Three kinds of entities are represented in this model, and they generally fall into three classes: *concepts* are particular ideas, *events* refer to actions with actors and objects, and *episodes* are series of events or actions.

Concepts are encoded by specifying, within the structure, the class to which the concept belongs, the characteristics that define the concept and, of course, examples of that particular concept. In the case of events, the representation centers around the verb that describes the action. Higher structures then relate various events one to another to form episodes.

To distinguish among different uses of a single concept or event, we can distinguish between nodes that define the type (or primary nodes) and secondary nodes that refer to the token. Thus, for example, the act "walk" may have among its tokens the uses:

John walks home, *and*

John walks the dog.

This structural approach also enters when we deal with episodes that are clusters of events or actions. Norman (1973) illustrates this with a representation of the episode:

John murders Mary at Luigi's.

It uses propositional conjunctions such as "then" and "while" that provide temporal relations within the structure. Encoding of the individual concepts involves not only nodes such as "Mary," "stabs," and "knife," but also specifies the structural conceptual relations as specified by the labels on some of the directed graphs. For example, objects, actors, times, and locations have their own conceptual representation.

The flow of action of an episode takes place in the memory system, whether or not the individual actually performs these operations or simply follows their representation (thinks about them), presumably representing them in consciousness for inspection, change, and consideration. The actual execution of the episode would follow a very similar search through the system, however, with additional specifying arguments and with an output to the action systems.

Norman suggests that the hierarchical structures of the memory system, whether they relate to concepts, events, or episodes, are built up on the basis of three general principles: first, *permanence*—once information has been entered in the memory structure it is not lost—in principle, nothing is forgotten; second, *generalization,* higher level nodes are developed that summarize or categorize information common to a number of lower nodes; and third, *discrimination,* a process by which nodes are subdivided with distinctive sets of features. Generalization is equivalent to concept formation; we encounter plumbers, physicians, and carpenters and develop the concept of professions. Discrimination is involved, for example, when we develop the conceptual subdivision that carpenters include furniture makers and building carpenters.

Additional arguments about the function of a semantic network in producing and encoding linguistic structures are of no central importance here, except to say that the processing involved in the understanding of a sentence, for example, requires consideration of extensive parts of the structure, of the logical notions such as implication and of the synthetic notions such as causality (i.e., considerations of the structure of the complete episodic set that is being experienced and analysed for its "meaning").

Finally, Norman points out that rules differ from concepts and acts in that they refer to a conditional set of actions; that is, actions that are performed subject to the prior satisfaction of other conditions events or actions. If I want to learn either abstract or concrete rules as, for example, "When winning stay with a particular choice, when losing shift to an alternative one," "In French, the position of the adjective relative to the noun depends on the required emphasis," or "Don't stop at a diner unless there are a lot of trucks parked outside of it," I have to know the proper conditions under which these rules apply, which in turn have a hierarchical structure of types and tokens as well as the appropriate acts to be performed. In that sense the rules may be treated like concepts and events in the memory structure.

Hierarchical organizations are a natural scheme for the development of the kind of networks discussed here. For example, consider a child learning about dogs. We assume that the central representation of "dogs" will develop out of the early instances and the early discriminations made about this concept. Assume that the first experience a child has is with a large, black dog that barks frequently. Thus the unspoken, prelinguistic (see Macnamara, 1972) meaning of this particular concept involves something moving, something black, and also something that because of sudden barking noises may have related to it some degree of autonomic arousal. This initial experience is complex (it is not a single node), and it is elaborated on subsequent occasions. However, the initial "dog" node and structure has connections to the arousal system as well as to a structure, presumably present prior to the first experience with a dog, that might make distinctions between large and small moving objects. As experience with dogs increases the central node of dog is discriminated into smaller ones, into nonblack ones, into ones that do not bark, and also into some new characteristics such as dogs that lick your hand, dogs that fetch things, and so forth. At the same time, there are characteristics of dogs (e.g., they are self-propelled objects) that will produce generalizations and coordination with high-level nodes, including the node relating to living things, or, for example, the common node between cats and dogs, which refers to them as tame domestic animals usually found in the home. Thus we assume that by discrimination and generalization, lower and higher nodes are developed from a central initial node in a hierarchical system. It should also be noted that Norman assumes that no forgetting or erasing of any information takes place. What does take place is relative degree of accessibility of certain information. In other words, any information once entered into long-term memory is available but may, in fact, not be accessible (see Mandler, 1967b).

Two other aspects of this model deserve particular emphasis in our present context. The first refers to the hierarchical structure of concepts. I have described this notion more extensively elsewhere (Mandler, 1967a). Generally, it assumes that there are multidimensional hierarchical structures that order concepts, their instances, and higher concepts of which the original concepts themselves are instances. Given a particular concept, further analysis may, depending on the search program used, yield lower-order instances, higher-order concepts, coordinate instances, or some combination of these. Nondirected search most often produces higher-order instances. For example, the question "What is a dog?" does not usually yield a single response; it sometimes yields reference to some collection of poodles, German shepherds, terriers, and so forth but, more frequently, it yields a higher-order concept such as "animal" or "living."

Second, we note that the initial characterization of the new concept or new node is important in the further development of the concept and its meaning in the sense of its relation to other nodes. Thus, if the initial instance is extensively processed, then despite development of that concept and its generalization and discrimination, reference will frequently return to that initial node. If the child's attention has been, for situational and organismic reasons, particularly drawn to the initial large, black, barking dog, then that will, to a very large extent, characterize his view of dogs and even the general meaning of pets.

It is not the purpose of this book to discuss in detail different kinds of cognitive models and cognitive structures. However, we must draw attention to the two dominant models of cognitive development: first, Piaget's, because it is the only well-worked-out system of cognitive development at the present time; and second, Freud's, because it pays special attention to the problem of emotional development. It should be obvious by now that most consistent workable theories are consistent with the kind of approach advocated here. There is no reason why both Piaget's notions of cognitive development and Freud's notions of emotional development cannot be included within the mental organization. Under different conditions and for different reasons, different kinds of these structures will be used and will be expressed in behavior and experience.

I shall not at this time deal with the development of emotionally relevant structures, such as Freud's notions of infantile preoccupations. How cognitive structures may be influenced and molded by specific infantile experiences, that is, by the kinds of mechanisms with which Freud was concerned, will be discussed more properly in Chapter 9 in connection with the development of individual differences.

Meaning Analysis

The concept of meaning analysis refers to the fact that any input to the cognitive-interpretive system is subjected to an analysis of its relation to existing structures. I use the term meaning analysis primarily as a communicative device, not to pretend an exhaustive analysis of the concept of "meaning." I do stress the relational aspects of meaning and could just as easily have used the term "relational analysis." The notion of meaning as relational has been mentioned earlier (cf. Garner, 1962).

I assume that all input to the cognitive-interpretive system undergoes such meaning analysis. It is one of the axiomatic characteristics of the whole system that all input is examined for its fit into relational structures. The system takes an item of input and, locating it in terms of its particular characteristics, attributes, and features, immediately notes (or activates) the relations of that particular item or set of events to other structures and sets of events. Thus the relation of a particular input to existing structures gives us an organization that is specific to that particular item and gives us the organization of that item within the existing structures or its meaning. Remember, however, that items, events, and situations are not taken in isolation, but that many of the relations of particular interest are these that exist to other inputs at the same time. A good example is the meaning analysis of polysemic words.

For example, the word "table" undergoes an entirely different meaning analysis when it occurs in the sentence, "I put it in the table," or "I put it on the table." The relational characteristics in the former case have to do with tables in books and papers, while the latter have to do with tables that are found in rooms and houses.

Broadly speaking, it may be assumed that the extent of a meaning analysis will depend on two major sets of variables: the mental structure of the organism involved, and the state of the organism at the time of input. Thus the more complex the mental structures, the more complex the meaning analysis, the "richer" the meaning, and the more implications a particular input will have for a variety of different past experiences (represented in structures) and other present inputs. We may assume that the meaning analyses performed by a rat between a black and a white cue will activate a relatively narrow range of relations, specifically the structures that have previously been established involving the relation of "black leading to food" and "white leading to no food." For a human subject a distinction between "black" and "white" may have similar implications (particularly if he has recently been a subject in a psychological experiment), but he has other relations that involve the event "black" at various levels of the semantic hierarchy, and such an analysis may range from simple brightness discrimination to the symbolic meaning of black. Similar elaborations of the complexity of the meaning analysis will, of course, hold between species and within species as a function of age and experience.

Of equal importance is the current state of the organism at the time of input. The assertion that all incoming stimuli undergo some meaning analysis may be true, but the degree of analysis can obviously differ. Presumably, the degree of meaning analysis is influenced by two nonindependent sets of variables: attention and task requirements. Considering task requirements, the degree of analysis to be performed is a part of the explicit or implicit instructions given to the individuals. For example, if I were to ask somebody whether or not a cow is a domestic animal, the degree of analysis would be relatively poor as compared to a question that requires the individual to tell me everything he knows about cows. The second question will elicit all the information that the first one does, but not vice versa. The complexity of response and the degree of analysis will be affected by the question. In short, it is highly likely that the system has a stop rule that goes into effect whenever the requirements of the tasks are apparently fulfilled. Anecdotal evidence is convincing, but there is also extensive evidence in the literature on memory and attention to suggest more rigorous and highly specified, limitations to the degree of semantic analysis that is performed. For example, in word recognition, it appears that the initial analysis to the question whether a word has previously been seen may involve the inspection of storage for the presence or absence of prior occurrence tags. However, when that particular search cannot be adequately answered to provide a stop rule, then a more extensive analysis in terms of memory retrieval is apparently performed (Mandler, 1972a). When we cannot immediately place a "familiar" face, we usually search for likely contexts in which we may have met that person before.

The degree or depth of semantic analysis may also be a function of the requirement of two or more tasks to be executed at the same time. For example, in an incidental learning situation, some tasks will be given a low level or depth of analysis that is adequate to the requirements of the task but not as extensive as it might otherwise be (e.g., Mandler and Worden, 1973). Other evidence, both on the depth and time-course of meaning analyses, can be found in recent work on semantic networks.

Attentional and task requirements are probably not independent. Stating the requirement of a task specifies not only what inputs ought to be attended but also what subroutines and structures ought to be brought into play in operating on the input. Thus the task requirement defines one aspect of the attentional problem. It is not my purpose here to discuss at length the rich and varied problem of attention (cf. Treisman, 1969). Suffice it to say that I assume that the degree and depth of meaning analysis will covary with the degree and intensity of attention. Even that may be a redundant statement, since the best index of attention may well be the degree of meaning analysis that a particular event has undergone. This is not saying anything new but emphasizes the fact that the literature on attention and the variables that influence attention are sources of insight as to the degree of meaning analysis that is likely to be performed. It is important to note in contrast, however, that meaning analysis and overt behavior are not necessarily correlated. In other words, it is not necessary to show an output from an action system in order to be able to say that a particular set of stimuli has been attended to. Low levels of meaning analysis may go on continuously (and the literature on dichotic listening supports this point most strongly) without any immediate reflection in behavior or experience. The notion that meaning analyses are part of the attentional armamentarium has influenced theories of discrimination learning (e.g., Sutherland and Mackintosh, 1971), and the dimensional analysis of stimuli in a choice situation becomes, in these theories, an important part of the model. But, even in the choice behavior of the rat, it has been shown that a meaning analysis (or dimensional or attentional analysis) of a set of stimuli may be performed and indexed by some measures such as response latency, while it may not influence some other actions systems such as choice (Mandler and Goldberg, 1973).

I have described meaning analyses entirely in terms of linguistic codes. This usage is primarily a simplifying device, since I do not intend to imply that meanings are entirely linguistic. On the contrary, I fully agree with Macnamara (1972), among others, who distinguishes between cognitive structures and the linguistic code, particularly in the early acquisition of language. If these cognitive structures precede linguistic codes and semantics, it is equally true that they continue to exist jointly throughout the lifetime of the individual. On the other hand, it is probably also the case that the linguistic code is the primary access the normal adult has to the structure of his experience.

At the same time, a structural view of "meaning" leaves us somewhat at a loss in trying to make any rigid distinction between connotative and denotative meaning or between sense and reference. It has generally been assumed that denotative or extensional meaning relates the perceptual world to the linguistic code, while connotative meaning is a more personal, frequently affective, or internal, intensional use of the term meaning. Denotative meaning is considered to be consensual, while connotative meaning is more individual and therefore more variable. The difficulty of making any strict distinction between connotation and denotation within a structural view should be obvious. While there will be structures that primarily relate perceptual events to language codes, there may also be structures that can be described without any reference to perceptual events. The "meaning" of a sentence or word will frequently involve the full range of structural relations of the concept addressed; there may be no "pure" denotations or connotations. If we accept the notion that much of meaning relations involve imagery and the quasivisual structures associated with it, then the "meaning" of the word "table" will involve not only its relationship to superordinate nodes such as "furniture" and "useful objects" but also perceptual features involved in the imagery of tables. While it is quite possible, of course, to restrict ourselves, particularly in the laboratory, to purely connotative judgments (e.g., Osgood, Suci, and Tannenbaum, 1957) by asking an individual how "good" or "bad" the "murderer" is, in daily functioning it is highly unlikely that these evaluative judgments are made in the absence of other analyses that relate to perceptual, categorical, and other aspects of the word or sentence. Conversely, evaluative judgments usually accompany "definitional" analyses.

Particularly from the point of view of a psychology of emotion, the "meaning" of an experience (be it linguistic or not) must include all the attributes and relations of an event or item, no matter where they may lead. These attributes and relations will include perceptual, affective, categorical, and imageal ones (referring to concepts, categories, and ideas). Some of these may be defined entirely within a semantic network, while others will require relations to perceptual, emotional, and other structures.

I now turn to my preference for the term "meaning analysis" to describe the cognitive evaluation of environmental situations. Other authors, specifically Arnold (1970b), Lazarus et al (1970), and Bowlby (1969), prefer the term "appraisal." My objection to appraisal is that it implies that we usually appraise something as good or bad. Arnold has made that point quite specifically; she considers appraisals to be in terms of "good" and "bad," to be followed by approach and avoidance, respectively. My objection is primarily to Arnold's metaphysical view that judgments of "good" or "bad" are somehow innate aspects of human consciousness. At the present state of knowledge, it is not likely that mechanisms of moral, affective, or ethical judgment have been built into people; therefore the implications of the term "appraisal" should be avoided as well. Meaning analysis, on the other hand, says that some analysis of the meaning of a situation is performed that, in many cases, may involve an appraisal as "good" or "bad," but it also may involve evaluations that are on different dimensions such as awe-inspiring, sexy, or funny, all of which may be independent of an implied ethical "appraisal" continuum. More important, "meaning analysis" refers to *all* the features of an event, not just the affective ones.

I should draw attention briefly to some of the central points of Piaget's theory, which has been summarized and developed by numerous writers in the past two decades. Probably one of the best expositions is Piaget's own relatively recent summary (1970). Piaget is primarily interested in the establishment of cognitive structures that develop out of a continuous interaction between the individual and his environment. The knowledge that the organism develops is a function of transformations performed on external objects and events. Structures change primarily by two processes, one of which is assimilation, the integration of environmental events into existing or developing structures. Accommodation, on the other hand, refers to the changes produced in an existing structure by an object or event that has been assimilated. Thus existing structures change as they assimilate new experience and adapt to that new experience by accommodation. In the current context assimilation and accommodation can be viewed as two different modes of analysis that generate changes in meaning.

Action Systems and Their Structures

Actions involve all the behaviors that act on the environment, be it social or not. From my point of view, they have two important characteristics. First, actions are activated by particular structures (action systems) within the mental organization. Second, they have certain consequences that, in turn, feed back into the system of organizations and structures and modify them. The output of these action systems has been of particular interest to psychologists of learning and motivation over the past several decades. The continuum of structures that underlie these action systems is of immediate interest. These structures may be ordered in the degree to which they are, on the one hand, developed in the individual as a result of his evolutionary and genetic history and, on the other hand, the extent to which they have been built up as a result of interactions and transactions with the environment and its response to outputs from the action systems. There is no intent to imply a dichotomy between "innate" and "learned" structures but, instead, to indicate an awareness that many action systems depend, for both their initiation and their effectiveness, on the evolutionary history of the species. Thus there are species specific action systems (see Bolles, 1970), situationally appropriate systems (Staddon and Simmelhag, 1971), situation specific adaptations (Rozin and Kalat, 1971), and many other structures that demonstrate the intricate interaction between the preparedness of the organism for certain situations and environmental pressures and demands. Bowlby (1969) has discussed some of the possible characteristics of these interactions in man.

However, we can assume that, whether a structure is preprogrammed or whether it is primarily influenced by the individual history of the organism, the functions of the central structure are essentially the same for well-developed behaviors. Thus it can be assumed that with extensive experience the structure that leads to the well-organized and highly integrated behavior known as "writing" is probably similar in its theoretical structure and functions to those that may be much less dependent on interactions with the environment such as "walking" or "eating."

The Organization of Action

The notion that even simple behaviors are not just chains of reflexes has occupied psychologists and biologists for some decades. In the following section I borrow heavily from Gallistel (1974) who has

presented the psychological-biological evidence for the central idea that
behavior or action sequences are centrally programmed (i.e.,
structured). Following the previous work of Weiss (1941), Von Holst
(1939), and Tinbergen (1951), Gallistel emphasizes the need to consider
higher processes that manage the direction of behavior. He postulates
the hierarchy of actions and behaviors, starting at the bottom, with the
"reflexes, endongenous oscillators, taxes, and other functional units of
behavior." Nodes at succeeding higher levels control combinations of
structures or coordinations represented at the next lower level. This
control is generated by appropriate inhibitory and disinhibitory signals.
Organized actions controlled by a particular node have functional
significance, but they do not necessarily, nor even usually, involve the
serial firing of the behavioral constituents. The nodal organization
"uses" the appropriate lower constituents so that a particular reflex, for
example, may precede another under one organization and follow it
under another. Gallistel considers the apices of these hierarchical
organizations of actions to be equivalent to the psychologist's use of
the term motive. Stimuli may be received at any level of the hierarchy,
but those that activate the apex of a hierarchy are generally equivalent
to motivational stimuli, concerned with survival functions, for example.

There are two distinct issues in the organization of actions: the
structure of action and the representation of action. The first addresses
the structure of action as presented by Gallistel. Leaving aside for the
moment the class of preprogrammed "innate" structures, in the course
of its transactions with the environment, the organism acquires new
complex action structures. These are typically built out of existing
units, at the lowest level of reflexes and taxes, but more generally out
of any existing organized action units. The conditions under which
these new action systems develop are, at least, complex and, to a large
extent, unknown in their specifics. For example, Gallistel suggests that
(primary) reinforcers function by inducing or generating the appearance
of previously established systems under new "motivational" contexts.
New sensory-motor systems develop on the basis of cognitive maps
and explorations of new environments. The distinction seems forced,
and the extensive literature on operant shaping suggests that new
action systems may as readily be generated by "reinforcement" as by
the information-seeking explorations of the organism. As we shall see
shortly, "primary" reinforcement is often the occasion for the
occurrence of highly organized responses and the system that is being
organized develops out of the extension of these existing "primary"
systems. In any case, it may be assumed that the continuing exercise
(execution) of a particular action system generates a more tightly
organized and invariant structure. For example, a rat learning a maze or
a human learning to drive from his office to his new home both

eventually develop well-organized action systems that at first are constituted of individual and unrelated subsystems. In the course of development much hypothesis testing (or so-called trial and error behavior) occurs. Potential subsystems may be tested behaviorally or cognitively before a particular combination is found and used. As it is used consecutively, with less and less variation (error), it establishes its own general structure and organization. But how do we acquire the representations or analogues of subsystems that can be cognitively or behaviorally tried out? This question brings us to the second issue in the organization of action—its representation. The distinction here is, for example, between the action system that organizes my use of knives and forks in eating a steak and the fuzzy cognitive representation I have of those actions.

I assume that once an action is executed, it becomes represented in a cognitive structure. In a previous attempt at understanding the structural representation of action I confused the issues of the development of action structures and their representation (Mandler, 1962a). I suggested a single "representational" structure for organized behavior arising out of the integration of a particular behavioral sequence. However, because of foolish youthful preoccupations, I assigned the role of generating the component units of the organized action to "associative processes." One and the same structure was used to *represent* the action and was implicitly involved in generating it. By recanting and disavowing any associationist tendencies now, I can also maintain the position on the representation of action that I took in 1962. I do need to add the importance of structures that *produce* action. I should also take this opportunity to acknowledge my ignorance that a highly similar, more influential, and better developed theoretical position on this issue by Piaget (1953; also Piaget and Inhelder, 1969) long predated my suggestions.

Many of our cognitive structures represent the internalization of action—the representation of action that makes possible its cognitive manipulation. Whereas much of this representation seems to be in the form of images (tactual and visual), there is no need to restrict the formal character of these structures to one modality or another. One study (Mandler and Kuhlman, 1961) demonstrated the development of the representation of complex response patterns. During early stages of training, experimental subjects could not reproduce the pattern in the absence of external stimulus support but, after moderate training, they reported tactual imagery and, after extended overtraining, they reported visual imagery of the overt pattern. In 1962 I noted that the development of so-called analogic structures of actions follows the elimination of errors. After the action systems that generate the structures have stabilized and performance is essentially asymptotic, the representation of the action will be essentially identical from occurrence to occurrence, and stable representations will develop.

Once a representation of action has been developed, these cognitive structures can be used for the elaborate choice and decision processes prior to output. In other words, what is manipulated cognitively is the representation of action and not, as I may previously have implied, the action structures themselves. As a matter of fact, I noted earlier that much cognitive activity is involved in the constructions of new action systems. During that phase, various separate action units are inspected and tested before they are incorporated into the new action system. Thus the construction of new systems is characterized by cognition and often by consciousness (e.g., when we consider various alternatives in learning a new skill). Once it has been established, the action runs off without cognitive intervention (i.e., by the activation of the appropriate action system). These new integrated actions will, in turn, become represented as cognitive structures.

One other relation between action systems and cognitive structures concerns the conditions under which the system can and does switch from a contemplated structure to the appropriate action system. What is the relationship between existing actions system and the cognitive structures that represent them? In the first instance, I assume that the mental organization always establishes a relationship between any two or more structures that are active at any given point in time. For example, a relation will exist between old memories of past meetings that are retrieved when seeing an old friend, and the perceptual structure that is operative in constructing the physical conditions of the current meeting with that friend. Given that assumption, a relationship will necessarily exist between an action system and its cognitive representation, since the action system is by definition active when the cognitive representational structure is being established. Furthermore, that relationship is unique in that only a particular action system and its cognitive structure have this relation, which might be called a pseudoisomorphism. Clearly, the two structures are not isomorphic— typically, the cognitive structure will be a degraded, abbreviated version of the action system itself. While verbal labels are only a poor approximation of the cognitive structure, they do convey the flavor of this abbreviated isomorphism. Consider the relation between "driving home," "making love," "preparing Beef Wellington," "writing my name," and the appropriate action systems. What is still obscure is the mechanism whereby the system goes from a cognitive consideration of a possible action system to its execution. Despite the lack of isomorphic structures, a single-action system may occur after only some partial activation of its cognitive representation or even in response to just a summary label (e. g., "Draw a dog," or "Tie your shoelaces"). To say that this sequence involves the activation of the relation between structure and action system only restates the hoary problem about the relation between thought and action.

In the remainder of this chapter I shall restate and develop some notions about action systems and observable organized response sequences.

Organized Action Sequences

I wish to stress in my view of mental organization a rejection of the emphasis on energies and drives, which was so popular in the first half of the century. I share with others the hope that a psychology without an economical substratum or energy concept might be possible and should be attempted. Thus Gallistel (1974) defines motives as nonenergic; "motivation is an internally patterned *signal*" that facilitates or inhibits the activity of lower behavioral units.

In addition to rejecting an energy model, I also believe that notions such as expectancies may often be unnecessary. In part, they are the result of the psychologist's fascinations with his phenomenal world. An expectancy may often be a construction that the human animal puts on his behavior but that can be explained without such concepts (cf. Skinner, 1957). This does not lead to a psychology without ends or goals, but the attempt is to talk about these "goals" without an appeal to conscious expectations. Similarly, variations in the intensity of behavior do not require energy concepts; we may talk instead about distributions of responses with different characteristics.

The development of new behavioral structures proceeds largely by response integration, the process whereby new response units are built out of previously discrete units.

The single most important feature of an organized sequence is its unitary nature. It is elicited or emitted as a whole, as a single unit: it is not simply a chain of responses. Consider an example: single letters or phonemes of a language are single units, but so are well-practiced words in that language. The letter A is just as unitary as the word "Cat," and there is good evidence that they function as equivalent units (cf. Murdock, 1961). To stay in the context of language, well-practiced phrases are also unitary (e.g., "How do you do" or "I love you"). Similarly, starting a car, unlocking a familiar door, and drinking out of a glass are single behavioral units. Now it is obvious that such units may be built into imposing proportions, such as driving home from the office. At the same time, some organized sequences are not rigid with respect to the units comprising them; the organism may have some element of choice at various time slices. Obvious examples that come to mind are taking a walk around the block or giving a prepared lecture.

Psychologists, in general, have not bothered too much with the definition of action, and some influential theorists such as Hull have taken it for granted that we know intuitively what the response units may be, be they innate or acquired. Others, like Skinner, have demonstrated a curious ambiguity in talking first at length about the acquisition of a topographically unique response but, once acquired, define it solely in terms of its consequences.

Of the several variables that might determine organization, there is one convincing antecedent condition for the development of organized sequences. It is the frequency of use of a sequence, with organization or integration developing gradually (cf. Mandler, 1962a).

I do not consider an organized response as a chain of constituent units with goal gradients, anticipatory goal responses, or expectancies within it busily driving the organism toward a goal. On the contrary, once started, any organized response has the same inevitability of completion that we readily accept in short, organized responses such as swallowing, lever pressing, kicking, or speaking a word. They are acquired in much the same way. There is nothing qualitatively different about learning how to write and learning how to strike a single typewriter key. There are, on the other hand, very potent organized sequences in an organism's repertory that are not acquired in this sense at all. These are preprogrammed organizations, innate, unconditioned, unlearned actions, such as sucking, and the consummatory facets of eating, drinking, copulation, and so forth.

Within the performance of an organized pattern there will, of course, be minor variations from occasion to occasion. The important point is that the band of variability around an organized sequence will not only be fairly stable but will also be much narrower than that around an as yet unorganized one. Similarly, there may also be quantitative differences, especially among sequences that differ in length in the sense that longer ones are more apt to be interrupted and may be less well organized (i.e., their band of variability may be wider).

I want to emphasize that the organization or integration of an action occurs after it has been "learned" in the traditional sense of the term (i.e., after errorless performance has been attained). The organization of the units that make up the new sequence—and that are themselves previously organized responses—cannot take place when errors still interfere with smooth performance. But, once organized, goal gradients and anticipatory goal responses become cumbersome and unnecessary. There is no necessity for cognitive goal-directed mechanisms of the type Tolman and Hull advocated, and there is some evidence that the goal gradient does, in fact, occur primarily during the early stages of learning or exploration (Hull, 1934; Pereboom, 1958) or with weak incentives (Crespi, 1942). I might add that organization probably proceeds from the "goal" backward but, since such a "goal" usually consists of the performance of a previously organized response, it is simpler to say that the process of organization of a sequence exhibits a gradient around its constituent preorganized units, the most obvious of which are consummatory responses.

Goals

In saying that these organized actions are not simply a bunch of means leading to an end, I am stressing that in the world of integrated responses there are no pure goals, no goals without means. There is often no need for invoking end states that are desired or anticipated; we may only need to specify behavior sequences that are performed. There are no differential goals and paths to them, only goal paths functioning as units. And what may be intended or anticipated are the organized sequences, not the pure goals.

Contrary to the intuitive and phenomenological view that acts are goal directed, that expectancies and goal anticipations are involved in the performance of an approach, we could argue equally intuitively that the phenomenal goal is never the pure consummatory act but always involves at least a small part of a complete goal path. It can hardly be argued that the phenomenal goal of going to a restaurant is the consummatory act of swallowing or digestive activity, or that the goal of riches is the folding of money into a billfold. What is envisaged as the goal always involves much more complex acts than that, sequences in which the "goal" only represents a minor part. But it is these apparent goals that are the goal paths, the organizations and plans that do—in contrast to the "goals"—play important cognitive roles.

Bowlby (1969) has discussed the difficulties with the concept of "goal" and has suggested that for behavioral systems such as the ones I have discussed here, other terms might be more appropriate. For example, he compares two kinds of such systems that have predictable outcomes; we might talk about a "goal" for one, but not for the other. Thus a system that through continuous feedback adjusts itself to environmental input as, for example, a ball player running to catch a ball, may be said to have a "goal," while another system in which a particular organized set of responses runs off smoothly (e.g., eating a meal) may not be said to have a goal. It is interesting to note in the last example the "goal" of eating cannot possibly be just one of its constituents such as restoring the blood sugar level, which is not discriminable as part of the action system, or finishing the meal, which is not always done, or any other number of possibilities. This difference is also related to the distinction between the cause and the function of a particular set of behaviors, a distinction that Bowlby, among others, has discussed and that will recur later in this chapter.

Bowlby prefers to use the term set-goal, by which he means "either a time-limited event or an ongoing condition either of which is brought about by the action of behavioral systems that are structured to take account of discrepancies between instruction and performance. ... A set goal is *not* an object in the environment but is either a specified motor performance, e.g. singing a song, or the achievement of a specified relation, of short or long duration, between the animal and some object in or component of the environment."

I believe with Bowlby that a withdrawal from the concept of goal is most appropriate. We might still use a goal-related concept in one context, which Bowlby also uses, namely the notion of goal correction. When an organism uses many different sequences to achieve some particular outcome, we might talk about that particular outcome as correcting the sequences that are used in order to complete the overall plan. One can then talk about the execution of a higher-order plan and its latter stages without even using the term goal correction. Maybe a term such as plan-directed (rather than goal-directed) correction might be appropriate. This is in keeping with the use by Miller, Galanter, and Pribram of the plan as the overall structure that serves as the umbrella or executive organizer of a hierarchy of subsystems.

Teleology and Organized Behavior

The implication that a mental system has certain adaptive functions and that its consequences act on the environment in order to create conditions that are adaptive, pleasureable, or generally sought by the organism raises the old teleological horror. There should be no reason for modern psychologists to worry about the mistaken views of teleology that have plagued philosophers and psychologists. However, for those still easily frightened, a discussion by Bowlby (1969) of the function of instinctive behavior is illuminating and instructive. Bowlby summarizes the general notions of *function* and its distinction from *causation* and concludes that "functions are the special consequences that arise from the way a system is constructed; causes are the factors that lead the system to become active or inactive on any one occasion." He goes on to note that for the individual organism, instinctive behavior is independent of function, while for a population of individuals the functions of a particular system must be fulfilled at least some of the time. Thus, while a particular system will have a predictable outcome for *individuals,* its adaptive function is a property of that system for the *population,* not for the individual.

Since we are here concerned primarily with acquired instead of preprogrammed or instinctive systems, the notion of adaptive function has to be interpreted in a wider and somewhat different sense. However, Bowlby's distinctions may be used to say that events such as goals, outcomes, and consequences occur as a result of the way a system is constructed, while the factors that lead a system to become active are conceptually different and may be considered to be the causal factors. As a matter of fact, Bowlby's distinction between individual and population aspects of instinctual systems can be generalized to acquired systems in looking at their specific occurrence and their general function. Thus, for a specific, unique action, the activation of the underlying structure is independent of its consequences or goals; it is "caused" by the initiating conditions. On the other hand, for a "population" of actions, these goals and consequences must be fulfilled at least part of the time.

Thus, just as instinctive behavior is maintained for the population, so the structure for a particular sequence of behavior is maintained for the individual, but the individual act is independent of its consequence for the organism and only dependent on the conditions that are necessary for its initiation. Getting into one's car and driving home from work is a single instance of a structure that is maintained because it has the "function" of spanning the distance between work and home. However, the organized behavior at any one time is independent of the function but is initiated by such factors as that it is five o'clock. This concept of consequences maintaining a system is, of course, similar to the notion of reinforcement within Skinner's system, although in a less restricted sense. Generally, it is a set of consequences (reinforcers) that establishes the behavior in the organism, but it is the controlling stimulus that initiates the specific action that is, in turn, not seen as goal directed.

Just as teleological discussions in the literature of biological systems have often mistaken the population characteristics of particular behavior for characteristics in the single individual, so does the function of a particular structure in an individual lead us to make teleological comments about a specific act. The acting individual may, on the initiation of the particular organized behavior, comment on that behavior as if the characteristics displayed were the characteristics of the population of acts instead of the unique action about to be performed. Since consciousness may have access to the structure of a particular act, output from the system may be of the form, "I am engaging in this act in order to reach a particular goal." In contrast we would say that while the function of the structure is, when completed, to have certain adaptive consequences, the only thing that can be said about the individual expression of that structure (the present and immediate action) is that it has been initiated and has certain predictable behavioral outcomes, but *not* predictable and, at best probabilistic, consequences. Here again, we are faced with the difficulty of making theoretical statements based on the commentary that consciousness and language systems provide about on-going behavior and the selections of structures. Thus the teleological expression of a goal, for example, "I'm going to leave now to go home and have dinner," is a commentary on the general structure but not, in any case, a "motivating" condition for the initiation of a particular set of behaviors. Presumably certain internal and external conditions (including blood sugar level and the sight of a clock) start a specific set of organized actions; the "goal" is often phenomenally perceived in terms of the class of behaviors of which this is an instance. In Bowlby's terms the behavioral system is constructed in such a way that it has the consequence of leading one home and to food; the system is activated by factors that are present at this particular occasion. The gloss provided by introspection is interesting but not causally relevant. Finally, the phenomenal experience of "goals" may be related to the general operation of stop rules, including Bowlby's set-goals. Since most, if not all, organized action systems include a stop rule, the registration of such a rule may, in the common language and in phenomal experience, be identified as the goal of the action. Stop rules terminate actions, as do "goals." But neither motivates or "causes" the initiation or performance of the act.

In this chapter I have skirted the role of consciousness in mental organization to the point of both elevating it to a central role and despairing of one of its consequences—introspection. In Chapter 3 I shall deal with these problems more directly.

Chapter III

Consciousness— A Special Function of Mind[1]

The concept of consciousness was abandoned as a proper object of experimental study about 60 years ago for a variety of reasons. The introspective method erred in assuming that consciousness could be made the datum of psychology or that verbal report was a royal road to its exploration. The failure of introspection engendered behaviorism and failed to provide any viable alternatives. Others, like the Gestalt school and the French and English enclaves, successfully defended their views of the conscious organism but had, for theoretical reasons, little grounds to mount a major analytic attack. The return of American psychology to a theory-rich as well as experimentally rigorous stance has given us the opportunity to develop the proper theoretical tools to return consciousness to its proper place in a theory of thought, mind, and actions. Most of the early steps that have been taken have been necessarily preliminary models and developments of experimental methods. In this chapter I will indicate the directions that these preliminary steps are taking. These steps will have been successful if they generate discussion and investigation and, eventually, theory, which will define and specify the role that consciousness plays in man's transactions with his world.

I hope to show that consciousness is respectable in the sense that it has become the object of serious and impressive experimental research; it is useful because it avoids circumlocutions as well as constructions, such as short-term memory and focal attention, that are more easily addressed by an appeal to consciousness as part of the apparatus of cognition; and it is probably necessary because it ties together many disparate but obviously related mental concepts, including attention, perceptual elaboration, and limited capacity notions.

[1]This chapter was preprinted with some changes in Mandler (1975b), I express my special appreciation to U. Neisser and C. R. Gallistel who commented most helpfully on a previous version of this chapter.

The Revival of Consciousness

The history of consciousness is strewn with philosophical, theological, and pedestrian semantic debris; the history of unconscious concepts has, by inherited contrast, suffered similarly. Having made the decision to recall the concept of consciousness to service, it is useful to start baldly with the distinction between conscious and unconscious processes. I do so with some sense of embarrassment *vis à vis* the contributions of others. Freud, in particular, has contributed much to the finer distinctions among shadings of the unconscious. However, if we are to make a fresh start within the experimental investigation of consciousness, we shall probably also have to rediscover these distinctions within the new realm of discourse. For present purposes the distinction among preconscious, preattentive, primary, and unconscious processes is premature. It suffices to distinguish those processes that are accessible to consciousness and those that are not. Neisser, for example, assumes that the product of preattentive (preconscious) processes are holistic, vague, and unelaborated. It is not at all certain that current research on reading and language production and comprehension will bear out this assumption. Miller (1962), following Freud, set a distinct boundary between preconscious and unconscious processes, implying that the latter are inaccessible. The evidence suggests that accessibility of unconscious processes shades from the readily accessible to the inaccessible. In what follows I shall have repeated occasion to use the various different terms of consciousness as they occur in context. However, the intent, from my vantage point, is to distinguish only between conscious and unconscious processes at this time. The latter include these that are not available to conscious experience, be they feature analyzers, deep syntactic structures, affective appraisals, computational processes, language production systems, action systems of many kinds, or whatever.

Much of what we know and say today about consciousness has been known and said in the past 100 years by Wundt, the Würzburgers, Lashley, and many others. I only want to summarize the high points of a modern view of consciousness as it has developed, or revived, during the development of a disciplined and highly structured new view of cognitive psychology.

The development of this viewpoint was tentative, as we would expect it to be against the background of the established dogma of behaviorism in the United States. In 1962, George A. Miller, one of the prophets of the new mentalism of the 1970s, started off his discussion of consciousness by suggesting that we "ban the word [consciousness] for a decade or two until we can develop more precise terms for the several uses which 'consciousness' now obscures" (1962). More than a decade has passed and we seem to be doing as prescribed without any intervening banishment. Most current thought on the topic was, as a matter of fact, well summarized by Miller.

Following William James, Miller stressed the selective functions of consciousness—the notion that only some part of all the possible experiences that are available at any point in time and space is selected for conscious expression. Miller also noted what I will stress again later, that "the selective function of consciousness and the limited span of attention are complementary ways of talking about the same thing." And, with Lashley, he reminds us that "[it] is the *result* of thinking, not the process of thinking that appears spontaneously in consciousness."

That last statement is important because it restates the new mentalism discussed in Chapter 2. "Thinking" or cognition or information processing, for the psychologist, refers to complex transformations on internal and external objects, events, and relations. These processes are not conscious; they are, in the first instance, theoretical constructions ascribed to the mental system.

The important advances in our excursions into consciousness must come through the usual interplay of empirical investigation and imaginative theory. The functions of consciousness are slowly being investigated, and the beginnings of theoretical integrations of the concept of consciousness into cognitive models are emerging.

As a prolegomenon to theory and better understanding of private knowledge, Natsoulas (1970) has examined the content of "introspective awareness." Although he does not present us with any conclusions, Natsoulas has provided a partial list of the problems that psychologists and philosophers encounter when they want to deal directly with these contents. We have, in general, not gone far beyond a listing, since it is obviously too early to argue for a specific model of private experience or consciousness—it does not exist, not even in the broadest outline. However, some of the necessary first steps have been taken to build some of the components that such a theory must accommodate. At the same time, psychologists are becoming sensitive to the need for a critical evaluation of common sense and philosophical notions about consciousness. Many phenomenologically oriented philosophers and psychologists are still wedded to a Wundtian idea that psychology should be the study of conscious mental events, whereas unconscious (mental) mechanism are to be left to some other world, such as physiology.

In modern theory one of the most influential books, Neisser's *Cognitive Psychology* (1967), is strangely circumspect about the problem of consciousness. Was it too early then to talk openly about the

Imperial Psychology's clothes? Not that Neisser avoids the subject; he clearly talks about consciousness, although we come upon it in circuitous ways. In his final chapter Neisser tackles the relationship between iconic memory and consciousness; he comes to consciousness through the attentive processes in visual perception and then to memory. He notes that the constructive processes in memory "themselves never appear in consciousness, their products do." And, in rational problem solving, the executive processes "share many of the properties of focal attention in vision and of analysis-by-synthesis in hearing." Noting the distinction between primary and secondary processes (cf. also Garner, 1974), he asserts that rational and therefore presumably conscious thought operate as a secondary process— elaborating often unconscious, probably unlearned primary process operations in the Freudian sense. The products of the primary process alone, preceding consciousness and attention, are only "fleetingly" conscious unless elaborated by secondary processes. By implication the elaboration by secondary processes is what produces fully conscious events. By tentative implication primary processes are "like" preattentive processes in vision and hearing; the conscious processes are "like" focal attention. The secondary processes elaborate and select. I shall present similar arguments from Posner and Shallice shortly. However, Neisser's contribution to the study of consciousness is in his discussion of preattentive processes and focal attention. When we turn to these processes, the clues from the final chapter open up a major contribution to the theory of consciousness. I apologize for the talmudic exegesis before coming to this point, but it does, I believe, illustrate the gingerly and skitterish way in which psychologists, until recently, have permitted themselves to talk about consciousness.

In Chapter 4, Neisser starts by taking the term "focal attention" straight from Schachtel (1959), a psychoanalyst whose history has not prevented a frank discussion of these forbidden topics. If you will, in what follows, permit the free translation of "attention" into consciousness, you will note why Neisser's contribution is important.

First, "attention . . . is an allotment of analyzing mechanisms to a limited region of the field." In other words, consciousness is a limited capacity mechanism. On the other hand, preattentive processes (i.e., processes that are not in attention, but precede it) form the objects of attention. Some of these preattentive processes (the primary processes of the final chapter) are innate. Many actions are under such preattentive control. Walking, driving, and many others are "made without the use of focal attention." There are processes that run off outside of consciousness (unconsciously), while others do not. "More permanent storage of information requires an act of attention." Transfer to permanent storage requires consciousness, as some decisional processes apparently do. And, harking back to another era, "the processes of attentive synthesis often lead to an internal verbalization." We often talk about the contents of consciousness.

In summary, Neisser's interpretation is in concord with much modern speculation about the role of consciousness. It is a limited capacity mechanism, often synonymous with the notion of attentional mechanisms. The processes that may enter the conscious state are secondary processes, secondary in elaboration and time to primary, preattentive processes that are unconscious, sometimes innate, and often the result of automatization. Consciousness is a state of structures that permits decision processes of some types to operate; it makes it possible for outputs from different systems to be integrated and for transfers to long-term storage systems to take place.[2]

Among the important attempts specifically to incorporate awareness notions into contemporary cognitive theory, Shallice (1972) has argued for the necessity of studying phenomena of consciousness if for no other reasons than that a number of concepts exist in current psychological theory that require the implicit or explicit postulation of some consciousness mechanisms. Among these are the postulation of conscious rehearsal in primary memory and the frequent equation of attention and consciousness (cf., for example, Mandler, 1974); others are methodological, as in experiments that require subjects to monitor private experiences (e.g., Sperling, 1967). In his theoretical development Shallice argues for an isomorphism between phenomenal experience and information-processing concepts. Specifically, he develops in some detail the notion that the content of consciousness can be identified with a selector input that first determines what particular action system will become dominant and then sets the goal for the action system.

Another approach, derived from problems of attention, has been mounted by Posner and his associates. They have focused on the mental operations that are characterized by interference effects or, in other words, by a limited capacity mechanism that may be related to the "subjective experience of the unity of consciousness" (Posner and Keele, 1970). By studying the processes that interfere one with another and showing how limited capacity is assigned to different functions, we can "connect the operations of this limited capacity mechanism to intention, awareness, storage and other traditional functions of consciousness" (Posner and Keele, 1970).

Shallice and Posner deny any attempt to specify a mechanism of consciousness or private experience that is coextensive with common language uses of the concept. The attempt is, so to speak, from the

[2]In a personal communication Neisser has indicated that he does *not* believe that consciousness is a useful concept for a stage of mental processing and that his avoidance of the concept has been deliberate rather than unconscious.

bottom up, trying to specify with some rigor some of the mechanisms that may be isomorphic with consciousness and trying to learn more about their operation within theoretical systems.

Posner and Boise (1971), in their ingenious study of the components of attention, have noted that "attention in the sense of central processing capacity is related to mental operations of which we are conscious, such as rehearsing or choosing a response . . .," Conversely, they noted that the contact between input and long-term memory is not part of this attentional (conscious) process and, in fact, the conscious component of the processing mechanism occurs as a result rather late in the sequence of "attentional" events. Posner and Synder (1975) have summarized much of these data and extended the distinction between conscious and automatic (unconscious) processes.

Posner and Klein (1973) have summarized their interpretation of the use of "consciousness" within the context of experimental investigations. They suggest that it refers to operations such as rehearsal or priming that require access to a limited capacity system. Although the conscious processes ususally occur late in the processing sequence and follow "habitual" or preattentive encoding, they are flexible and may occur early under time pressure. Also, in a bridge to other similar views, these processes are seen as setting up required responses "without depending upon the actual release of the motor program" (Posner and Klein, 1973).

The recurrent theme of readiness for and choices among actions has also been invoked by Festinger et al. (1967). They have suggested that the conscious aspect of some perceptual phenomena partly depends on preprogrammed sets of efferent (action) programs that a particular input puts into a state of readiness for immediate use.

The limited evidence from the experimental studies and from informed theory points to extensive preconscious processing that is, under some circumstances, followed by conscious processing. Much of behavior however is automatic and does not require conscious attention. Typically, such actions are called habitual, automatic, or preprogrammed. Typically, also, they tend to be ballistic in form and are run off with little variation.

It is far beyond the scope of this chapter to discuss the problem of automaticity and the kinds of structures that occur automatically in contrast with those that require attentional, conscious work. I have discussed the issue of action systems in Chapter 2. I allude to the problem here simply to note that much of "learned" behavior and actions can be integrated into new central structures, which then become functional units represented cognitively as single chunks and manipulable consciously in the constructions of new plans and new actions. At the action side of consciousness, relatively little work has been done to describe how the limited capacity system is used in integrating representation of overt actions into larger units. Just as consciousness deals with chunks of incoming information, so must it deal with chunks of efferent actions.

In the arena of perceptual events the topic of automatic processing or encoding confronts us repeatedly as the converse of conscious processing. Posner and Warren (1972) have discussed the variety of such automatic processes involved in coding mechanisms. Generally, what is automatic is very much like what Neisser calls preattentive, parallel processes. In contrast Posner and Warren note that conscious processes are more variable and that constructions in consciousness provide the new mnemonic devices needed to store material in long-term representations. It is here that we face the insistence that new encodings for long-term storage depend on a functioning conscious system.

LaBerge (1974) has addressed the issue of automatization in a novel way—asking not only about the relation between automatization and attention, but also about the process whereby certain coding systems become automatized. He concludes that during postcriteria performance, a gradual withdrawal of attention from the particular components of a task occurs. Under this process of decreasing attention (consciousness?) the part of the processing involved in coding the particular perceptual material is being made automatic. Eventually, much of the perceptual processing can "be carried out automatically, that is prior to the focussing of attention on the processing." LaBerge also implies that this postcriterial, overlearning process produces the integration of new, higher-order units or chunks. He is obviously addressing the development of preattentive processes and also the functional unity and autonomy of these units, particularly when he notes that often "one cannot prevent the processing once it starts." There is a useful similarity between these propositions about the development of automatic encodings and our discussion of the representation of action systems in Chapter 2.

We have here a possible distinction between two kinds of unconscious (preattentive, primary) structures: those that are innate or preprogrammed, and those that, although initially in the conscious state, become, by some process such as overlearning, automatic and unconscious. Although the latter are easily brought into consciousness, it is also intuitively likely that this might be difficult, if not impossible, for the former.

It seems to be agreed that the conscious state enters into the flow of processing under certain specifiable but, at present, still not specified conditions. Certain processes operate on conscious information generated by nonconscious (preattentive) processes. However, it bears

repeating that there are important nonconscious, postattentive processes
that are operative subsequent to information generated by conscious
processes. Many of these involve actions that operate often without
conscious attention. These actions and their representation systems are,
as we have seen in Chapter 2, as complex and as finely structured as
the preattentive perceptual systems. Unfortunately, partly by accidents
of history, cognitive psychologists tend to be somewhat careless about
specifying how organisms come to act.

In summary, current thought has concentrated on the consciousness
of the perceptual or encoding side of information flow. Some attention
has been given to its functions in memory storage and retrieval. Much
is still to be done at the output side. Current notions have focussed on
the functions of consciousness as selecting encoded sensory information
and preparing choices among appropriate action or response
alternatives. Many other functions of consciousness still await detailed
analyses or may be incorrect assignments to this particular system.

Conscious Contents and Processes

Talking about consciousness, in the absence of a well-developed
theory and its relevant terminology, is most difficult and constrained
by the vagaries of ordinary language. The common usage frequently
talks about consciousness as a space, a place, or even a homunculus. I
do not want to imply any of these allusions, but I will often use
common expressions that may convey the wrong impression. Thus
does the common language make liars of us all. What I do want to say,
as a preliminary approach to an understanding of consciousness, is that
consciousness is a mode of processing that affects the state of a
structure. Given that conscious mode, the "contents" of consciousness
are those structures and their products that are in the conscious state.
Consciousness is limited in capacity because of the limitations on the
conscious-processing mode. But consciousness is not a special place or
space or area of the mind.

My own interest in consciousness arose partly from some
considerations of the limits of attention and consciousness (Mandler,
1974). In that presentation I argued for a direct translation between
focal attention and consciousness. I suggested that some of the
so-called short-term memory phenomena are best assigned to the
limited capacity mechanism of consciousness, and that the limitations
of that single conscious system, in terms of dimensional analyses, may
serve as a bridging concept for George A. Miller's puzzle about the
similar limitations that he noted for short-term memory and absolute
judgment.

The limited capacity of "short-term" memory, the immediate
memory span, and the limitation in absolute judgment task to some

seven values or categories can be ascribed usefully to the limited capacity of conscious content. The limitation refers to the limited number of values on any single dimension (be it physical, acoustic, semantic, or whatever) that can be kept in the conscious state.

The main points of the argument relevant to the present topic concern certain distinctions among the concepts of attention, consciousness, and short-term memory. In the first instance, I want to restrict the concept of consciousness to events and operation within a limited capacity state, with the limitation referring to number of functional units or chunks that can be kept in the conscious state at any one point in time. This concept has much in common with what has been called *focal attention*. Attentional processes are the mechanisms that deal with the selection of objects or events that occur in the conscious state. Second, I want to assert a distinction between short-term memory and consciousness. The limited reach of consciousness has a respectable history, going back at least 200 years (cf. Mandler, 1974). But it is not a memory system—it does not involve any retrieval. What is in the momentary field of consciousness is not remembered; it does not have to be recalled. Other short-term memory phenomena that do not involve immediate consciousness can remain under the rubric of a *memory* concept.

None of the foregoing denies the utility of the conception of different memory systems, whether long term, working, or operational. It is probably most reasonable to consider these different "systems" on a continuum of depth of processing, as proposed by Craik and Lockhart (1972). Different types of analyses require different processing depths and processing times. But the information that, so to speak, can be "read off" the contents of consciousness is not memorial as such. Depth of processing determines how and what can be remembered. If processing time is short or encoding "superficial," and if the code decays rapidly—it will be shallow; if processing is extended or if encoding is "complex," information adequate for long-term retrieval or reconstruction will be stored. Within certain limits, the storage processes—at whatever depths—can only take place on conscious material; conversely, retrieval usually implies retrieval into the conscious field. But the memory *mechanisms* and the process that generates consciousness are two very distinct kinds of mental events.

Posner, who has contributed much to recent investigations of the structure of the limited capacity system of conscious events, suggested as early as 1967 that "operational" and "short-term" memories should be considered as different systems. The operating systems may vary à la Craik and Lockhart in their time course and their products, but they should not be confounded with the immediately given content of consciousness. The confounding of these two systems in early investigations and theories is understandable, given the very brief time course of some memory processes and the rapid changes in the focus of consciousness (attention). However, within consciousness, many different kinds of operations may be performed; consciousness is not limited in the complexity of the information it draws on—only in the amount. Consciousness is modality independent and, depending on the task facing the individual, may involve very complex and abstract operations. In general, I will prefer to use the term *consciousness* to focus attention (although they may have to be interchanged), but I will differentiate strictly between consciousness and short-term memory processes, which deal with storage and retrieval (cf. Craik and Lockhart, 1972).

I do not intend to invoke a separate processing stage or system to accommodate the concept of consciousness. Consciousness, in the first instance, refers to a state of a structure. Certain operations and processes act on these structures, which constitute conscious content. Cognitive structures, or schemas, may, under certain circumstances, become conscious (i.e., enter the conscious state); when they do not, they are, by definition, unconscious. Limited capacity refers to the number of such unitary structures that may be conscious at any one point in time. But there is not a separate system that contains the conscious contents. Instead, structures in the conscious state differ from others in that certain operations—such as storage, retrieval, and choice (see below)—may be performed on them.

It is not the intent of this chapter to discuss the origins of consciousness. It is a characteristic of the organism that certain structures can become conscious, but it is a function of human interactions with the environment that determines which structures do, in fact, become conscious. Piaget (1953) has discussed these interactions extensively and stressed the transactions among perceptions of the self, the environment, and the development of consciousness. The development of consciousness is not, from my view, some magical burgeoning of internal awareness but, instead, it is dependent on specific organism-environment interactions. These involve to a large part the internalizations of actions (cf. also Mandler, 1962a). More important, however, the conditions of personal and social development determine what can and what cannot be represented in consciousness. Depending on these conditions, different individuals, groups, and cultures will have different conscious contents—different social and cultural consciousness, different realities.

Finally, conscious contents can be spoken about. I shall discuss later the lack of any one-to-one correspondence between consciousness and language, but this should not obscure the important relationship between private conscious events and language. It is by the use of the latter that we primarily communicate our own private view of reality;

it is, in turn, by the use of language that—in the adult, at least—many conscious structures are manipulated and changed.

With these primarily definitional problems out of the way, I address first some of the ancient and admittedly complex and very special problems that the concept of consciousness poses for any psychological theory. I shall not propose any radical solutions; instead, I suggest that the problem of the private datum can be approached reasonably and analytically, rather than frantically or mystically. Next, I shall sketch some of the possible uses of consciousness in cognitive theory, followed by some suggestions for the adaptive functions of consciousness. Finally, in the last section, I present the broader problem of the flow of consciousness and its relations to limited capacity, with particular attention to special states of consciousness.

Consciousness—A Special Problem for Mental Theory

The individual experiences feelings, attitudes, thoughts, images, ideas, beliefs, and other contents of consciousness, but these contents are not accessible to anyone else. Briefly stated, that is the special problem facing psychologists. There are no evasions possible. It is not possible to build a phenomenal psychology that is shared. A *theory* of phenomena may be shared, but the private consciousness, once expressed in words, gestures, or in any way externalized, is necessarily a transformation of the private experience. No theory external to the individual (i.e., one that treats the organism as the object of observation, description, and explanation) can, at the same time, be a theory that uses private experiences, feelings, and attitudes as data (cf. Gray, 1971a). Events and objects in consciousness can never be available to the observer without having been restructured, reinterpreted, and appropriately modified by structures that are specific to the individual doing the reporting. These structures may even be specific to the kinds of experiences, feelings, and attitudes that are reported. The content of consciousness, as philosophers and psychologists have told us for centuries, is not directly available as a datum in psychology.

How are we to deal with the contents of consciousness? Can the perennial problem of private datum and public inference at least be stated concisely in order to indicate the magnitude of the problem and possible directions for future development?

We are faced with a phenomenon that might be called the uncertainty principle of psychology. Adrian (1966), for example, noted that "The particular difficulty that the questioner may influence the answer recalls the uncertainty principle in physics, which limits the knowledge we can gain about any individual particle."

There are two related problems in the study of consciousness. The first is more fundamental than the question that Adrian addresses. It is not only the case that the nature of the interrogation may affect the reported content of consciousness but, more basically, the act of examination itself may affect the individually observable conscious contents. This conjecture is reasonable, even at the level of processing capacity, since the conscious act of interrogating one's conscious content must occupy some part of the limited capacity. As a result, the available content is altered by the process of interrogation.

Given that the act of interrogation changes the content of consciousness, the source or origin of that inquiry becomes of secondary importance. The second problem to be faced is the fact that the contents of consciousness are not simply reproducible by some one-to-one mapping into verbal report. Even if these contents were always couched in language—which they surely are not—some theory of transmission would be required. As a result, we are faced with the individual's awareness of the structures that are in a conscious state, on the one hand and, on the other, with the psychologist's theoretical inference about those contents, based on whatever data, including introspective reports, are available. Both knowledges may be used as relevant to the construction of a psychology of cognition, although it may, in principle, be impossible to determine, in any exact sense, the relation between these two interpretations of consciousness.

Private experiences are important aspects of the fully functioning mental system. It is possible to get transformed reports about those events, and it should be possible to develop appropriate theories that relate contents of consciousness, their transformations, and their report. However, it is not possible to build a theory that makes direct predictions about private experience, since the outcome of those predictions cannot be inspected by the psychologist-observer.

This position does admit the development of private theories, by the individual, about himself. To the individual his experience *is* a datum and, as a consequence, his theories about his own structures are, within limits, testable by direct experience. These individual, personal theories-of-the-self are both pervasive and significant in explaining human action, but they cannot—without peril—be generalized to others or to the race as a whole (cf. Mandler and Mandler, 1974).

People's reports about their experiences, their behavior, and their actions are very frequently, and may always be, fictions or theories about those events. But only those reports are available to us. Even the introspecting individual who says that his experience conforms to certain predicted aspects is making statements about derived correspondences resulting from mental transformations. Indirect scientific predictions about experiences are possible, but the test of those predictions is one step removed from the actual experiences, as are all predictions about the values of theoretical entities. If the behaviorist revolution, with all the negative influences it has had on the development of a fully theoretical psychology, has had one positive effect, it is this realization that even the complete acceptance of the importance of private experience does not thereby make it a possible end point for a scientific theory.

Some Uses of Consciousness

One of the important processes in which consciousness intervenes is in the testing of potential action choices and the appraisal of the situational givens. The relation between choice and consciousness has, as we have seen, motivated much of the recent research. The analysis of situations and appraisal of the environment, on the other hand, goes on mainly at the nonconscious level. In any case, the outcomes of these analyses may be available in consciousness, and the effect of potential actions on the present situation can be estimated and evaluated. Potential choices are given the opportunity to be evaluated against potential outcomes in consciousness. This delay produces reflective consideration and may, in fact, be responsible for greater "freedom" of action (cf. Mandler and Kessen, 1974).

Much of what is often considered to be the meaning of the commonsense term "thinking" is what takes place in consciousness when the outcome of different structures, and even in some cases their composition, are evaluated and decisions are made. It is possible for the cognitive system to call for the testing of specific outcomes while temporarily blocking output from the system as a whole, to compare the consequences of different outcomes and to choose outcomes that produce one or another desired alternative. The notion of choice would be entirely within the context of modern choice theories (e.g., Luce, 1959; Tversky, 1972) and the choice itself, of course, would go through some "unconscious" cognitive structures before a "decision" is made. However, consciousness permits the comparison and inspection of various outcomes so that the choice systems, which may, in fact, be "unconscious," can operate on these alternatives.

It appears that one of the functions of the consciousness mechanism is to bring two or more (previously unconscious) mental contents into direct juxtaposition. The phenomenal experience of choice, as a matter of fact, seems to demand exactly such an occurrence. We usually do not refer to a choice unless there is a "conscious" choice between two or more alternatives. The attribute of "choosing" is applied to a decision process between two items on a menu, several possible television programs, or two or more careers, but not to the decision process that decides whether to start walking across a street with the right or left foot, whether to scratch one's ear with a finger or the ball of the hand, or whether to take one or two sips from a cup of hot coffee. I would argue that the former cases involve the necessity of deciding between two or more choices presented to a choice mechanism at the same time, whereas the latter involve only the situationally predominant action. However, these cases may be transferred to the conscious choice state if and when certain conditions of possible consequences and immediate adaptability supervene. Given a hot cup of coffee so labeled, I may "choose" to take one very small sip, or I may "choose" to start with my right foot in a 100-meter race, given certain information on its advantage to my time in the distance. In other words, consequences and social relevance determine which choices are conscious. More important, however, the mechanisms of choice (including the various theories of choice behavior) are not conscious. It is presumably the operation of these mechanisms on material in the conscious state that give the epiphenomenal experience of free choice, the appearance that someone (the agent) is doing the choosing. He or she is but, by the operation of unconscious mechanisms, which therefore gives the appearance of voluntary choice among the conscious alternatives. Mental mechanisms "choose" among both conscious and unconscious events.

The so-called mentalism that philosophers talk about often refers to these "thought" processes, the outcome of unconscious mental processes that are evaluated in the "conscious" system. However, to mistake conscious mental events for much more complex nonconscious structures is surely in error and leads to the kind of naive mentalism shown in the works of some philosophers of the mind.

Evaluative activities often act on conscious content, but evaluative activities also may take place at an "unconscious" level. Clearly, many cognitive structures that lead to certain outcomes and the anticipation of these outcomes (a scanning ahead of a particular structure) may switch the system from one structure to another. However, these changes are not available to direct inspection and are only available to indirect inspection by the process of hypothesizing their constitution and testing these hypotheses.

If the only difference between these two kinds of evaluative actions and choices is that some take place in consciousness and others do not, the end result would be a rather puny achievement for so imposing a mechanism as consciousness. I would propose initially two arguments for the distinction between conscious and unconscious evaluations and choice. First, many relational processes operate primarily, if not exclusively, on conscious content. I have already indicated this particular argument in the case of simple choice. However, there are other relational operators that seem to do their work primarily on conscious content. In addition to choice, these include evaluation, comparison, grouping, categorization, and serial ordering. In short, practically all novel relational orderings require that the events to be ordered must be simultaneously present in the conscious field. This applies to choice as well as to relational concepts stored in memory, for example. Needless to say, there are many relational judgments that do not require conscious comparisons. To say that "a dog is an animal" makes use of established structures and does not require a new relational operation. However, to say that "Rex looks like a cross between a dachshund and a spaniel" might require conscious juxtaposition. Once relations (be they superordinate, subordinate, opposites, or whatever) have been established and stored, subsequent evaluations are frequently unconscious.

The second argument for the importance of consciousness suggests that choice and other processes that operate on conscious content are dependent on those structures that *can* enter the conscious state. Only the structures that can become conscious can be subjected to choice activities. Thus situational and social relevance determine the content of consciousness and the "ideational" operations that can be performed on the individual's reality.

The Possible Adaptive Functions of Consciousness

We may also look at some of these uses from the point of view of their adaptive significance. Probably because of the unpleasantness of the past 50 to 60 years, relatively little has been said about the adaptive functions of consciousness. Miller (1962) has described them in general terms and Gray (1971) has called for a more intensive look at the evolutionary significance of conscious systems. In general, however, American psychologists particularly have shied away from looking at the functional significance of consciousness. This is at least surprising, since we are faced with a characteristic of the human species that is without exception. Given the weak evidence that psychologists have accepted as indicants for the evolutionary significance of such vague concepts as aggression and intelligence, why avoid a phenomenon as indisputably characteristic of the species as consciousness? The answer lies partly in the behaviorist dogma that consciousness is epiphenomenal and, by implication, has no adaptive significance. It is partly in opposition to the dogma that I want to suggest some possible directions in which speculations and investigations about the adaptiveness of consciousness might go.

There are various functions that the consciousness system may perform, all of which may be said to have evolutionary significance and all of which have varying degrees of evidence for their utility and theoretical significance.

1. The first and most widely addressed function of consciousness considers its role in choice and the selection of action systems. Decisions often are made on the basis of possible outcomes, desirable outcomes, and appropriateness of various actions to environmental demands. Such a description comes close to what is often called "covert trial and error" behavior in the neobehaviorist literature. This function permits the organism more complex considerations of action-outcome contingencies than the simple feedback concept of reinforcement does, which alters the probability of one or another set of actions. It also permits the consideration of possible actions that the organism has never before performed, thus eliminating the overt testing of possible harmful alternatives. In this sense the process is similar to the TOTE system of Miller, Galanter, and Pribram (1960).

2. Within the same general framework as the first function, consciousness makes possible the modification and interrogation of long-range plans rather than immediate action alternatives. In the hierarchy of actions and plans in which the organism engages, this slightly different function makes it possible to organize disparate action systems in the service of a higher plan. For example, in planning a drive to some new destination, we might consider subsets of the route or, in devising a new recipe, the creative chef considers the interactions of several known culinary achievements. Within the same realm consciousness makes it possible to retrieve and consider modifications in long-range planning activities. These, in turn, might be modified in light of other evidence, either from the immediate environment or from long-term storage.

3. In considering actions and plans consciousness participates in retrieval programs from long-term memory, even though these retrieval programs and strategies themselves are usually not conscious. Thus, frequently, although not always, the retrieval of information from long-term storage is initiated by relatively simple commands—in program language rather than machine language. These may be simple instructions such as "What is his name?" or "Where did I read about that?" or more complex instructions, such as "What is the relation between this situation and previous ones I have encountered?" This process has the adaptive function of permitting simple addresses to complex structures.

4. Comments on the organism's current activities occur in consciousness and use available cognitive structures to construct some storable representation of current activity. Many investigators have suggested that these new codings and representations always take place in the conscious state. Processes such as mnemonic devices and storage strategies apparently require the intervention of conscious structures. Certainly many of them, such as categorization and mental images, do.

Once this new organization of information is stored it may be retrieved for a variety of important purposes.

First, in the social process, prior problem solutions and other memories may be brought into the conscious state and, together with an adequate system of communication, such as human language generate tremendous benefits to cooperative social efforts. Other members of the species may receive solutions to problems, thus saving time, if nothing else; they may be apprised of unsuccessful alternatives or, more generally, participate in the cultural inheritance of the group. This process requires selection and comparison among alternatives retrieved from long-term storage, all of which apparently takes place in consciousness.

Second, both general information and specific sensory inputs may be stored in propositional or analogue form. The rerepresentation at some future time makes possible decision processes that depend on comparisons between current and past events, and the retrieval of relevant or irrelevant information for current problem solving.

5. Another aspect that consciousness apparently permits is a "troubleshooting" function for structures normally not represented in consciousness. There are many systems that cannot be brought into consciousness and, probably, most systems that analyze the environment in the first place have that characteristic. In most of these cases only the product of cognitive and mental activities are available to consciousness; among these are sensory analyzers, innate action patterns, and language production systems. In contrast, many systems are generated and built with the cooperation of conscious processes, but later become nonconscious or automatic. These latter systems may apparently be brought into consciousness, particularly when they are defective in their particular function (cf. also Vygotsky, 1962). We all have had experiences of automatically driving a car, typing a letter, or even handling cocktail party conversation, and being suddenly brought up short by some failure such as a defective brake, a stuck key, or a "You aren't listening to me." At that time the particular representations of actions and memories involved are brought into play in consciousness, and repair work gets under way. Thus structures that are not species specific and general but are the result of experience can be inspected and reorganized more or less easily.

Many of these functions permit the organism to react reflectively instead of automatically, a distinction that has frequently been made between humans and lower animals. All of them permit more adaptive transactions between the organism and its environment. Also, in general, the functions of consciousness permit a focusing on the most important and species relevant aspects of the environment. The notion that attentional mechanisms select personally relevant materials and

events is commonplace in attentional research. The processes that
define such relevance are generally unknown, although we can assume
that an adaptive function of selection into consciousness exists.
However, there remains the unexplored mystery of the processes of
information reduction that select some aspect of the surround.

The need for a rapid reduction of all the sensory information that is
available to an organism at any given point in time and space is
obvious. If we were conscious of all the information available at the
sensory surface, we would never escape from the blooming confusion
generated by our environment. Consciousness (or attention) is highly
selective. The sensory systems themselves are, of course, selective in
the first instance. The evolutionary process has generated organisms
that register only a limited amount of the information available in their
environment. How these limitations from the environment to the
sensory surface have developed has been the subject of some biological
speculations. The reduction from the sensory surface to consciousness
is even more spectacular, but we have few clues for the evolutionary
reason of this reduction. We know that it exists (e.g., Miller, 1956;
Mandler, 1974), and attention theorists have been concerned primarily
with the filtering mechanisms that reduce the sensory information to
the few chunks of information that reach consciousness. But why that
number should be 5 or 6 or 7 and not 3 or 12 is still shrouded in
mystery.

The Limitation of conscious Capacity and the Flow of Consciousness

One of the most perplexing results of experimental studies of,
consciousness has been the counterintuitive notion that mental
contents that enter the conscious state seem to be discrete, relatively
short, and quite transient. How does this contrast with consciousness
in the common discourse? There it is described as continuous, flowing,
and extending without break throughout our waking hours—and just
as flowing and continuous in our dreams. William James aptly called it
"the stream of thought, of consciousness, or of subjective life." How
can we reconcile these two impressions?

Before tackling that particular problem, consider the role of
consciousness in our perception of time, or better, duration. For this
purpose, I shall adopt the theory of time duration proposed by
Ornstein (1969). This review relates the time experience to "the
mechanisms of attention, coding, and storage" (1969). Ornstein's
central thesis is that storage size is the basis for the construction of the
duration of an interval. The notion of storage size derives directly from
recent theory that emphasizes the compact organization of information

in memory and experience. The more different unrelated units there are, the greater the storage size, the more highly organized the units, objects, or events are, the fewer units or chunks, and the smaller the storage size. As storage size of the material in consciousness increases, the duration experience lengthens. What changes storage size are increases or decreases in the amount of information received, changes in the coding or chunking of input or, as Ornstein has shown experimentally, influencing the memory of the interval after it has passed. As Ornstein summarized in a later book (1972), "the more organized . . . the memory . . . the shorter the experience of duration."

Generally, then, the experience of duration (in consciousness) is a construction drawing on immediately pressing factors (such as attentiveness) but primarily on our stored long-term memory. Duration is constructed, first in the momentary consciousness, and second in the retrieval of events and codes that are recalled during the "construction" of a past interval. The contents of consciousness thus determine the experience of duration. Restricting these contents shortens duration; expanding them by, for example, increasing the complexity of an experience, lengthens duration. Vigilance, which increases expectancy of some event, will lengthen duration; Ornstein uses the example of the "watched pot." On the other hand, condensing some experience into a very brief code ("I made breakfast") condenses the duration. Ornstein and others note that our Western linear mode of constructing duration is not the only mode, and that present-centeredness is not only possible but, in fact, the mode for cultures other than ours. The concatenation of limited conscious capacity, on the one hand, and of the same consciousness serving as a vehicle for constructing experience of duration, on the other, brings us back to the disjunction between discrete consciousness and the flow of consciousness.

There is, in principle, no objection to constructing a flow model of consciousness out of the discrete units of attention or consciousness. The metaphor that comes to mind is a simplistic view of modern conceptions of light, which may be described either in terms of particles or in terms of waves. Again borrowing from physics, we then may metaphorically speak of the quantum of consciousness on the one hand and the flow of consciousness on the other. Another possible metaphor is that of the illusion of moving pictures, which consist of individual frames. Neither metaphor probably does justice to the phenomenon, as no metaphor ever does. In particular, it is likely that instead of individual quanta or frames, the flow of consciousness frequently may involve the successive sampling of materials across a continuous retrieval of connected material from long-term storage. Such a phenomenon would depend on the retrieval strategies being used on long-term storage as well as on the nature of the material being sampled. In the case of consciousness of externally generated events (e.g., somebody else's speech), the overlapping moving model may be the most appropriate, whereas in attempting the retrieval of a specific chunk of knowledge, the retrieval may be discontinuous.

Because of the limited capacity characteristics of discrete consciousness, I shall use the figure of speech of the conscious frame. We still carry with us the unsolved problem of the content of that slice of consciousness. For the time being we can only allude to the probability that it involves units or chunks of unitary aggregates of information.

Regardless of one's view of the conscious frame as sampling discrete, overlapping, or continuous elements of mental content or environmental input, our view requires a continuous interchange between long-term storage and the conscious state. In the case of an exclusively internal dialogue between the two, material is brought into consciousness and then returned to long-term storage either in essentially unchanged form or after some operations may have been performed on it while in consciousness. Thus the memory of a friend brought into consciousness may be combined with a new insight that he resembles a recent acquaintance, and then the information is returned with the new relationship coded with it. Or information from storage is brought (within consciousness) in conjunction with new information currently being processed from the environment (e.g., "Joe has grown a beard") and then returned to storage newly coded. Many experimental studies of memory require exactly this retrieval from storage and combination, in consciousness, with new information, such as that the word belongs to a particular list or category, or occurs at a particular serial position. The distinction between internal and external information is not a very clean one. Clearly, external events do not enter into consciousness as "pure" perceptions; instead, they are coded and identified in terms of existing preattentive structures before they enter consciousness.

In general this position joins the long tradition of cognitive and phenomenological psychologists in asserting the importance of the role of consciousness in developing knowledge of oneself and the environment. I do not think that consciousness is primary or sufficient; it is one mode of processing. Just because some evaluation or knowledge does not enter the conscious state does not permit a pejorative evaluation of such "automatic" or "unconscious" processing.

Conscious Stopping

One special reason why the view of the conscious frame is useful is that it permits a consideration of special conditions; when the flow of consciousness stops, single frames enter into consciousness and remain there. Experimental psychologists have paid some attention to this phenomenon, as in the concept of maintaining or primary rehearsal, in which material is repeated but does not enter into long-term storage (Craik and Watkins, 1973; Woodward, Bjork, and Jongeward, 1973). However, the major source of knowledge of this phenomenon comes from esoteric psychologies and meditative methods.

The best objective presentation of these methods is once again provided by Ornstein (1972). He reviews meditation techniques dispassionately and positively. However, in reading Ornstein's description of these methods, a recurrent theme may be discerned. The achievement of the special kinds of conscious states that are claimed to occur seem to depend, without exception, on the unique attempt to stop the flow of ordinary consciousness—to concentrate on the frame, to hold it fixed in the focus of consciousness. The very difficulty of achieving the initial, apparently trivial, exercises of these techniques suggests the difficulty of stopping the flow. It requires total attention to a single, restricted set of limited thoughts or perceptions. In Zen, the exercises start with counting breaths and then go on to concentrate on the process of breathing. Yogic meditation uses the *mantra,* "sonorous, flowing words which repeat easily." Some of the Sufi practices are seen as an "exercise for the brain based on repetition." The Christian mystic St. John of the Cross says (quoted in Ornstein, 1972): "Of all these forms and manners of knowledge the soul must strip and void itself and it must strive to lose the imaginary apprehension of them, so that there may be left in it no kind of impression of knowledge, nor trace of thought.. . .This cannot happen unless the memory can be annihilated in all its forms.. . ." Or, as Ornstein points out, many prayers are monotonous, repetitive chants. In summary, "[The] common element in these diverse practices seems to be the active restriction of awareness to one single, unchanging process, and the withdrawal of attention from ordinary thought" (Ornstein, 1972). And again: "The specific object used for meditation is much less important than the maintenance of the object as the single focus of awareness during a long period of time. . . ."

I suggest that the "object of the single focus" must be no more than a frame of consciousness; in fact, it is restricted by the very limits that the limited capacity mechanism has been shown to exhibit. We could not meditate on an event that, at first, contains more than five to seven chunks. The observations that Ornstein and many others have reported suggest that it is possible to stop the flow of consciousness to keep a single frame of consciousness in focus for extended periods of time. However, such an experience should be a very *different* form of consciousness; the normal form is the flow. We thus experience this new consciousness only after the extensive practice it requires. But we must also experience a very different content of consciousness. Given that the single "object" is held in consciousness, many new and different aspects of it then may be discovered.

Consider the possibility that at first any such object consists of several related qualities (or chunks). Presumably, as these various attributes are related one to the other, the new relations form a more compact perception, and the number of chunks, as it were, is reduced. This opens up the possibility of new chunks or attributes to enter into the single frame. New relationships are discovered and again coalesce. Under these circumstances we may go through a process of structuring and restructuring, of discovering aspects of objects or events that would not normally be available during the flow of consciousness. Once this ability has been achieved, we should, in principle, be able to use the special consciousness to stop the flow of events, examine new nuances, and then continue. Thus a limited set of attributes within a single frame is available at first; then new aspects enter, and old ones drop away. The complexities of a rose, a face, or a cake "become conscious." This seems to be taking place in what Ornstein calls the "opening up" of awareness, which follows the "turning off" phase and provides the individual with a different state of comprehension of ongoing actions and events. Quoting Ornstein (1972) again: "The concentrative form turns off the normal mode of operation and allows a sensitivity to subtle stimuli which often go unnoticed in the normal mode.. . . It also produces an *after-effect* of 'fresh' perception when the practitioner returns to his usual surroundings." All I wish to add to Ornstein's insightful discussion is the possibility that modern psychology may define the process wherein this attentiveness occurs and also the processes that generate new perceptions and sensitivities. Meditative techniques provide us, in this fashion, with new insights into a mechanism that otherwise seems mundane and restrictive. There need not be anything mysterious about meditation, nor anything pedestrian about an information-processing analysis of consciousness.

The enriching of knowledge though meditative experiences or, as we might call it, conscious stopping, should be put into the proper context of the ordinary, normal means of enriching experience. Without doubt, we enrich our experience and knowledge about the world around us without resorting to meditation. We can, without special preparation, perceive new facets about the world, about other people, and even about ourselves as we gain new perspectives, new ways of structuring our experience. A main difference between the normal and the meditative enrichment is that the former deals with an open system, and the latter deals with a closed one. Our enrichment in knowledge and appreciation of a lover, a novel, a science, an occupation always

occurs in new contexts, sometimes widely different, sometimes only
minutely so. But the relationship between the object or event and
ourselves is changed continuously by our mutual relations with the rest
of the world. The new information is, in a way, always acquired in
new contexts. What seems to distinguish this usual accretion from the
meditative one is that the latter is a closed system; we are restricted to
those relationships among qualities and attributes that are given in that
object or situation. This restriction of possible relations presumably
provides not only the illusion but possibly also the reality of depth of
perception that the special experience provides. In contrast, artists and
scientists, for example, apparently achieve the same depth of
perception of special objects or events without the meditative
experience.

Ornstein's notion that the experience of duration is constructed,
based on the storage size of the cognitive structures that constitute an
interval, may be applied directly to the flow and frame aspects of
consciousness. In the open system flow time experience is constructed
across frames out of cognitive structures that will—to varying degrees
—occupy the capacity of the limited capacity frame. Consider listening
to a lecture on difficult but interesting material. As the speaker
proceeds, information is transmitted at a great rate, taking up the full
capacity of each frame of consciousness. In Ornstein's terms storage of
information is near a maximum. As a result, the duration experience
increases. In contrast, the redundant speaker makes fewer demands on
each frame; the very ability to approach a difficult subject slowly and
cumulatively permits us to use less of the full capacity of the frame, or
—another possibility—the capacity is filled less frequently in physical
time and fewer frames are expended. In any case, the experience of
duration is more extended in the former than in the latter case.

It is interesting to speculate that Ornstein's storage metaphor may be
directly translated into the frame locution. Since consciousness is
necessary for the transfer of information to long-term storage, complex
(many chunks and relations) information requires more frames for the
transfer function, as does rapidly presented information (more chunks
per unit physical time). It appears that the storage metaphor is quite
consistent with the frame-flow notion of consciousness. In the latter
mode the construction of time depends on the sheer number of frames
of consciousness activated or utilized during a specified interval.
Parenthetically, this position also indicates the independence of the
conscious frame from physical time. The specious present, the limited
capacity mechanism, does not have a time constant. Frames are
replaced under a variety of conditions, all of which seem to depend on
using up their capacity; a new perceptual dimension, another class of

stimulation, a sudden demand for focusing (attention), and many others will demand a shift to another content of consciousness, which is perceived as another *moment* of consciousness.

Finally, I note the drastic changes in time perception that take place as a result of meditative experience. Given that the flow of frames is radically altered, we would naturally expect a similar and unusual change in duration experiences. The direction can be either way. Holding a single unit of consciousness and impeding the flow may collapse the duration experience, whereas the eventual ability to manipulate the flow of consciousness may change the usual duration experience with its apparently rather constant rate of change into a more variable ebb and flow of "short" and "long" durations. Instead of the flow of frames during normal states, during meditation the change from one conscious content to another occurs infrequently in physical time. The slow changes in perceptual structures that I suggested earlier for the meditative phase thus produce unusual duration experiences.

It is intriguing to speculate that the action of hallucinogenic or "mind-expanding" drugs has a similar locus and effect. Changes in perceptual processes coexist with changes in the experience of duration. It has been argued that these drugs often produce in the instant the experiences that meditative methods generate with extensive practice. It is possible that some drugs actually slow the flow of conscious frames, and that some of the lasting effects of these drugs may be due to structural changes in control of the flow of consciousness.

Chapter IV
Mind and Emotion

In this chapter I shall briefly describe the aspects of the general system of mental organization that are responsible for the production of the subset of behavior and experience often called "emotional." Again, the purpose is to explain thought and action and not to explain or analyze common language concepts, be they modern or ancient, although there is a specific subset of behaviors and experience that has a large overlap between the ordinary notion of emotion and the more refined use of that term by psychologists. Specifically, I shall discuss those interactions between the arousal system and the cognitive-interpretive system, that produce a set of behavior and experiences that overlaps with the concept of emotion. Given that warning and having bounded my interest, I shall use the terms "emotion" and "emotional behavior" fairly freely, as long as it is understood that I am primarily interested in certain specifiable outcomes of the parts of the mental system.

I shall avoid saying two things in this context: first, that this is a theory of emotion, and second, that mental states are unanalyzable events. It is important to emphasize the latter: mental states are to be explained as any other part of a theoretical system; they have no special status. This is my main point of contention with psychologists and philosophers who so often are entranced by their own and other people's minds—when they admit their existence.

My first disavowal is obvious. I do not claim a theory of emotion, but I do believe that many of the parameters discussed below are, in fact, operative when we talk about "emotions." My efforts, as everybody's, are impervious to examples of experiences and behaviors that are emotion in common parlance but do not fit the system. No system can or should aspire to such pretensions.

I do know one fact about this system and about all the other systems of "emotion"—they are all, to some extent, wrong. The joy is to try to be a little less wrong next time around.

What follows is first a summary statement about arousal, cognition, and consciousness, since these are active in the generation of the particular experiences and actions that I want to subsume under "emotion." Following this summary, I shall develop in detail particular functions of the cognitive-interpretive system and of consciousness. In subsequent chapters I shall discuss the relation between this point of view and others, the evidence available, the functions of arousal, the special relationship between interruption and emotion, the ubiquitous case of anxiety and, finally, some further extensions of the principles generated in the earlier chapters.

Mental Organization and "Emotion"[1]

Arousal

The particular human behaviors and experiences of interest to us occur subsequent to the activities of the autonomic nervous system, particularly its sympathetic division. I shall refer to this activity as arousal. Autonomic nervous system activity acts on visceral receptors. The resulting effective event is the perception of autonomic activity, which—except for some special states such as sexual arousal—is registered as undifferentiated arousal, varying primarily in intensity.

Some of the conditions that lead to automatic arousal are known in detail but not in principle. In the human being many of these conditions depend on cognitive transformation. However, a broad category of such conditions that also appear to have reasonable adaptive and evolutionary backing can be found in the interruption of ongoing plans and actions. Interruption and its consequences will be discussed fully in Chapter 7. It refers to the blocking or interference with any well-established action sequence or cognitive plan. One of the consequences of interruption is autonomic arousal.

Autonomic arousal has two main adaptive functions. One is embodied in the principle of homeostasis and the physiological readiness of the organism. The other is a signal to the mental organization for attention, alertness, and scanning of the environment.

[1]I have presented an earlier view of the production of emotion in Mandler (1962b). The present treatment is a descendant but not a copy of that previous statement. I should also note that the theoretical notions presented then and, by definition, those presented here were to a large part a result of what I learned from the insights produced by Schachter's work on cognitive and physiological determinants of emotional states. A proper appreciation of the influence of his work on current views of emotion will be found in Chapter 5.

The latter function demands interpretation and analysis of the environment by the various sensory and cognitive systems following autonomic activation. This information-seeking activity may inquire either about the sources of autonomic arousal or generally about the present state of the environment and the organism.

Cognitive Interpretation

Cognitive interpretation of the situation and of the organism's own actions and thoughts involve interpretive structures, some prewired reactions to classes of events, and evaluation of the perception of self, its state, and actions. Among the classes of stimuli that may generate automatic cognitive reactions are expressive movements that carry with them messages arising out of the species' history. However, interpretations of the situation and reinterpretations may alter such reactions.

Among the perceptions that influence the cognitive interpretation of the environment and situations is the class of actions that are appropriate or inappropriate to the situation. The perception of the unavailability of appropriate actions—the cognition of helplessness—is often coextensive with the commonsense description and experience of anxiety.

The experience of emotion and the conditions for many emotional behaviors are the interactional result of autonomic arousal and cognitive interpretation. The former determines the special visceral quality of these experiences as well as their intensity, while the latter affects the quality and category of the experience.

Consciousness

Emotional *experience* occurs by definition in consciousness. Both the perception of arousal and the results of cognitive interpretive activities are registered and integrated prior to or in consciousness. Output from consciousness is frequently coded by our language systems into socially sanctioned and culturally determined categories. These categories subsume relatively large subsets of these "emotional" experiences; their usage is determined by conscious content as well as by the initial interpretation of the surround. In other words, verbal expressions of emotion depend on prior mental states and on direct environmental categorization.

One set of the cognitions operating in human beings is concerned with the further interpretation of their own experiences and actions. These hypotheses about the system's own operation—issuing in consciousness—are not necessarily equivalent to an accurate description of the events or to a testable theory about these events. Many components of these self-descriptive systems may, however, occur outside of the conscious system and, in turn, determine evaluations and actions.

The Interaction of Arousal and Cognitive Interpretation

We assume that the two major systems involved in emotional behavior are arousal and interpretation, specifically meaning analysis. Many of the processes involved will be elaborated at greater length in Chapters 5 and 6, but the major assumption, to be documented later, will be discussed here. Emotional behavior has, as one of its necessary concomitants, the production of autonomic nervous system arousal. This arousal is nonspecific and merely sets the stage for emotional behavior and experience; the particular quality of the emotion is determined entirely by the meaning analysis, which the arousal and, more important, the general situation and cognitive states engender. The joint action of both of these systems, arousal and meaning analysis, has outputs to consciousness as well as to action systems, including language output. Thus arousal provides the emotional tone for a particular cognition, and cognition provides the quality to the emotional state.

Specific events relevant to "emotional" experience have two functions: first, they set off arousal; second, they induce a particular meaning analysis of the situation in which the individual finds himself.

As far as arousal is concerned, events may produce arousal under one of two possible conditions. First, there may be a preprogrammed, automatic release of autonomic nervous system arousal. Second, that arousal may be mediated by a meaning analysis that transforms an otherwise innocuous stimulus into a functional releaser of the autonomic nervous system. Thus there are some classes of stimuli, for example, tissue injury, loud noises, interruption of ongoing plans and behavior, and sudden loss of support, which are automatically wired to the autonomic nervous system and produce an immediate reaction in that system. On the other hand there may be objects and events that are initially innocuous, such as animals, radiators, and guns, but which, on the basis of past experience, have become, in one language, conditioned stimuli for autonomic arousal or, in our terms, are transformed into functional autonomic releasers. The complexity of the human mental organization suggests that this dichotomy is not as simple as it sounds but, rather, that there is a continuum from innate to experiential factors, which are needed for a particular event to produce arousal. For example, we know that tissue injury by itself may sometimes not be a releaser for autonomic arousal (see Melzack, 1973).

But, in general, we can think of a continuum from automatic to cognitive paths that produce the input to the arousal system.

Only perceived arousal has psychological consequences, although we will note some effects of arousal on attention in Chapter 6. The arousal system leads back into the mental system, which perceives the state of arousal and feeds that back to a meaning analysis on the one hand and to consciousness on the other. However, the perceptual system may be nonoperative (e.g., because instructions or past experience have increased the threshold, or the perceptual system may be turned off, by pharmacological means). In that case, no psychological consequences ensue.

Meaning analysis presumably takes place automatically for any input that is perceived or attended. The perception of arousal sets the stage for additional analyses, a "search" for a structure that can assimilate both the external input and its analysis and the perception of arousal. Given a particular fit between the perception of arousal and a meaning analysis, a particular structure is activated and is put into a state of consciousness. When such a structure has been found, a stop rule goes into effect, and the search terminates. It is fairly obvious that there are many different stop rules in operation in our mental organization. Probably the most useful one is the search within the system for an "appropriate" structure and the stopping of the search once such a structure has been found. By "appropriate" I mean any structure that can take the inputs operating at any one time, in this case the perception of arousal as well as the meaning analysis of the situation, and that can accommodate some reasonable set of these inputs. We do not know at the present time how much of the inputs need to be accommodated by a particular structure in order for the stop rule to go into effect. In the case of instinctive behavior Bowlby (1969) has discussed some of the various stopping and starting conditions. These include many hormonal as well as environmental and other factors that are primarily involved in starting a particular instinctive sequence as, for example, the arousal of the autonomic nervous system. Also, in the case of instinctual behavior sequences, the conditions that terminate these may come from a variety of sources, most frequently from the completion of a particular sequence, as in the execution of a consummatory act. However, there are other terminating stimuli or stop rules that may be extraneous to the behavior observed. Some of these stop rules may be changes in the condition in which the individual finds himself, which then terminate the search for an appropriate structure.

Concerning the outputs from the various structures that are eventually involved, we are interested essentially in two action systems, one general and one concerned with language in particular. Action systems are of two types, particularly in the case of emotional behavior. One of them involves the automatic release of particular action systems, as in the case of sexual behavior or defensive aggression; the other includes action systems that are put into effect because certain transformations of input have taken place. In any case, there will be central structures ("motives") that will activate action systems, which will vary in the degree to which they have been influenced by past experience.

As far as output to the language system is concerned, we deal with what is often described as verbal emotional behavior. It may begin with statements such as "I feel" and may frequently make reference to the unobservable private events that we have summarized as conscious and that have varying degrees of contact with mental structures. Emotional verbal behavior varies from highly specific references to autonomic nervous system reactions such as "I can feel my heart racing" or "My stomach feels tight" to analogical discussions about the state of one's internal economy. As Skinner (1957) has sensitively discussed, the conditions under which we learn to make these referential statements are complex, since the events that control this kind of behavior and its consequences are not as available to the social environment as, for example, the contingency between the visual appearance of red objects and learning to refer to them as "red." Thus emotional statements that make references to unobserved events can be expected to be vague and to show large variance from individual to individual and even within individuals from situation to situation.

Verbal emotional behavior that is not directly descriptive typically involves a classification or interpretation of (1) the environment, or (2) the behavior of the individual. In the first class are statements such as "I feel so good the world looks beautiful to me today" or "I feel as if everybody is after me". The second type is often related to referential statements, but it also describes one's own behavior as, for example, "I have never been so happy in my life" or "I must look terrible" or "I wish I could stop running away from this situation." All of these tend to be either descriptions of one's behavior (i.e., feedback from action systems) or descriptions of tendencies or structures that may or may not be completely realized. In the area of psychotherapy extensive work has been done on the analysis of verbal behavior, and the analysis of the emotional utterances of patients is an important potential source of insight into the classification of emotional output.

I have made reference to nonverbal expressions of emotional behavior. It should be noted that along with Darwin, many psychologists have drawn attention to the similarity between certain emotional behaviors in man and in animals, and also to the possibility of classifying some of these emotional behaviors in terms of preprogrammed, instinctive categories. I shall discuss these in Chapter 6.

Another aspect of nonverbal emotional behavior that occurs as a result of autonomic arousal consists of the symptomatic aspects of arousal such as blushing, rapid eye-blinking, and even failure to control elimination. A classic aspect of related emotional behavior is the so-called startle response, studied extensively by Landis and Hunt (1939), a very stable pattern of action that includes head movements, widening of the mouth, and muscle contractions.

The most important aspect of the *quale* of an emotional experience and its accompanying behavior is the interpretation of the environment, the events that are the occasions for particular emotions. Some environmental events may automatically produce arousal and may also be subject to very little in the way of complex meaning analysis. These so-called "unlearned" emotional stimuli will be discussed again in Chapter 6, where I consider the particular characteristics of arousal, but I assume that when a stimulus has an invariant effect on the autonomic nervous system, its interpretation by the meaning system is usually also fairly constant and invariant. Thus, for lower animals, the instinctual response to species—specific "fear" stimuli—presumably involves the interpretation of the stimulus as threatening, which may be just as automatic as the arousal occurring at the same time. In many human cases some releasers also have fairly invariant interpretations. Consider, for example, the feeling of loss of support or sudden intense stimulation (which sets off the startle response).

However, even here the action of the cognitive interpretive system may be important. For example, loss of support has just been considered as an instinctive condition for an essentially negative emotional reaction, yet it is a condition for euphoria for many people when it is experienced on a roller coaster. The interpretation of the roller coaster as a positive event and the autonomic reaction that takes place at the same time produce a positive emotional response in this particular case.

The roller-coaster effect also illustrates another important aspect of meaning analysis. One of the inputs that is analyzed for the "meaning" of a particular situation is our own behavior. If we see ourselves in control of a particular situation the emotional reaction is more likely to be positive than negative. Thus the seeking out of autonomic stimulation, as in the case of the roller coaster, is a condition for positive rather than negative evaluation. Contrast this with the child who does not want to go on a roller coaster but is forced to do so; the reaction is likely to be negative. With the increasing observation of his own control of the situation, that he can "choose" to go on the roller coaster, the situation changes from negative to positive. I shall discuss this question of "control" further when dealing with the problem of anxiety and the question of helplessness.

I have now made repeated reference to the fact that one of the sources for interpretive evaluations is the person's own behavior and actions. This point of view fits well into so-called self-attribution theories of social behavior (e.g., Heider, 1958; Kelley, 1967) and more behavioristic analyses that call attention to the control of a person's action by his own behavior (e.g., Bem, 1967). These theories usually assume that some automatically engendered actions form the basis of evaluations by the actor. Our attitudes may be judged by observing our own behavior under certain conditions. These formulations fit well into the present schema, but two reservations must be entered with respect to those theories that require action prior to evaluation. First, not all, or even most, evaluations are based on self-attribution. If they were, we would be dealing with a cumbersome system. Actions have to be generated automatically, and these actions are then evaluated by the organism and form the basis of his often conscious self-perceptions and attributions. For example, some event generates my evasive action, and my perception of that action produces my evaluative attitude. In contrast, I would insist that many self-attributions are not the product of actions but may well be generated directly by cognitive structures. In other words, *one* of the sources of interpretive evaluations stems from the analysis of our own actions. It is an important source, particularly in emotional behavior, but it is not the only one. Second, it is important to note that only those actions of the agent that are, in fact, processed and perceived form the basis of these self-evaluations. In other words, we need to attend to and be conscious of our own actions in order for them to be the basis of evaluations. The clinical and theoretical literature of psychoanalysis is full of examples of individuals who are not conscious of their own actions or their meaning. In the course of therapy, these persons often learn appropriate self-attribution. Prior to such "insight," these individuals attribute or misattribute characteristics to themselves that may be generated by actions but are often directly derived from their existing long-term self-images.

Finally, I should note the continuous feedback involved in self-perception and emotion. Some cognitive interpretation of the environment produces arousal and the perception of that arousal together with some cognition of the situation generates "emotional" experience. But then the evaluation and perception of our own new "emotional" states changes and colors the original cognitive interpretation. Our original reactions of fear and joy feed back into subsequent evaluations.

Meaning Analysis and Emotion

Chapter 2 dealt with the function of meaning analysis in the mental system as a whole. I shall now relate the problem of meaning analysis to the inputs that are dominant, attention demanding, or situationally relevant in the emotional complex.

First, it should be obvious that the very complexity of inputs in the emotional situation is exactly the factor that make for the complexity and richness of emotional experience and emotional meaning. The structure of a particular input and its relation to other contemporary inputs as well as to existing mental structures provide the "meaning" of the situation. In the emotional situation I have postulated two major sources of input: cognitive evaluations and arousal. Since, in the context of our present discussion, these are necessarily contemporaneous, the meaning of the situation, or its emotional significance, will be the total structure or relationship of these various inputs and their mental consequences.

There are two possible interpretations of the cognitive-arousal interaction during meaning analysis. One could be described as passive, and the other as active. The passive interpretation suggests that at the time of inputs from both the interpretive structures and the perception of arousal, these sets of structures come into relation to each other and result in a total relational network, which is the *quale* of the emotion. Thus, if there is perception of autonomic arousal and evaluation of a particular situation as positive and joyful, then the set of relations produced by these two inputs and their interaction produces the emotional feeling of joy or elation. The experience would be different if the situation and its evaluation were the same, but with no input from the perception of arousal. In that case we would make essentially a "cold" positive evaluation of a situation without feeling of emotional intensity. Similarly, if there were only arousal with no specific evaluation in any positive or negative direction, then we would have an emotional experience that would best be described as excitement without content. However, even that situation generates some uncertainty and a search for meaning, arguing against the passive system. In summary, a passive system would take various inputs and produce a new mental organization consisting of the various input elements, but it would not involve any active organizational or structural activity on the part of the mental system.

The last sentence indicates the direction in which an active system would go. For an active system we assume that inputs from either the cognitive-interpretive system or the perceptual-arousal system are fed into existing structures based either on past experience or possibly even on innate factors. There would have to be subroutines that are question-asking within the system. These subroutines would determine which existing structures provide a "best fit" for the new input.

Instead of a passive aggregate of the various inputs and their interpretations, the active system fits the new information into previously existing structures that best accommodate the current events. For example, when the perceptual-arousal system is activated, it would be fed into previously existing arousal structures, which relate it to cognitive inputs and structures that would then produce a previously experienced (established) emotional structure. In the absence of these other cognitive inputs the system might request evaluational input in order to complete its requirements.

For example, arousal in the presence of a New Year's Eve party would be channeled into an emotional interpretation based on previous parties. If one usually had a "bad time" at parties, that evaluation might require (ask for) new interpretations based on predominantly positive signals received at the current party. Because of a "bad fit," the active system asks for more inputs and information.

Since we must always be careful not to invoke new homunculuslike structures, it should be noted that this is an easily simulated system. At the lowest level we could produce a structure that is sensitive to inputs from arousal-perception, but that does not complete its output until it has found input at the evaluative-interpretive level, which would require input from very specific systems that are appropriately labeled. The previous discussion of meaning analysis implied that there will be continuous searches on the basis of previously experienced structures in order to complete the meaning analysis if the task requires such an analysis at a very deep level or to an extensive degree. Similarly, we can imagine that the cognitive evaluative system also withholds output either to experience or to external systems until it has examined input from the arousal system. In general, and in view of the discussions in previous chapters, it is more likely that the system is an active one.

It should be noted however that there is an asymmetry in these systems. The cognitive-interpretive system presumably will look only at a rather restricted range of possible inputs and, if they are absent, may then go to output. On the other hand, if the arousal system is *dependent* on cognitive-evaluative inputs before outputs are possible, it has two characteristics. First, it presumably will search an extensive system of structures that make up the cognitive-interpretive system and second, it is highly likely to find some such evaluative output. Semantic analysis—independent of the particular emotional situation— is continuously proceeding in the active, awake organism; thus there will always be some input from the cognitive system that will have to suffice for the completion of the output circuit for the arousal system.

Until now I have talked as though the input to the cognitive and the arousal systems are disparate sets of events. They are not. The most

frequent situation, of course, is one in which the same set of events are
both operating as functional releasers of the arousal system and as
events to be evaluated by the cognitive system. A near collision while
driving a car has both a negative cognitive evaluation and an arousal
function, and the two of them interact in the usual and expected
fashion.

We may not need to make a choice between the passive and active
models of meaning analysis in emotional behavior and experience.
Instead, we can assume that both kinds of systems operate and that
there may be a developmental shift from the passive to the active
system. Thus a particular passive system is organized through a
concatenation of circumstance, and a new structure is developed. On
subsequent occasions any of the components of this passively
established system may occur in the life of the individual. The
previously laid down "passive" organization now becomes a possible
structure to evaluate the event and may work as an active system. It is
difficult to specify, although easy to speculate about, the experiences
that produce new structures out of these passive concatenations. In the
previous example, a long series of bad party experiences may have
(passively) established a structure that is then (actively) selected. That
structure is, in turn, rejected when another evaluation is more
appropriate. Thus the sheer frequency of similar experiences may
provide the process, whereby passive organizations become
autonomous within the mental system and can work as active systems.
In any case the malleability and variability of the young child in
emotional expression and experience suggests that the fortuitous
concatenation of events produces variable emotional structures in the
child but, with the development of more stable structures relating
arousal to cognition and evaluation, inputs from either one of the
systems are more likely to be channeled to one or the other of now
well-established structures. In the discussion of individual differences
in Chapter 9 I shall suggest exactly this kind of development in the
early acquisition of emotional structures.

Is there any *a priori* system that permits the prediction of specific
evaluations of "objective" situations? Except for some life-sustaining
and life-threatening situations, the individual structures, on the basis
of past experience, vary widely. There is one pragmatically useful
categorization of emotional situations. This purely operational solution
lies in the area of social induction. There is good reason to believe that
the most powerful environment for the induction of certain kinds of
behavior is to have that behavior exhibited by others. As we shall see,
the Schachter experiments show quite clearly that people tend to be
euphoric in the presence of a euphoric model or angry in the presence
of an angry model. Experiments by Nowlis (e.g., Nowlis and Nowlis,

1956) on mood demonstrate the general point that the mood represented by the majority of a social group influences the mood of all its members.

In the same area, philosophers (e.g., Peters, 1969) and psychologists (e.g., Arnold, 1969, 1970b) have argued that emotions follow an initial appraisal of an object as "good" or "bad." One might suggest, and I shall have more to say about this later, that the case may be exactly the other way around: that an event generates some particular meaning analysis (whether together with or disjointed from arousal) and that the final emotional expression and its quality then lead back to an assessment of the event as being "good" or "bad."

The intuitively appealing notion that we make emotional appraisals on some antecedent continuum of *good* versus *bad* has received relatively little critical attention. What are the psychological processes that generate the phenomenal judgment of "good" and "bad"? To relegate them to some physiological "central" decision system (e.g., Arnold, 1960) is unsatisfactory because it delays a reasonable description of processes and, at least for me, is unacceptable on both metaphysical and nativistic grounds. Schneirla (1959) has suggested that fundamental approach and withdrawal tendencies should be viewed as basic to positive and negative behavioral and phenomenal evaluations—a view consistent with much of the behaviorist literature, as well as with some modern views of fear and anxiety (e.g., Bowlby, 1973). It is not unlikely that classes of stimuli and events exist that act on preprogrammed (innate) structures which, in turn, generate generalized approach and withdrawal action structures. Among such events might be extreme heat and cold, sexual stimuli, and certain smells. Whenever new events are encountered and attended to in conjunction with these conditions, the analytic evaluative structure might assimilate this new set of events (a process known descriptively as classical conditioning). The phenomenal experience of evaluating something as good or bad might be no more than the conscious accompaniment to (commentary on) such withdrawal and approach actions. Furthermore, once general evaluative linguistic structures of "good" and "bad" are established, they may act independently in conjunction with other new events. A child learns what "bad" means (i.e., there exists a structure in his semantic network that is active when evaluating that and similar terms related to withdrawal actions). He may then be instructed what events are bad and encode this new information, thus producing subsequent appropriate evaluation. Given arousal and the cognitive evaluation of the situation, a negative emotional reaction might be established. I note in Chapter 8 that this process cannot be simply based on some simple conjunction between pain and previously neutral events. Finally, "good" and "bad" evaluations may be related to the adaptiveness of the appropriate cognitive structures. I shall return in Chapter 7 to the possibility that "bad" is what cannot be accommodated or assimilated.

We can now apply the foregoing arguments to some of the possible processes that operate when a particular input goes through meaning analysis and either does or does not produce some degree of arousal. Arousal, in turn, would be the condition for emotional behavior and experience in concert with the separate, although not necessarily independent, meaning analysis. I am concerned here primarily with the process whereby particular inputs do or do not lead to arousal. I shall not deal with the conditions under which arousal is directly tied into specific input structures, the prewired ties between certain events and arousal. (I shall discuss what these conditions for autonomic arousal might be in Chapter 6.)

First, I assume that there is a set of structures that provides an analysis of inputs, of whatever modality, and an initial identification so that a meaning analysis can proceed. As an example, and at a very simple level, we might say that one analyzer system is concerned with the phonological analysis of certain acoustic inputs (e.g., words). The sounds that are received by the receptors when somebody says the word "table" are analysed in such a way that a specific structure in the analyser system is activated that uniquely defines the phonological properties of that particular acoustic input. These acoustic inputs rarely act in isolation, and others, whether they are visual, cognitive, or whatever, are operating at the same time. One set of such analysers deals with the contextual cues at the time of input. For example, the contextual cues with the input "table" might identify that word "table," which is further classified as a piece of furniture, while another contextual input might identify a different node for the same acoustic analysis: that the word "table" is to be identified as something to be found in books. It should be obvious that from this point of view these are not two meanings of the same word but two different words, and they are uniquely identified by the total analysis of the input situation.

We now assume that we have arrived at a point that is a specific but, for the time being, unanalyzed node in long-term storage. Meaning analysis now proceeds up and down the hierarchical, categorical structure to give further interpretation of this event. An event can be preliminarily and superficially noted, but its meaning (full structure) may not be available until some kind of meaning analysis has taken place. Whether these meaning analyses occur inevitably or need a program input that requests a meaning analysis can be left open for the time being. However, the meaning analysis of the event that has arrived at some lower node need not be full or complete. It is intuitively obvious and empirically demonstrable that the degree of meaning analysis of incoming material that we undertake is rarely complete and often just adequate to the requirements of the particular situation (cf. Craik and Lockhart, 1972). In contrast to theories that suggest an immediate, automatic, and full analysis of each item in terms of its semantic features or attributes (e.g., Katz and Fodor, 1963), this description suggests that many of the semantic features may not be activated in the analysis of a particular item at a particular time.

We now assume that there are certain nodes at various levels of the hierarchical structure that are direct releasers or triggers for autonomic arousal. Assume that some node two steps removed from the original analytic node is such an arousal node. Thus there is an analysis of an event at some relatively superficial depth that will produce arousal and, in connection with the cognitive appraisal of the situation, a *specific* emotional reaction.

Next consider the possibility that some higher order node—if reached in the process of analysis—would produce ideational or action conflict. In that case, access to such a node might be blocked—the occurrence of repression to be discussed later in this chapter.

In addition, there will be nodes encountered during meaning analysis that may or may not lead to an emotional experience. It may be that in the analysis of an event, and of surrounding items, a downward or upward analysis may be optional. In other words, analytic requirements are ambiguous and allow either superordinate or subordinate elaboration of a concept. There may even be a conditional process such as, "Under condition A complete structure upward, but follow downward trees under condition B." Whenever the downward analysis occurs, an arousal node will be reached and emotional arousal and experience will follow; if it does not occur then emotional experience will be absent. These sometimes emotional experiences may depend on a variety of contextual and intrapsychic factors. For example, thinking about a 2-year old child may be painful (conflictful), but a remark about preschoolers in the context of a discussion of education will produce an analysis in the direction of "children" and no emotional consequence. The same remark in the context of relating examples of preschool behavior may lead to the "2-year old" node and emotional consequences.

Consider the case where the original analytic node involves the identification of a Siamese kitten. At a very low level, there may be an emotional arousal related to the node that is equivalent to the concept "cat." (Note again that the labels of nodes do not identify them; they are simply used for purposes of exposition.) Thus, at a very low level, as soon as a Siamese kitten is identified as a cat, an emotional response may occur.

An example involving a type of repression addresses a memory store about the person's mother once having been very upset when he brought a stray cat home. This involved and complex interaction with the mother produces conflict contingent on the idea of "bringing stray cats home." Thus repression would require that in the case of stray kittens or cats, we should not complete an analysis that leads to the structure about bringing these stray animals home. Since such an analysis is not necessary for a meaning analysis of the Siamese kitten, we could then further identify cats as pleasant, cuddly, domestic, and innocuous animals.

Finally, an analysis could generate the identification of the kitten as a cat, a cat as a domestic animal, and then a downward analysis that says domestic animals also include dogs. If we once had a very bad experience with a particular dog, thinking about the cat as a domestic animal and hence about dogs might lead to the particular memory node that relates to that particular unpleasant experience, which then triggers arousal and emotional experience. But it is not necessary that every time we see a Siamese kitten we need to be reminded of that particular experience with the dog. Whether we are or not may depend on random factors or on situational factors, which will make an analysis to the arousal node or its equivalent more likely. For example, we might see the Siamese kitten in a context that is very similar to the one in which we had our unpleasant canine experience.

In summary, whether a particular input will lead to some emotional experience will depend on whether the arousal switch has been triggered, and whether that switch has been triggered depends on the particular meaning analysis that the input has undergone. If a node that leads to arousal is involved in the meaning analysis then arousal and emotional experience will presumably take place, but a variety of factors determine whether the arousal switch will or will not be triggered.

Consciousness and Emotion

It should be obvious by now that I am as concerned with the expression of emotion in private experience or consciousness as with behavioral indices of the "emotional" complex. Some special aspects of consciousness and emotion deserve specific attention. Once again it should be stressed that, whereas for the individual, events in consciousness are sensitive and unique indications of the state of his mental organization, these are not available without transformation to the observer and particularly to the observing psychologist. The examination of consciousness is a theoretical enterprise, and it is not a high road to the raw constituents of feeling and emotion. Nobody has ever had access to the "raw experience" of another individual, and my point of view says it is impossible in principle. Language and even nonverbal communication, in gestures and bodily attitudes, cannot possibly give full expression to the felt emotional experience. Our action systems are crude instruments when it comes to describing the fine distinctions among emotions that we can inspect in consciousness. This does not deny that, because of the essential identity of mental structures (but not their content) from individual to individual, much of private experience is made of the same stuff across individuals, but it does suggest that similarities may be due to similarities in language and action systems that are, after all, to a very large extent influenced and molded by the social community.

Thus the phenomenological analysis of emotion requires two basic steps: first, humility, in the light of the imperfection of the system, and second, a theory that will provide us with some testable propositions about the transformations from consciousness to action systems.

These concerns need to be restated because consciousness ranks high when problems of emotion and visceral-cognitive interactions are explored. I shall argue later that visceral arousal and its interpretation comprise an important auxiliary signal system in the organism's transactions with the environment. It is one of the functions of consciousness to make it possible to evaluate environmental conditions and action alternatives more effectively. But these evaluations and decisions often occur prior to any observable behavioral output. In other words, one of the important functions of the "emotional" complexes is that their crucial input occurs sometimes at the level of the evaluative functions of consciousness. There may be conditions where there are no direct behavioral "observable" outputs of these "emotions" at all; their primary function is that they are experienced, that they contribute to the evaluation of the current state of the organism, and that they influence a final set of decisions as to actions and behaviors but, from a behavioral point of view, they may not be expressed at all. Granted that we might ask an individual what his particular emotional tone or feeling might have been or was (thus activating an additional output) and then presumably obtain some reasonable facsimile of the internal event; in the real world these questions are not typically asked. On the other hand, at the subjective level, the individual is often well aware of the "emotional" reactions that enter into the complex determination of much of his behavior but are never expressed directly. The importance of human consciousness to the study of emotions is that many of their important determining functions may take place only in consciousness.

In a sense this position comes full circle in the context of my rejection of the nineteenth-century position that placed feelings and ideas prior to actions. Under some conditions, the present discussion places consciousness of emotional states prior to action or inaction. There is, however, one important difference; the emotional contents of consciousness that I espouse do not posit feelings and ideas as primitives. On the contrary, emotional consciousness is seen as developing out of more basic and more general processes involving arousal and cognitive structures. Just as some action may be a prior condition for some other behavior in the flow of human acts, so may some conscious state. At least this type of analysis pushes the building blocks of emotional consciousness back to the same constituents as those that control other aspects of human action, and eventually to the individual and social conditions of development.

One other important interaction between emotion, consciousness and actions needs to be explored—the concept of repression. As classically used, it refers to the absence from consciousness of important memories. In other words, it involves memory, consciousness, and emotion.

The relation between memory models and emotional activity goes back to fundamental principles first systematically specified by Freud and elaborated and summarized by Rapaport (1942). It is useful to recall that some primary tenets of contemporary memory theory and, in particular, the distinction between storage and retrieval, can be found, in somewhat different language, in Freud. As Rapaport summarizes it, for example, Freud viewed "remembering as emergence into consciousness, and forgetting as non-emergence." Freud's contribution is of particular interest in respect to repression and its representation in an information-processing model.

First, recall Freud's notion of affect, which is a "process of discharge, the final expression of which is perceived as feeling." More specifically, "affectivity manifests itself essentially in motor (i.e., secretory and circulatory) discharge resulting in an (internal) alteration of the subject's own body" (Freud, 1925a).

For Freud affects cannot be unconscious; they are, by definition, represented in consciousness, even though their source may not be "known" to the individual (i.e., unconscious). And Rapaport makes the important point that Freud never taught that the disagreeable is forgotten. This is of central importance for a cognitive model and particularly for our point of view. Semantic (memory) representations are not disagreeable as such; it is only if they lead to conflict arousal, and interpretation that they may become disagreeable. Or, as Rapaport puts it, "What Freud discovered was the function preventing the emergence into consciousness of an unconscious idea, which if it became conscious, would give rise to conflict."

Repression, with its essential "function of rejecting and keeping something out of consciousness" (Freud, 1925b), operates to prevent retrieval, not of unhappinesses, but of mental contents that would produce conflict in consciousness. Among these conflicts are reality situations that prevent the execution of actions that follow from these contents, or conflicts between different cognitions as, for example, between a particular mental content and its social unacceptability.

At the risk of alienating the psychoanalytically oriented reader, I might say that repression keeps out of consciousness those meaning analyses that would, if present, produce the interruption of either action or plans. And, as we shall see in discussing the major mechanisms of interruption, the mental mechanisms that Freud proposes for "screen memories" that may be "allowed" into consciousness are not that different. When we consider substitution or alternative response sequences in action, we can easily see their cognitive parallels in the psychoanalytic concepts of displacement, condensation, and symbolization.

Other aspects of the interaction between consciousness and "emotion" will be discussed appropriately in later chapters. One recurring theme will be that presentation of arousal and meaning analyses in consciousness takes up at least part of the limited capacity of the conscious system. In that sense emotion becomes a disrupting and interfering set of events. On the other hand, when emotional response helps in the adaptive evaluation of some environmental events, its contribution to more adaptive behavior may frequently outweigh its interfering function.

Chapter V
New Insights and Old Theories

Having said earlier that I am not concerned with explicating the concept of emotion as it is used in the common language but, instead, in developing a psychological rationale for a set of experiences and behaviors that define our range of intent, it is now appropriate to broaden the range of discourse and to retract, for purposes of discussion, the constricting apsects of that particular definition. There is a good reason for such a temporarily liberating move. Previous efforts toward theories of emotion have, in most cases, tried to specify the functions and processes that give rise to palpable emotions, defined by the common language and common experience.

In my brief review of some of the more visible theories of emotion and emotional behavior, I shall marshal another argument against any attempt to develop a theory of "emotion." The previous argument has been about the purposes of psychological theory and has argued that it is more appropriate to develop psychological theory that is independent of the quasiinsights of the common language but that makes psychological sense in describing, explaining, and predicting the thought and behavior of organisms. Beyond that goal, it is *not* my aim to develop a theory of emotion in the sense that a theory of learning or memory or visual perception might be developed. All such theories, and many others in psychology, attempt to specify unique processes, hopefully to be molded in a mathematical or logically precise language; processes and mechanisms that may, in fact, have rather precise neurological correlates. These mechanisms are transforms and rules that state how some specified form of behavior may be integrated and stored in the action repertoire, how certain experiences may be temporarily processed in a short-term memory buffer, how and under what conditions they are transferred to a long-term storage, or what transformations take place peripherally or centrally on sensory input to the visual system. It is my belief, or probably an axiomatic supposition, that emotion is not a process or mechanism of that order. Rather, it is a conglomeration of mechanisms and processes. This point of view argues also against any theories of emotion that are independent of or different from a more general analysis of human processing systems. The processes and mechanisms to be used exist independent of the fact that one of their outputs is so called emotional behavior. And it is for this reason that I would quarrel with attempts to produce emotional theories based on particular and specific "emotional" mechanisms.

The Belief in Fundamental Emotions—a Human Vanity

I shall sketch three major sources for the belief that the search for the complete and separate theory of emotion is proper—all rooted in historical notions about the nature of man. The first deals with the irreducibility of ideas and feelings—the idealism of Western philosophy; the second deals with the invariance of the products of evolutionary mechanism; and the third deals with our intuitive sense of certainty about experience, whether it is based on phenomenology or language analysis.

It is a refreshing and peculiarly twentieth-century enterprise to ask about the *origins* of emotional feelings and experiences, to be concerned with antecedents instead of with givens. We readily forget that the psychologist-physiologist-philosopher of the nineteenth century (and his predecessors) typically inquired about the consequences of ideas (and feelings) and rarely concerned himself with the origin of ideas, as such. Philosophy and psychology (such as it was) took for granted states of mind and irreducible ideas. The concern was primarily with the consequences of mental acts, with the result of feelings and affections and with their combination. These elemental ideas and feelings were the property of rational conscious man, possibly even his birthright and distinctiveness. To ask for their origin required the postulation of processes that were nonconscious. It was easier to take them for granted and, more important, they were the mark of the philosophical idealism that dominated much of Western science.

Nowhere did this commitment to the fully fashioned psyche appear more dramatically than in the field of emotion. Contrast our two most illustrious forebears in the field, Charles Darwin and Sigmund Freud. Both were committed natural scientists, the former less a philosophical idealist than the latter, and yet it was Freud who saw emotions as emerging out of mechanisms and processes that were, in the first instance, not irreducible givens. For Darwin the *expression* of emotions was of interest, but it was the expression of something that remained an unanalyzed *a priori*. Joy, anger, pain are the ideas and feelings that *result* in expressive movement, and only rarely does Darwin even speculate about the antecedents of these feelings. When he does, his observations are usually embarrassingly commonplace: "If we have suffered or expect to suffer some wilful injury from a man, or if he is in any way offensive to us, we dislike him; and dislike easily rises into hatred" (Darwin, 1872).

The need to rely on some given emotional states that are beyond explanations is not a feature of the nineteenth century alone but, often in simplified forms, has remained with us as metaphysical postulates of fundamental unanalyzed reactions. The metaphysics of *a priori* judgments or appraisals have even found their way into contemporary physiological speculations, with neurophysiological structures given the task of making these *a priori* judgments.

Another source of the belief in an unanalyzed emotional substratum is the unassailable finding that some of our expressive behavior, as so much of our other behavior, has evolutionary rather than contemporary origins—it is natured rather than nurtured. Here it was, of course, Darwin who demonstrated in detail how these expressions transcend species boundaries. Contemporary ethologists have shown us how lower animals exhibit these behaviors under specified environmental and hormonal conditions. However, the notion that these *expressions* are unavoidably tied to certain prewired conditions in *man* denies the plasticity of man, or even that of nonhuman primates. It is part of our humanness that we are not bound to evolutionary patterns of behavior, that we can exhibit these inherited patterns under conditions unknown to our forebears or inhibit them when their expression may be maladaptive—or unavoidable in lower animals. To assert this plasticity in no way opens the back door to a misleading voluntarism, but it does deny the utility of using expressive behavior as the invariable demonstration of rigid stimulus-response chains or—in the modern case —of inferred internal hypothetical states. Man, in contrast to lower animals, may deliberately exhibit some emotional sign—in the absence of the internal or external releasers that provide the evolutionary links to these emotional expressions. I may frown in order to frown without "wanting" to *express* anything at all.

I also want to reject—and will do so extensively in Chapter 6—the currently popular ethological journalism that wants to make laws of nakedness, apedness, territorialism, and aggression out of unsubstantiated extensions of animal behavior patterns to man, but also I need to place our inherited expressiveness into context. Expressive movements can be seen as any other indicators or behaviors, frequently to be interpreted in terms of *possible* antecedent cognitive and perceptual reactions. They are not invariant, nor should they—as

in the most extreme popular version—be made the basis of all
motivation and emotion (e.g., Tomkins, 1962, 1963).

The third major source that motivates a search for the "true"
emotional theory arises out of our common language, out of folk
psychology and philosophy. It is related to the myth-making
tendencies of human individuals, societies, and cultures, which I
discussed in Chapter 1. To recapitulate, the fact that the common
language has established broad and rather vague categories of emotions
easily leads into the belief that these categories represent real and
underlying dimensions of thought and experience. As for all such
common language orderings, it is an empirical question whether these
categories are useful. More important, the folk belief that emotions—
commonly labeled—are primary feelings does not represent a
psychological theory. It is a useful way for talking about experience
and actions, but its scientific value is doubtful.

Theories of Emotion

After a brief survey, I shall discuss in detail the most recent and
influential position—Schachter's contribution. Since it is closely related
and antecedent to my own views, it requres a more extensive
exposition. Thereafter, I shall spend some time with the James-Lange
theory and Cannon's critique thereof as well as relevant evidence,
primarily because of the historical influence of these two approaches
on my explication of emotional behavior. Other theoretical notions will
be sketched in more superficially and will be discussed when necessary
in other chapters.

Nothing as complex as emotional behavior and experience is likely to
be determined by a single set of inputs or stimuli and, similarly, no
unidimensional theory of emotion may be all right or all wrong. What
is preferable is an analysis that admits a variety of determinants for
any particular act and a variety of acts that may arise out of a
restricted number of determinants. Again it was Freud, who should be
read more carefully by some contemporary philosophers, who insisted
on the overdetermined nature of behavior. However we might describe
our own actions; whatever fictions we make up to explain the reasons
why we did one thing or another, it is highly likely that there were a
variety of determining factors at work that produced the experience or
the action with which we are dealing. The human organism is a
complex system because it is open to so many "causes" at any one
time, because its outputs may be a function of internal processes
generated by the cognitive-interpretive system, external events that are
or are not consciously apprehended, that are or are not transformed, as

well as by its own reactions to its outputs, its response to its own behavior. The inputs to the system that produce arousal, those that give rise to a particular characterization of the situation, and those that occasion a particular action may all be different subsets of all the events acting on the organisms at any one time.

Unfortunately, few extensive and objective reviews of theories of emotion exist . Without claiming objectivity for the current effort, it would have been most useful if we could point to an extensive review and evaluation of existing theories that draws new conclusions from such an effort. A recent book by Strongman (1973) surveys the field and provides useful summaries, but it does not break any new ground. A surprisingly complete summary of current theories of emotion and feeling is a book by Ruckmick published in 1936. Very little, apart from physiological speculation, has been added to Ruckmick's exposition since then. It is primarily the impetus that emotional theories received through Schachter's work that provides a contrast between the 1936 review and a current purview of the situation. There have been some minor reviews of theories of emotion (e.g., Goldstein, 1968; Izard, 1971) but most books on the topic either were designed to present a particular point of view or integration of the existing data or are collections of less ambitious efforts. The most important additions are the collections of papers edited by Arnold (1970a) and by Black (1970). Still important, and in the same tradition, are the two volumes on feelings and emotion edited by Reymert (1928, 1950). Among the more important presentations from a personal point of view are Arnold (1970b), Duffy (1962), Izard (1971), and Plutchik (1962).

The following discussion of various theories of emotion is not a survey of all theories of emotions that have ever been proposed. Their number is legion, many of them have been forgotten, and none of the ones that we ignore has been of major influence in generating either scientific acceptance or intensive research (especially outside the theorist's laboratory). It will also be obvious from the general attitude that motivates this volume that I am not concerned with theories that are primarily addressed to neurological mechanisms. Thus, while we shall consider Cannon's criticism of James, we will not consider Cannon's theory, since it is concerned with the direct action of neurophysiological mechanisms. Similarly, the elaborate and somewhat opaque theory presented by Arnold (1950, 1960) is primarily one that appeals to neurophysiological mechanisms.

My major concern will be with the theoretical statements that are important forerunners of my emphasis on the interaction between arousal and cognition and on the emotional consequences of the disruption and interruption of actions, cognitive structures, or plans.

The Schachter Contribution

The poverty of psychological theory about emotional phenomena was brought into sharp focus in 1962 with the publication by Schachter and Singer of the first of a series of experiments that demonstrated unequivocally the utility of a new two-factor approach to problems of emotion. Prior to that time, theory in emotion harked back to William James, concentrated on neurophysiological theories that provided few psychological insights, or was concerned with the differentiation of physiological states subsequent to emotional arousal. In his prior work Schachter (1959) had been concerned with problems of emotion in the area of affiliation and anxiety. However, it was not until the publication of the 1962 paper that he stated unequivocally his commitment to a two-factor theory of emotion, stressing physiological arousal on the one hand and cognitive appraisal on the other. Schachter's work has been collected in a single volume (1971), which provides more details of his theoretical and empirical work (see also Schachter, 1966). At the present time I shall only summarize the most important parts of his theoretical ideas and experimental evidence.

While Ruckmick (1936) had stressed the interaction of visceral and cognitive factors in the production of emotion, and others, for example, Hunt, Cole, and Reis (1958) had specified how different emotions may be tied to specific environmental-cognitive interactions, the major antecedent of Schachter's work was an essentially anecdotal study by Marañon (1924). Marañon found that when he injected a large number of patients with adrenalin, approximately one third of them responded with a quasiemotional state. The rest reported little or no emotional response and simply described their physiological state of arousal. However, the patients who gave emotional reactions typically reported what has now become the classical description of the "as if" emotion. They would report that they felt "as if" they were afraid or "as if" something very good was about to happen. In other words, they reported not the full range of emotional experience but something closely akin to it. In some few cases Marañon discussed their recent emotional experiences with the subjects, such as a death in family, and then the patients reported full rather than "as if" or "cold" emotion. Thus it appeared there were three kinds of reactions in Marañon's experiment: a description of the physiological arousal, an "as if" emotion, and a full emotion, if appropriate cognitive support was available.

Considering these and other data Schachter put forward three general propositions.

1. Given a state of physiological arousal for which an individual has

no immediate explanation, he will 'label" this state and describe his feelings in terms of the cognitions available to him. . . .

2. Given a state of physiological arousal for which an individual has a completely appropriate explanation . . ., no evaluative needs will arise and the individual is unlikely to label his feelings in terms of [any] alternative cognitions available. . . .

3. Given the same cognitive circumstances, the individual will react emotionally or describe his feelings as emotions only to the extent that he experiences a state of physiological arousal (Schachter, 1971).

In other words, both physiological arousal and cognitive evaluation are necessary, but neither is a sufficient condition for the production of emotional states. In addition, it is assumed that physiological arousal produces an evaluative need, such that an appropriate explanation is sought by the individual. In the first set of experiments Schachter and Singer gave subjects injections of adrenalin under the cover story that these were vitamin compounds that would affect visual skills. In another condition subjects were given the same instructions, but the injection was a placebo, that is, an injection of saline. Following the injection, subjects were either informed of the consequences of the injection (i.e., they were given correct information about the effects of adrenalin, without of course having been told that they were given an adrenalin injection), or they were not given any information about the affects of adrenalin, or they were misinformed.

In the informed condition they were told that they would feel palpitations, tremors, and similar descriptions of sympathetic nervous system discharge. In the misinformed condition they were essentially given a description of parasympathetic symptoms—that their extremities would feel numb, they would have an itch and a slight headache—none of which would be expected as a sympathetic result of the adrenalin injection.

Following the injection and the various types of information, the subject was left in a waiting room together with what was ostensibly another experimental subject, who was actually a "stooge" of the experimenters. Then, depending on whether the subjects were in a *euphoria* or *anger* condition, the stooge would engage in euphoric behavior, playing with paper airplanes, playing basketball with the wastebasket, and engaging in other euphoric, happy behavior, or in angry behavior, becoming more and more insulting, asking personal and insulting questions, and eventually leaving the room in anger.

Schachter and Singer's primary interest was in the subjects' behavior during the interaction with the stooge as a function of having received adrenalin or not (i.e., experiencing physiological arousal), whether they had an "appropriate" explanation for that arousal, and finally what the environmental-cognitive cues for an emotional "explanation" were.

Subjects were observed through a one-way mirror during their sojourn in the waiting room and they gave a self-report of their mood following the waiting-room experience.

The results were essentially in keeping with the two-factor theory coupled with an evaluative need hypothesis. First all the adrenalin-injected subjects that were included in the analysis showed significant increases in ANS arousal as measured by changes in heart rate. More important, the degree of information about the physiological consequences of the injection was negatively correlated with the degree of self-reported emoitonal state and with the degree of emotional behavior induced by the stooges' behavior. Thus the misinformed group, which presumably had the highest evaluative need while under the influence of adrenalin, since the information they had been given about the physiological effects and their actual experiences were completely uncorrelated, showed the greatest degree of self-reported euphoria as well as behavioral signs of the "appropriate" emotion.

At the other extreme, the informed group, who had no "evaluative need," showed the lowest degree of either self-reported or behavioral euphoria, with the ignorant group in between. Similar results were found in the anger condition.

In summary, the data suggest that if a state of physiological arousal is induced, and if the individual has no immediate explanation for it, he will then label his state in terms of the environmental-cognitive information available at the time. Conversely, if the state of physiological arousal is completely explained in terms of antecedents such as an injection, then the individual will not use other environmental-cognitive information to label his internal state. Subjects who were injected with adrenalin and told what to expect were essentially unaffected by the behavior of the stooge, while subjects who were given incongruous information were maximally affected by the stooge.

In a subsequent study Schachter and Wheeler (1962) showed that when subjects in a similar situation were given injections of adrenalin or chlorpromazine, differential reactions were produced. Chlorpromazine blocks autonomic reactions and should have physiological effects opposite to arousal caused by adrenalin. Schachter and Wheeler showed that subjects injected with adrenalin reacted more to the humor of a slapstick movie than subjects injected with a placebo and, in turn, the subjects injected with chlorpromazine were least reactive to the humor of the film.

I have given only a quick summary of the experiments conducted by

Schachter to demonstrate the possibility of independent manipulation of physiological arousal and cognitive evaluation. This is, of course, the central argument of my thesis. The physiological arousal that generated differential degrees of euphoria and anger was the identical injection of adrenalin; this supports a claim that the physiological arousal that is functional in emotional states is a general sympathetic nervous system reaction and not a specific pattern. As far as we know, coupled with the Marañon experiments, Schachter's is the only experimental evidence of the functional stimulus at the physiological level—the nature of arousal. At the cognitive level, clearly one of the best ways to induce a particular cognitive state is to generate an unequivocal state of the environment. Thus the subject looks about him and says that this must be a euphoric or angry situation because the only evidence he has is what other people in his environment are doing.

The relative independence of physiological and cognitive factors demonstrated by Schachter is somewhat overshadowed by the necessary artificiality of the experimental situation. After all, physiological arousal is rarely if ever artificially induced by the injection of adrenalin but, instead, is caused by environmental events, and I shall discuss what some of these might be in the following chapter. The positing of an evaluative need might be necessary for the analysis of Schachter's experiments, but is perhaps less interesting in an analysis of the determinants of emotional states in the day-to-day life situation of an individual. It is relatively rare that we are in a state of arousal that is independent of cognitive factors, and I have already indicated some of the interactions between the functional releasers of ANS arousal and their cognitive interpretation. Thus the notion of evaluative need is best handled in terms of a meaning analysis. The consequences of the artificial induction of physiological arousal should represent only part of a more general view of emotional induction in everyday life.

As far as the Schachter and Singer experiments are concerned, the meaning analysis model is fairly straightforward. Given autonomic arousal (subsequent to the injection of adrenalin), its perception— intense as it is—will activate a large number of structures that were previously relevant to the integration of autonomic arousal. In the case of the misinformed subjects, who did not expect that particular arousal-perceptual system to be active, the perception of autonomic activity starts the appropriate search for evaluative cognitive inputs before it can produce an output. This set of inputs is clearly given by the stooge who defines the cognitive boundaries of the situation and thus the appropriate emotion results. In the case of the informed subjects, however, there is a prior structure set up as a function of the instructions. That structure says there will be input from the perceptual arousal system, and that input is to be interpreted (given a meaning analysis) in terms of the specific situation that the subject has been told about: that the injection will produce certain perceptual results. While this may be an old structure, it is certainly a highly effective one in that given the input from the perception-arousal system the interpretation, or its meaning analysis, is ready made and output is completed. The arousal and the appropriate structure relevant to the perception of physiological indices together generate a stop rule that terminates further cognitive analyses.

I disagree with Schachter's interpretation of and stress on the discrepancy between subjective arousal experience and the label provided by instructions. It is more likely that autonomic arousal has certain consequences that generate and terminate the search for cognitive structures. I do not believe a discrepancy interpretation and the postulated evaluative need are necessary, but this disagreement does not in any way detract from the importance of the Schachter experiments to the development of a reasonable explanation of emotional behavior.

Finding an "appropriate" structure and invoking a stop rule will, of course, rely to a large extent on previous experience. For example, emotional quality may be stored with some concepts, events, and episodes, just as temporal or geographic information is stored with them. This may form the basis of finding an appropriate structure for these events whenever they occur together with ANS arousal.

Plutchik and Ax (1967) have offered a critique of Schachter and Singer (1962) that primarily focuses on aspects of the study that might have been done better. They point to some differences in the levels of heart rate of different groups, cavil that the placebo groups only found their place in the theoretical structure after some internal analyses, argue that indices of self-report are inadequate and that the data have been inadequately presented, and insist that greater care could have been taken in the procedures used. Most important, however, is their general rejection of Schachter's conclusions without providing adequate supporting data. They say that "one general source of difficulty in this kind of research is the naive notion that emotion is completely defined by what a subject says, even though the whole history of clinical psychology indicates that a person's verbalizations can be markedly influenced by overt or subtle suggestions." It is difficult to understand that particular criticism. Neither Schachter and Singer nor anybody following in their footsteps have suggested that emotion "is completely defined by what a subject says," but it is the case that if we want to know what people feel, *one* way to find out is to ask them, and it is difficult to find nonverbal ways of finding out how people feel. Even questionnaires and adjective checklists are verbal self-reports. However,

Plutchik and Ax go on to maintain a position for which there is no good evidence, in contrast to the Schachter and Singer position for which, they admit, there might be some evidence. They suggest that it is difficult to show physiological differentiation of emotions because of the confounding of individual and stimulus response specificities, the problem of the law of initial values (which says that physiological response is a function of the level of response prior to stimulation), and confusion over the matter of "independent criteria for emotions." They wind up by saying "it is likely that emotional expression, verbal or otherwise, is the result of a subtle interaction of cognitive factors with physiologically differentiated states." I shall shortly examine this argument in detail; it claims that different emotions are generated by different patterns of autonomic discharge. Unfortunately, the authors give absolutely no evidence that emotional expression, verbal or otherwise, is under the control of "physiologically differentiated states." They point out that Schachter and Singer's evidence does not deny "the possibility that both the cognitive and physiological systems are differentiated with regard to . . . arousal states." This is quite correct; any hypothesis is entertainable, including the most outlandish one. However, what makes an hypothesis useful is some evidence to support it. Plutchik and Ax present no such evidence, and I shall show in Chapter 6 that no such evidence is available.

Misunderstanding of the *causal antecedent* role of physiological patterning demanded by his position led Ax (1971) to produce the specific criticism of Schachter's studies that they "never looked to see if the resulting emotional states did or did not have different physiological concomitants!" Schachter might well have found such "concomitants," but their appearance is irrelevant to the causal argument about general sympathetic arousal (see the next chapter for further discussion).

The important contribution that the Schachter experiments have made is the unequivocal statement of a theory of emotion that postulates two independent and interacting factors: physiological arousal and cognitive evaluation. Schachter and his associates were not particularly concerned with the specification of the conditions that produced the physiological arousal in the first place, they preferred to use an artificial induction of the physiological arousal. The historical heritage and received wisdom of ascribing emotional states to differentiated physiological arousal was derived primarily from James and dominated emotional theories. The recognition, best found in Ruckmick (1936), that cognitive factors are of primary importance in determining emotional states had never been put in appropriate apposition. Schachter cut the Gordian knot, and his specific statement of the interactional hypothesis made possible new approaches to the theoretical and empirical study of emotional states. More important, that hypothesis, in light of other previous and subsequent data, can now be maintained independent of any flaws in Schachter's original experiments.

The James-Cannon Controversy

The notion that there was something dual about emotional states dates back to Aristotle who, in *DeAnima,* distinguished between the matter and the form (or idea) of emotion. Presumably the former could be identified as the visceral component and the latter as the psychological experience. However, until William James used this dualism, psychology continued to stress the primacy of ideas in determining psychological states and behavior. It was not until 1884 that James stood psychology on its head, although unfortunately only in the area of emotion, and suggested that emotional feelings are a result of bodily responses. He suggested that we feel afraid because we are avoiding a situation, that we feel sad because we cry, and not vice versa. "Our feeling of the [bodily] changes *is* the emotion" (James, 1884).

Many of James' critics, particularly Cannon (1927), have deliberately or inadvertently restricted the Jamesian theory to visceral action. What William James did say was that "we feel sorry because we cry, angry because we strike, afraid because we tremble, and not that we cry, strike, or tremble, because we are sorry, angry or fearful, as the case may be. Without the bodily states following on the perception [of the exciting fact], the latter would be purely cognitive in form, pale, colorless, destitute of emotional warmth" (James, 1884). Thus, in contrast to Lange, to whom I shall turn next, all bodily reactions "colored" the emotional experience. James made the probably incorrect and, from our point of view, unnecessary assumption that "every one of the bodily changes, whatsoever it be, is *felt,* acutely or obscurely, the moment it occurs." Finally, in a footnote, James entertained two possible courses that would make these bodily changes felt: "*After* they are produced, by the sensory nerves of the organs bringing back to the brain a report of the modifications that have occurred or *before* they are produced, by our being conscious of the outgoing nerve-currents starting on their way downward towards the parts they are to excite." He opts for the former alternative, but in the next chapter shows how, in modern language, we can also fruitfully entertain the latter possibility.

Finally, it should be stressed that James was concerned with internal, experiential effects of emotional sequences, rather than with emotional behavior. In discussing a case of generalized analgesia and its relevance to his theory he says that such patients ought to be "interrogated as to the inward emotional state that co-existed with the outward expressions of shame, anger, etc." The insistence on the experiential locus of the emotion is important in reference to his later critics.

Recall again the fundamental importance of James' thought. He rejected the primacy of thought and feeling that had been with philosophy and psychology at least since the Greeks. James insisted that after the initial perceptual apprehension of an event or object, it produces bodily consequences (including the visceral, the skeletal, and the muscular), and the perception of these consequences in turn lend emotional feeling to the object or event. Apart from the revolutionary shift from the *a priori* feeling to the produced feeling, his insistence on self-perception as an important determiner of experience and action (and emotion) has stayed with us to this day and has in recent years found renewed expression in cognitive studies of emotion (Schachter and Singer, 1962) as well as in behavioristic approaches, which use self-perception to explicate important social phenomena (Bem, 1967). James was falsely credited with saying that emotional feeling is defined by the perception of differing *visceral* patterns and these alone—an ascription that generated decades of research trying to find the particular visceral patterns that were assumed to be associated with each and every discrete emotion. Given what James did say, would he have approved of this search for the discrete emotion—and only in the viscera?

The man who probably would have approved was the Danish physiologist C. Lange (1885), whose major impact came in 1887 with the German translation of his work. Lange said that "we are indebted to the vasomotor system for the entire emotional part of our mental life." The psychological aspects of emotional experience of behavior, the "motor abnormalities, sensation paralysis, subjective sensations, disturbances of secretion, and intelligence" are secondary effects that "have their cause in anomalies of vascular innervation." Thus Lange should be credited equally with the revolutionary thought that feelings could be derived from some antecedents and he can, partly because of being linked with James, be given credit for much of the tradition of fruitful, although often misdirected, Psychophysiological research.

The most important and devastating attack on James came from Walter B. Cannon (1927, 1929), whose five major criticisms were used to defend his own neurophysiological theory of emotion. However, the subsequent history of the psychology of emotion depended more on James' position and Cannon's criticism and has shown relatively little influence of Cannon's own theory. Cannon's theory will not be discussed here mainly because it is a physiological theory that suggests how the functions of certain brain structures may determine emotional states. Since it does not lead to any specific psychological consequences, the theory is of no particular interest in the present context. Cannon pointed out the following in criticism of James.

1. Even when the viscera are separated from the central nervous system, emotional behavior may still be present. Thus, in cases of sympathectomy or vagotomy, where no visceral response can occur, emotional states may still be observed.

2. There does not seem to be any reasonbale way to specify visceral changes that differ from emotion to emotion. If James were correct, rather sharp and well-differentiated patterns of emotional reactions need to be found.

3. The perception and feedback from autonomic nervous system discharge is so diffuse and indistinct that one must assume that the viscera are essentially insensitive and could not possibly serve the differentiation function that James' position requires.

4. Autonomic nervous system responses are very slow and their slow speed, in order of 1 to 2 seconds, would suggest that emotion should not occur within shorter intervals. Introspection and some observations seem to suggest that such long latencies are not typical of emotional reactions.

5. When visceral changes are produced by artificial means as, for example, by the injection of adrenalin, emotional states do not seem to follow as a matter of course.

All of Cannon's criticisms are valid from a strict Jamesian position. However, if we adopt the position suggested in the current context, specifically that rather global visceral changes, and specifically their perception, are important in the production of emotional states, then the James-Cannon controversy takes on a different tinge, and we'arrive at a position somewhere between the two of them. I shall summarize here my previous arguments about the relevance of Cannon's criticism not just to James but to a modern theory of emotion (Mandler, 1962b), A similar, extensive discussion of the peripheral (Jamesian) versus central (Cannon's) view of emotion has been presented by Schachter (1970).

As far as Cannon's first point is concerned, that emotional behavior may be present in the absence of visceral activity, it apparently is true, if arousal has *previously* been organized in a structure involving environmental conditions and emotional behavior. Experiments by Solomon and his associates (e.g., Solomon and Wynne, 1954; Wynne and Solomon, 1955) have shown that an intact sympathetic nervous system is necessary for the normal acquisition of an avoidance response in dogs, but that the maintenance of such a response does not depend on autonomic functioning. It has also been demonstrated that, during the acquisition of an avoidance response, probability of responding is related to changes in heart rate, but that the maintenance of the avoidance response is independent of that particular index of visceral functioning (Black, 1959).

A more modern and promising technique for investigating the role of the sympathetic nervous system (SNS) is the procedure known as immunosympathectomy. Following the discovery of a nerve growth factor by Levi-Montalcini about 15 years ago, an antiserum derived from the nerve growth factor protein, which removes significant portions of the SNS, became available (Levi-Montalcini and Angeletti, 1961). Typically, the antiserum is injected in newborn animals (usually mice) and destroys from 80 to 90% of the SNS, apparently without affecting other aspects of the animals' functioning. Much of the behavioral research has been conducted by Wenzel, who has also provided the most complete summary of current knowledge in the area (Wenzel, 1972). As far as total activity is concerned, immunosympathectomy (IS) seems to have little effect. Emotionality in an open field test, measured by defecation, does seem to be affected by IS. Experimental animals also show greater variability in agonistic (aggressive) behavior. More important for the current discussions, IS retards avoidance of shock, whether in a passive or active situation. In addition there was some suggestion in several studies that IS produced greater reactivity to some external stimuli, particularly auditory ones. Wenzel (1972) summarizes the findings to date by suggesting that the "immunosympathectomized animal [is] . . . somewhat less reactive to *threatened* aversive stimuli, . . . but also somewhat overreactive to certain *actual* stimuli. . . ." "The results obtained . . . are compatible with the hypothesis that sympathetically innervated responses may play a mediational role in avoidance learning." In other words, "emotional" avoidance behavior apparently requires the operation of an intact sympathetic nervous system.

I have wandered far from Cannon's original question, but so has subsequent research. Cannon's original assertion is not as obvious as it was then, since neither in sympathectomies nor even in the case of immunosympathectomy is it clear that *all* functioning parts of the SNS have been removed. Even as little as 1% may, hypothetically, mediate avoidance behavior. James' insistence on awareness of the emotional state clouds the issue even further, if animal behavior is considered as evidential to the controversy.

I have suggested (Mandler and Kremen, 1958) that after extensive experience of autonomic discharge (and its perception), autonomic imagery may develop. There is no reason why the phenomenon of imagery need be restricted to the visual or auditory systems. Just as extensive experience in these areas may lead to the perception of objects and events in the absence of external stimulation, so can past experience lead to the perception of autonomic discharge in the absence of actual discharge. Thus visceral events are necessary for the acquisition of emotional states but apparently are not necessary for their future occurrence. Such occurrence may take place because of structures that directly relate environmental events to emotional behavior. The actual arousal is bypassed after extensive, repetitive occurrences of the event-arousal-cognition-action chain, leading to an event-cognition-action chain, or the perception of arousal may occur without the actual presence of arousal. Note that when James talked about the perception of bodily states, Cannon took that to mean their occurrence. For James occurrence and perception were essentially indivisible. Psychologists have subsequently pointed out that there may not be, in fact, a discrepancy between these two positions (cf. Valins, 1970, and others). As far as the actual controversy was concerned, the point is crucial, because for James occurrence and perception were coextensive and Cannon's critique about emotional states in the absence of the *occurrence* of visceral states was, of course, a highly relevant criticism. From a modern point of view it is a less important criticism when we consider that the occurrence and the perception of a particular state are not coextensive and that, given as complex a cognitive system as man's, perceptions may occur in the absence of the actual occurrences.

In his discussion of the James-Cannon controversy Schachter has summarized an important study by Hohmann (1966) that bears on the question whether visceral activation is necessary for emotional experience. Hohmann investigated patients who had varying degrees of spinal cord injuries. The patients were divided into five groups, according to a continuum of degree of visceral innervation and sensation. The higher on the spinal cord a lesion, the less the degree of visceral sensation. Hohmann found that the height of the lesion was related to the differentiation of emotional experience before and after the injury; the higher the lesion, the greater was the loss of emotionality subsequent to injury. This was true for states of anger, fear, grief, and sexual excitement. The less intense the autonomic arousal after the injury, the more the patients reported a loss of emotionality from their preinjury state. The patients' descriptions of their subjective states bear a striking similarity to the "as if" descriptions of Marañon's subjects. Where Marañon's subjects had "as if" emotions in the absence of the appropriate *cognitive* cues, Hohmann's subjects report responses to emotional situations that had the same "as if" character but, presumably, in the absence of autonomic *arousal*. As Schachter points out, Marañon's subjects "report the visceral correlates of emotion, but in the absence of veridical cognitions do not describe themselves as feeling emotion." On the other hand, the patients in Hohmann's study "describe the appropriate reaction to an emotion-inducing situation, but in the absence of visceral arousal do not seem to describe themselves as emotional" (Schachter, 1970). The degree of visceral arousal determines emotional states. In answer to Cannon, separation of the viscera and the central nervous system significantly affects emotional behavior and experience.

As far as Cannon's second point is concerned, I will support his position in Chapter 6. Visceral changes do not differ from emotion to emotion as far as current knowledge goes. In contrast to James and, in partial agreement with Cannon, I assume that visceral changes that are perceived and that form the basis of emotional arousal are global perceptions of sympathetic nervous system discharge and that the quality of an emotion is determined by entirely different factors. Thus the central notion of James' position is both theoretically and empirically rejected—emotion is not a perception of a specific pattern of autonomic discharge.

The same argument, of course, applies to Cannon's point three. There is no need for a very sensitive perceptual apparatus within the autonomic nervous system in order to perceive the global arousal that we postulate to be necessary for emotional production. As long as what is perceived is a general degree of arousal, then such perception can be both cumulative and relatively insensitive. No fine perceptual system is necessary in order to register general autonomic arousal.

Cannon's fourth criticism is important both for a Jamesian position, although there are few defenders left of that, and for the current point of view. It is the case that autonomic responses are slow, and it also appears, at least introspectively, that emotional reactions are much faster than the 1 to 2-second latency of the autonomic nervous system. We could reject the introspective report and say that the immediate reaction is a startle response, which is not a true emotional state. However, there are other possibilities. One is that in the adult we are usually dealing with an organism that has had extensive emotional experience. The structures that organize environmental events and emotional states are well developed and eixst prior to the time that the psychologist initiates his investigations. Thus emotional stimuli are familiar stimuli that may directly produce some aspect of the emotional response. What seems necessary for such an argument is the proposition that "emotional" responses can occur in the absence of arousal. It is likely that the notion of autonomic imagery is again the important aspect that may bridge the time between the onset of environmental events and feeling state of emotion. Presumably autonomic images are no more durable than visual and auditory ones, but they may be sufficient to produce the appearance of the perception of autonomic arousal, which lasts long enough until the actual autonomic arousal takes place approximately 1 or 2 seconds after the stimulus onset. I shall have further opportunity to discuss the difference between delayed onset of emotional behavior in inexperienced individuals: young children.

Finally, Cannon's last point that artificial production of autonomic nervous system response does not seem to produce emotion addresses itself primarily to experiments like Marañon's. But, from the current point of view and, of course, from the point of view that engendered Schachter's original experiments, this is not at all surprising. If arousal is only part of the emotional pie, then we would not expect artificial production of visceral arousal to produce emotion unless there is a cognitive input that specifies the emotional state. Visceral changes of a diffuse character, as produced by the injection of adrenalin, do in part determine emotional states. However, these states only occur if the meaning analysis specifies the cognitive factors that give a particular quality to the emotion. If, on the other hand, the meaning analysis (e.g., in Marañon's and Schachter's experiments) relates the arousal to some other environmental set of events (e.g., the effects of the injection), then emotional responses and emotional states would not be expected to occur.

Just as an increase in visceral arousal should, under the proper circumstances, produce a higher probability of emotional experience and behavior, our position also demands that a decrease in sympathetic nervous system activity should—in the absence of environmental changes—decrease the probability of emotional consequences. Unfortunately, most pharmacological agents that provide for a reduction in visceral activity usually also have marked central nervous system effects. One of the few exceptions is practolol, which blocks cardiac receptors (thus reducing heart action) with little attendant action on other sympathetic receptors. More important, very little practolol enters the central nervous system, thus restricting its actions to peripheral effects. Bonn, Turner, and Hicks (1972) have shown that psychiatric patients characterized primarily by extreme anxiety showed significant improvement when administered daily doses of practolol— thus demonstrating that some emotional disorders and, more important, emotional reactions, may be regulated by apparently entirely peripheral management of the sympathetic nervous system.

The discussion of James' position and Cannon's criticisms has not been presented in order to defend one or the other. The controversy has been extremely fruitful in generating relevant research and in specifying the theoretical issues more clearly. It also places the present position and current research in its proper historical context. James' contribution still is important in that he led us to understand the relevance of autonomic arousal in the production of emotion, and Cannon's criticism is equally important in pointing out that emotions are *not* "nothing but" the perception of visceral arousal. Whereas Cannon would not have been particularly happy about an arousal-cognitive interpretation of emotion, neither does such a position support James' original position.

A fairly extensive review of the evidence on the James-Lange theory (i.e., on physiological aspects) has been published by Fehr and Stern (1970). Unfortunately, it is generally uncritical and also fails to come to grips with the *causal* role of visceral patterning. However, it contains useful further discussions of the issues raised in this chapter.

A Contemporary Jamesian

Probably the only modern equivalent of a Jamesian theorist is M. A. Wenger (1950, 1956). Wenger (1950) places his theory of emotion on two foundations. First, he assumes that emotional behavior involves changes in the activity of the autonomic nervous system; and second, he assumes that emotional behavior is related to "frustration, anticipated frustration, satisfaction, or anticipated satisfaction of a need." The latter, of course, simply sets the conditions, as well as possibly the interpretations, under which a situation will elicit autonomic reactions. As I shall note, this listing of the four emotional conditions is an early forerunner of the tendency of modern behavior theorists to reduce all emotions to three or four types. On the other hand, Wenger is sensitive to the complexity of emotional behavior and does not restrict the emotions to the four types of eliciting conditions but, instead, suggests that emotional terms such as fear or jealousy refer to organismic reactions, which are the emotional reactions *plus* other organismic reactions. However, in line with modern behavior theorists, he refused to speculate about emotional *experience.*

For Wenger the perceptions of visceral discharge act as drive stimuli. These internal events may determine both emotional behavior and verbal report, which implies some contact with emotional experience. However, emotional experience is seen as a result of emotional action, not an integral part of it. In 1956, in collaboration with Jones and Jones, Wenger put the point more succinctly by saying that "emotion is activity and reactivity of the tissues and organs innervated by the autonomic nervous system. It may involve, but does not necessarily involve, skeletal muscular response or mental activity." His direct contact with James can be seen again in the 1956 book when he says that "change in emotional behavior is altered activity or reactivity in part of one, or more, . . . organs innervated by the autonomic nervous system." Thus Wenger considers autonomic nervous system activity, or visceral response, as the "emotion," with the "emotional complex" involving both the stimulating conditions and the resultant skeletal and mental activities. However, differences in emotions are thought to be associated with differences in patterns of autonomic activity.

Some Behaviorist Positions

The search for an adequate definition of emotion and its classification within existing theoretical frameworks has also appealed to behavioral psychologists and even radical behaviorists. Starting with J. B. Watson's statement that there are only three *basic* emotions—fear, rage, and love—the analysis has become somewhat more sophisticated, although unfortunately no more enlightening.

Radical behaviorists—the descendants, although unfortunately not the intellectual children of B. F. Skinner—have suggested a quadripartite division of the emotions, usually after asserting that it is really not the business of a behavioristic psychology to try to use such mentalistic terms as emotion. Having said that, they accept the fact that, after all, psychologists and people have classified some behavior as emotional. The suggestion that is generally made (e.g. Millenson, 1967) is that all emotions can be defined in terms of the consequences of positive reinforcement, negative reinforcement, and withdrawal of termination of those two. Thus the occurrence of these four classes of events, or of stimuli that have been paired with them classifies emotions and, if we want to become more sophisticated, some combinations of these four events and their conditioned stimuli may produce the occasion for "mixed" emotions. Generally, then, the argument goes that positive reinforcement is classified as joy, negative reinforcement possibly as frustration or anger, while the termination of negative reinforcement is classified together with joy or is sometimes called the emotion of relief.

There is no question that a community will tend to classify states of the environment that are easily distinguishable and differentiable, or at least as easily distinguishable to the public at large as they are to psychologists, and tends to use the common language to give these states relatively common names. Unfortunately, there are some difficulties with such a simple analysis, primarily because the occurrence of positive reinforcement and of conditioned stimuli for positive reinforcers does not usually produce the response of joy. Neither does the removal of a positive reinforcer necessarily produce anger or frustration, particularly if the organism has been reinforced previously for finding alternative ways of reinstating the positive state of events.

As I shall demonstrate later, whether or not a state of arousal occurs differentiates these diverse states. Thus the removal of a negative reinforcer is not equivalent to the occurrence of a positive reinforcer simply because the former usually involves arousal, while the latter may not. The removal of any "expected" event is an interrupting event and, therefore, it is a condition for arousal. There are some positive reinforcers that also have arousing properties (in the autonomic sense), but clearly they are not all of that type. The best way to look at the operant view of emotions is to consider the fact that the division of the world into positive and negative reinforcers and their termination may be interesting, but it may not be the emotional world that is divided. Another consideration must enter into the argument; does this kind of event lead to autonomic arousal?

There have been other attempts to deal with the topic of emotion in terms of classical models of animal and human learning. In these treatments the description of the conditions under which behavior occurs and its reinforcement or lack thereof is used to "explain" emotional behavior. Granted that few of these explanatory attempts are concerned with subjective feeling states, they do imply that certain conditions of reinforcement do, for all practical purposes, correspond to such subjective states. For example, Mowrer (1960) has spoken of "hope" as the conditioned form of positive reinforcement.

One recent such attempt has been Gray's (1971b, 1973) delineation of three definable emotional systems based on specified relations among reinforcing stimuli and response systems. He distinguishes (1) approach, where the reinforcing stimulus is the conditioned stimulus for reinforcement or nonpunishment; (2) stop, where the reinforcing stimulus is the conditioned stimulus for punishment and nonreward; and (3) fight-flight, where the reinforcing stimuli are unconditioned punishment and nonreinforcement. Gray initially differentiates emotions from other motivational states in terms of a common language distinction and suggests that we call states such as fear, disappointment, hope, and anger emotions, while hunger, thirst, and drowsiness are not. He suggests that the latter are internal states that are caused by changes internal to the organism, while "emotions are internal states . . . principally caused by events external to the organism." Gray needs a rather forced argument for this distinction; when emotional states arise with "no precipitating environmental event," or when "drive states become dependent on specific environmental events," he considers these states to be pathological and outside of the range of argument. This distinction between normal and pathological states goes against both the history of psychopathology and common sense. After all, there is no normal organism that does not at one time or another exhibit so-called pathological states, nor is the so-called pathological organism necessarily qualitatively different from the normal organism. By appealing to pathology, Gray excludes such phenomena as free-floating anxiety and abnormal eating behavior from the distinction between emotions and drives. Free-floating anxiety appears in most so-called normal individuals, and eating without hunger can occur in response to environmental stimuli even in nonobese individuals. The major distinction between these "unusual" emotions and drives then seems to be the rate of onset of the state rather than the external and internal source of elicitation.

Bindra (1970), among others, has also argued against a simple external-internal distinction between emotions and motives. To conclude my rejection of this particular distinction, it should be noted that Gray has particular difficulties with sexual behavior when he says that we do not regard "feeling sexy" as an emotion, since the emphasis is on internal causation, while we do regard "being in Love" as an emotion, with the emphasis being on a particular object in the environment. Granting the difficulty of classifying sexual arousal and romantic love under the same rubric, a topic to be discussed in Chapter 9, I doubt whether anybody would question that extreme feelings of sexual arousal or lust, even in the absence of love, are emotional in character. Furthermore, the eating behavior of the ravenous individual both has the appearance of emotionality and often its subjective feeling tone.

As far as Gray's three emotional systems are concerned, his primary concern with neurological structures may have obscured the psychological concerns that are our primary emphasis. For example, the distinction between unconditioned punishment and nonreward and signals for punishment and nonreward may not be as important from a psychological point of view as the distinction between fight and flight, with the former more frequently related to aggression and anger, while the latter is more closely related to fear and terror. On the other hand, punishment that interrupts an ongoing response sequence, and the conditioned stimulus for punishment, which functions as a signal for impending interruption, may have similar psychological emotional consequences (see Chapter 6).

Another version of an "emotional" analysis from a behavioristic point of view has been presented by Brady (1975). Using the appetitive-aversive dimension as a first approximation to the fundamental characteristics of respondent and operant behaviors, Brady suggests four combinations of superimposing classical "Pavlovian" conditioning on ongoing instrumental performance. These paradigms are used as first approaches toward a scheme of four general categories. These categories are defined by the operations performed, although Brady suggests some possible commonsense parallels of internal "feelings" for each of these classes that control emotional behavior.

1. Appetitive operants and respondents (possibly related to "joy").

2. Appetitive operants and aversive respondents (the well-known "conditioned emotional response" and possibly related to "fear" and "anxiety").

3. Aversive operant and respondents (possibly related to inward-directed "anger").

4. Aversive operant and appetitive respondent (possibly related to "relief").

While I would applaud the escape from the confinement of the commonsense language that Brady espouses, it is difficult to know whether the gamut of human behaviors can be properly expressed in terms of external respondent and operant relations alone. These behavioral schemas serve well for post-hoc explanations; they rest on highly artificial laboratory experiments, and they avoid becoming entangled with human consciousness. As a final point, we can argue even from a behavioristic point of view that emotions and feelings cannot be reasonably distinguished, as I have argued (Mandler, 1967c) in comment on Brady's (1967) position.

Another Cognitive Theory

Since I am primarily concerned with discussing a cognitive theory of emotion, a cognate position developed by Lazarus, Averill, and Opton (1970) is of direct relevance. At one point in the introduction to their theoretical position, Lazarus et al. make the point, with which we are in complete agreement, that "each emotion [is] characterized by its own specific pattern of response, which includes physiological, behavioral, and cognitive components." However, they apparently maintain the importance of different physiological patterns as determinants of emotion. In their critique of Schachter, for example, they say that Schachter attributes little theoretical significance to differences among the emotions along the physiological continuum, and they class him together with other theorists who have been concerned with the activation or intensity dimension as explaining the physiological aspects of emotion. Unfortunately, Lazarus et al. failed to make the distinction between physiological patterns in emotional expression or response on the one hand, and physiological patterns as controlling stimuli for emotional behavior and experience on the other.

However, the general position is really unaffected by that particular attitude toward the problem of physiological differentiation in controlling emotion. Lazarus et al. see emotions as "response syndromes which are relational," which means that they imply an object or the analysis of a total situation.

While acknowledging the importance of adaptive, evolutionary processes, they point out that cognitive factors in the expression of complex syndromes such as "aggression" seem to override any simplistic way of looking at its evolutionary significance. Similarly, they note that, from a cultural point of view, different cultural backgrounds change the perception or appraisal of emotional stimuli.

Central to the cognitive position espoused by Lazarus et al. is the notion of appraisal and reappraisal. Specifically, impulses to action are generated by a particular appraisal by the individual of the situation and by his evaluations of the possibilities for action that are available. In other words, all external inputs are subject to transformations, and the specific transformation that is given to a particular input is its appraisal; it characterizes the environment and will lead to different kinds of actions and experiences, not to speak of arousal, depending on the kind of transformation invoked, in light of the individual's prior experience and biological makeup. While insisting on the specificity of physiological changes, they also point out that the "cognitive subjective component of the emotion reflects an essential element of the total reaction, that is, the passive danger or threat, or in positive emotional states, an appraised sense of security, mastery, or a desirable bond between individuals." In addition, motor-behavioral components undergo similar differentiations.

The central question addresses the nature of these cognitions or appraisals (or, in our terms, structures, plans, and transformations) that give rise to different emotional reactions. They consider two kinds of determining conditions for these cognitions: situational and dispositional conditions. The former refer to environmental factors and the latter to the psychological structure of the individual, presumably his past experience and biological inheritance. Furthermore, these dispositions include tendencies to search out certain stimuli, to filter stimulus information in terms of both species-specific structures and the individual's own idiosyncratic needs.

The appraisal of the situation, in terms of Lazarus et al.'s notions, includes an evaluation of the outcome: to what extent the individual can cope with the situation and what the consequences of such coping reactions are. As they summarize it, "cognitive processes thus create the emotional response out of the organism-environment transaction and shape it into anger, fear, grief, etc."

The coping reactions are of two kinds. One is direct action, with its effect on the environment which, in turn, affects the appraisal of the situation. The other coping process is cognitive in that it involves further evaluations or reappraisals. In our language, a coping reaction would be a reaction to a particular situation that may be executed and have certain effects as a result of the structures invoked, or it may result in a change of the structures themselves, whereby cognitive or mental restructuring (or reappraisal) may result. Finally, they note the importance of specifying the cognitive factors that are involved in particular emotional responses. Thus "the important theoretical and research task in a cognitive theory of emotion is to identify the nature of the relevant cognitive processes, to establish their determinants in the stimulus configuration and in the psychological structure of the individual, and to link these to emotional arousal and reduction as well as to the quality of the emotional experience."

In summary, suffice it to say that there is relatively little disagreement, apart from the specificity of physiological patterning, between their position and the one advocated here. What I hope to do in part of this book is to specify some of the conditions that produce arousal and emotional experience, transformed and mediated by complex cognitive structures.

Theories Stressing Plans and Perceptions

In Chapter 7 I shall advance the proposition that *one* important functional releaser of autonomic arousal involves the interruption of organized response or action systems and of plans and expectations. Since arousal caused by interruption or disruption sets the stage for much of emotional behavior and experience, I shall next review briefly some theories that have described emotions in terms of such factors.

One of the most influential theorists who has discussed emotion in terms of consequences of disruptive or interruptive events is D. O. Hebb (1949). Hebb restricts his discussion of emotion to what he calls "violent and unpleasant emotions . . . and to the transient irritabilities and anxieties of ordinary persons as well as to neurotic or psychotic disorder." He specifically does not deal, under this particular rubric, with subtle emotional experience nor with the positive pleasurable emotions. Hebb's theoretical work derives initially from his observations of rage and fear in chimpanzees. He first discovered that the animals would have a paroxysm of terror at being shown a head detached from the body, that this terror was a function of increasing age, but that also various other unusual stimuli, such as other isolated parts of the body, produced excitation. Such excitation was not specifically tied to a particular emotion, instead, it would be followed sometimes by avoidance, sometimes by aggression, and sometimes even by friendliness. Hebb assumes that the innate disruptive response that is the emotional disturbance is the result of an interference with a phase sequence, which is Hebb's term for a central neural structure that is built up as a result of previous experience and learning. I shall not discuss the physiological aspects of Hebb's theory, but it is quite clear that a translation of his phase sequence into our structures is easily possible and that we are talking about the same kind of theoretical entity. Hebb's insistence that phase sequences first must be established before they can be interfered with, that the particular emotional disturbance follows such interference and the disruptive response, identifies his theory as an important precursor for our current speculations. In particular it should be emphasized that Hebb's theory does not require any specific emotional physiological pattern, but does require an acquired pattern of response as a result of the disruption of a phase sequence. Such disruption, from his point of view, may take place because two phase sequences are in conflict and therefore, in our terms, one or the other structure cannot be completed, or the environmental evidence (i.e., the sensory support for a particular phase sequence) is inadequate, so that, again in our terms, a particular structure cannot be completed because it is (for environmental reasons) not relevant to the particular input. However, while Hebb does not talk about specific physiological antecedents for specific emotions, neither does he put any great emphasis on the physiological consequences of interruption, specifically that the disruption of the phase sequence has specific, perceivable consequences in an arousal system. Finally, Hebb distinguishes between emotional disturbance and other emotional states—a distinction which we have abandoned. His rejection of emotional experience as a causal factor is one that we share, but it seems to be reasonable to generate a system that predicts and explains the experience, as well as the more observable aspects of the emotional system.

I have previously commented on the important influence of the book by Miller, Galanter, and Pribram (1960) on modern mentalism and cognitive psychology. It is of some relevance to note their comments, brief though they are, on the relation between Plans and emotion. Miller, Galanter, and Pribram treat the problem of emotion relatively briefly, as might be expected from a book primarily concerned with cognitive structures, but they do suggest that emotional behavior and experience is related to the disruption or interruption of Plans. For example, they note that when "a successful Plan suddenly becomes useless, the reluctant desertion of that Plan is accompanied by strong emotions." This phrase suggests that emotionality accompanies the desertion of Plans, but does not directly ascribe emotional consequences to the interruption or disruption of Plans. However, in another context, they say "the [emotional] activation appears to result directly from the suddenness in the alternation of Plans. . . ." Here it appears that they do ascribe the emotional experience at least to the degree of interruption of an existing Plan. Thus Miller, Galanter, and Pribram are precursors of the current position on the importance of interruption as a condition for emotional behavior. Since they were primarily concerned with cognitive structures, it is not surprising that they do not consider the problem of emotional experiences other than negative or disruptive ones, such as joy and pleasure, nor do they deal with the interaction between arousal and cognitive structures in detailing particular emotional experiences.

Miller, Galanter, and Pribram do describe briefly three possible consequences of an interrupted or disrupted Plan. One of them is the reinstatement of the old Plan and the perseverance, against environmental evidence, in maintaining existing cognitive structures. The extreme such case would be a paranoid state. The second possibility is to maintain the general structure of the Plan, the strategy, but to change the tactics. Thus the underlying, unconscious, and often irrational structure would be maintained, but different behavior would be employed in its service. The extreme case would be a schizophrenic reaction. Finally, they note the possibility that the strategy may be given up (i.e., the central structure may be changed), but that the individual may hang on to the tactics, in which case isolated bits of behavior, without adequate central structural support, are maintained, which is, in the extreme case, seen in the occurrence of compulsive and obsessional behavior. Just as the general structure of their notions of the Image and Plans is congruent with and a precursor of the notions presented here, the three possibilities of changing Plans are consistent with some of the discussions of psychotherapy I shall present in Chapter 9.

Another theorist who has discussed emotion, or anxiety and fear, in terms of structures and plans, although he did not use those terms explicitly, was Kurt Goldstein (1939). Goldstein's major contribution was to see anxiety as an individual's subjective experience that he was in a catastrophic condition. The impending catastrophe is perceived whenever the organism feels that it cannot cope with a particular situation and therefore feels its existence threatened. Goldstein interprets the symptomatology of brain-injured patients as an attempt to avoid the catastrophic situation. Thus the compulsiveness and even the seeming irrationality of the patient's behavior is seen as an attempt to avoid catastrophe or to bring order into his environment. Goldstein was one of the early psychological writers to deny that pain was inextricably linked up with the experience of anxiety or fear. Instead, he perceived anxiety as a general objectless experience that surrounds the individual.

In 1921 J. R. Kantor noted that "emotional reaction is not a positive response to a stimulus but rather a failure of a stimulus-response coordination to operate. What happens is that the organism is left in a crucial situation (in the most striking cases) without certain expected or desirable means of adaptation, either because of not having a response system for the particular stimulating circumstances or because of some failure of such an acquired response system to operate. Emotions are therefore essentially 'no response" activities." For Kantor emotions had no functional utilitarian purposes. Emotional situations were seen as chaotic and could be avoided by substituting an appropriate response for the one that was not available. The parallel between my point of view and this partial description by Kantor will be obvious. It was unfortunate that Kantor insisted on a negative view of emotion, common to the general view of looking at problems of emotional behavior as problems of undesirable and avoidable behavior and experience.

There is another subset of theories of emotion that is useful because it is primarily descriptive, without developing any extensive attempt at describing mechanisms. Probably the best example is Schlosberg's (1952) work on the dimensions of emotional expression. However, Schlosberg did not claim his to be a theory of emotion, but a useful approach for measuring and describing emotional behavior in the expressive realm. Another example is Plutchik's (1962, 1970) theory in which he describes a three-dimensional model of the emotions with an attempt to place all emotions, essentially derived from the ordinary language, along the dimensions of intensity, similarity, and polarity. Plutchik is also concerned with the functional, evolutionary aspects of emotions. Finally, Davitz (1969) produced a descriptive model of the language of emotion that provides some insights into the structure of our emotional descriptors without, of course, claiming to be explanatory.

I have reviewed both current and historical theoretical analyses of problems of emotion and placed them within the context of my own approach. In subsequent chapters central concepts of that appraoch such as arousal and interruption will be explored in depth and, as appropriate, related to other theoretical views.

Chapter VI

Arousal–
The Cognitive
Biology of Emotion

This chapter deals with the arousal system and its ramifications. My special interest derives from the notion that it is specific and measurable arousal that, combined with the cognitive interpretive system, lends the special "emotional" quality to certain experiences and actions. I shall first briefly describe the autonomic nervous system, which provides the physiological background of psychologically perceived arousal. Then, I shall present some speculations about the evolutionary role and current significance of the autonomic system primarily within the context of its interaction with an acting, adjusting, and thinking organism. That section will conclude with some of the current evidence for the cognitive consequences of autonomic activity. I shall further discuss the specific stimulation from the autonomic nervous system that is psychologically functional. Next I shall consider current knowledge about the stimuli that produce autonomic arousal, followed by a discussion of two reputedly instinctive sets of emotional action systems: aggression and facial expression.

I intend to use the concept of arousal differently than most arousal theorists have employed it. Arousal, as used here, refers to specific measurable events that occur *external* to the mental system; in a more ancient language, arousal is stimulation. While the arousal system is responsible for producing that stimulation, which is, in turn, perceived by the mental apparatus, arousal is external to the system, just as other environmental events that receive cognitive interpretation are external.

The difference between this environmental-cognitive use of the concept of arousal and previous applications (e.g., Berlyne, 1960; Duffy, 1962) is that the former endorses a psychological system that does not rely on energy concepts. The belief that the actions of organisms require some economy of energy in order to spring alive or,

111

in a larger sense, to be motivationally justified, is relatively recent. Notions of energy flow did not become central to psychological theories until the late nineteenth century and, in particular, with Freud's primary insistence on an energy economy. After that, concepts of arousal, drives, motives, and their cognates became indispensible in the explanation of action. Although biologists tended to be wary of these constructs that have so little empirical grounding (e.g., Hinde, 1956), the necessity for such mechanisms seemed to be self-evident.

However, recent years have seen a questioning of this necessity and, at least as an attempt, it seems worthwhile to proceed with an energyless psychology that relies a little bit more on such observables as autonomic functions and less on hydraulic fictions. From another point of view, Kessen (1971) has shown some of the advantages of deenergizing our view of early infant development. He makes the distinction between "hot" theories that "root thought in impulse" and "cold" cognitive theories, such as Piaget's. In the sense of that distinction, this presentation aims to be cool.

The Autonomic Nervous System

The autonomic nervous system and the somatic nervous system may be roughly differentiated by their respective functions. The autonomic nervous system is generally concerned with those functions that may be loosely called visceral, with the muscles of the heart, the smooth muscles of the intestines, blood vessels, stomach and the genito-urinary tract, and with the glands that are activated by the nervous system. In contrast, the somatic system includes among its functions the conveyance of information from sense receptors, their transformation, and the conveyance of information to the striped musculature of the body and limbs. And, while the pathways of the two systems can frequently be easily differentiated in the peripheral system, in the central nervous system both autonomic and somatic systems are closely interrelated and, at the present state of knowledge, frequently cannot be distinguished.

My major focus here is the peripheral autonomic system, primarily because I am concerned with the actions of the autonomic nervous system (ANS) that are discriminable by the psychological system (i.e., that are psychologically functional). The action of the peripheral ANS provides direct input to receptor organs, thence to the central nervous system, and generally to mental organization.

Thus, for our purposes, and in keeping with pshysiological knowledge, we can consider the ANS as an output system, and our special concern is, in part, with the differentiation of that output. Of additional interest is the fact that the ANS tends to act in a more or less total fashion; its output is less differentiated than that of the somatic system, so that it is less usual—as is obviously frequently the case in the somatic system—that only specific parts of the ANS will be reacting to stimulation.

However, there is a division of the ANS that is separable, and that does show generally differentiated but not wholly separate action. That is the distinction between the sympathetic and the parasympathetic divisions of the ANS. Again, I am not concerned with the neurophysiological distinction (whether anatomic or functional) between these two divisions but with the differences in their possible perceptually differentiable outputs.

Generally, the sympathetic system is concerned with bodily mobilization and the expenditure of energy, while the parasympathetic system is concerned with the conservation of bodily energy and resources. The two systems are antagonistic but not independent and, depending on the demands of particular environmental and internal situations, they will be in varying degrees of balance.

Because of the mobilization aspect of the sympathetic system, it is often considered to be the emergency system that reacts to bodily threat and danger as, for example, in flight or fight. Visceral blood vessels are constricted, thus channeling the blood supply to the muscles and the brain; heart rate is increased; stomach and intestinal activity is slowed down; the pupils of the eyes widen; the rate of metabolism is increased; and the sugar content of the blood is raised. The function of most of these effects in preparing the organism for immediate and alert reaction is obvious.

The parasympathetic system, on the other hand, renews and conserves bodily resources. Blood vessels are dilated and, as a result, blood pressure is lowered; heart rate is inhibited; stomach and intestinal activity is increased as is salivary secretion; waste materials are disposed of by action of the bladder and colon; the pupils of the eyes are constricted; and the rate of metabolism decreases. The parasympathetic system is also effective in the reproductive system, as in lubrication and tumescence, although it should be noted that the sexual response is a prime example of the interaction of the two systems. For example, contraction of the prostate prior to and during ejaculation is sympathetically innervated.

The fact that no exact line can be drawn between sympathetic and parasympathetic actions of the ANS has its roots partly in the phylogenetic history of the two systems. Pick (1954, 1970) noted that the autonomic nervous system is only gradually differentiated into a sympathetic and a parasympathetic system. The initial and early development suggests that ANS activity is first directed toward the accumulation and preservation of energies and that "the ability of the autonomic nervous system to mobilize and spend energies for the purpose of defending the organism from environmental exigencies is a comparatively late acquisition in the evolution of autonomic nerves" (Pick, 1970). Thus the sympathetic division apparently developed as an antagonist of the phylogenetically earlier parasympathetic functions. With the slow evolutionary differentiation of the two divisions of the ANS, it is not surprising that the functions of these two systems are not always clearly separable. I shall note presently that parasympatheticlike functions may regularly accompany sympathetic recruitment and may have important roles in behavioral adjustment. The interactions of the two systems become even more dramatic under some conditions of extreme physical stress when some higher organisms, including man, "do not activate the sympathetic for combat or for flight; they 'freeze' or even die instead of using every resource for flight or for escape. . . . [An animal] which ordinarily reacts to stress with a profuse sympathetic discharge resorts to phylogenetically older responses whenever the stimulus is too excessive" (Pick, 1970).

One other distinction must be made in discussing the ANS: a distinction between two closely related adrenal hormones or catecholamines, both of which are secreted in the adrenal gland. I mention them because they may have psychologically functional consequences. They are epinephrine and norephinephrine (sometimes called adrenalin and noradrenalin). Both have sympathetic effects, primarily by raising blood pressure. However, epinephrine acts by increasing heart rate and increasing heart output directly, while norepinephrine acts by vasal constriction and thus produces a decrease of volume, which increases heart rate. In addition, both catecholamines increase sugar levels in the bloodstream, epinephrine more effectively than norepinephrine. There are other important differences between these two hormones, such as their role as neurochemical transmitters, but these are of no direct concern to us, since they do not have any psychologically functional significance. It is possible that ANS discharge may be differentiated in terms of the primary action of either epinephrine or norepinephrine. If that is possible—and there is no hard evidence available at present—then two kinds of sympathetic activity (epinephrine and norepinephrine dominated, respectively) may play a differential role in emotional arousal, just as sympathetic and parasympathetic discharge do. However, the psychological difference between these two sympathetic patterns is obviously going to be slight. It is mentioned primarily because there is some evidence (e.g., Funkenstein, 1956; Brady, 1967) that differential output of the two hormones may distinguish certain emotional patterns. But, to stress again, there is no evidence yet that these two patterns control or direct differential emotional behavior or experience.

The Behavioral and Cognitive Functions of Arousal

The Adaptive Significance of ANS Arousal

The specific evolutionary aspect of emotional behavior and experience can be divided into two broad general areas. First, there are the preprogrammed, species-specific behavior adaptations that function for the population of a particular species and often have well-known adaptive significance. Among these are some defensive behaviors, sexual acts, and attachment patterns. Many of these are considered to be, in one form or another, prime examples of emotional behavior, such as anger, aggression, lust, and reactions to separation. A respectable ethological literature exists (e.g., in the work of Hinde and Tinbergen, the early works of Lorenz, and others) that has investigated the necessary and sufficient internal and external conditions for the appearance of such behavior in lower animals. However, little is known —as shown later in this chapter—about the internal or external stimuli that set the conditions for such behavior in man or the specific action patterns that are derivative from the evolution of the species. Most of the work on human action patterns in this "emotional" area is still carried on by analogy and does not carry us significantly forward beyond Darwin's original work on emotion in animals and man. While there are exceptions, and the most notable is Bowlby's work on attachment behavior (1969), we can only assume that some of the conditions and behaviors seen in mammals, particularly the subhuman primates, is applicable to the human case. Thus, I can say little more than that the flight, fight, and freeze reactions under specified conditions of threat are typical of mammalian behavior. Similarly, some generalization can be built on the observation of sexual behavior in primates, and some quasiethological work has been done in this area on humans by Masters and Johnson (1966). In any case, in the ordinary language, we describe much of this behavior as emotional because it provides the occasions for describing individuals as fearful, loving, lustful, and so forth. However, there are other preprogrammed patterns of behavior that seem to be specific to man and about which we know, from an ethological point of view, relatively little. Among these are laughter and crying, which seem to be typical of, if not exclusive to the human species.

We have assumed that all of these behavior patterns are necessarily "emotional" within the context of a psychological assessment of human beings. In fact, such behavior can often be seen as "cold" and unemotional. Even the peculiarly human responses, such as laughter and crying, are often seen—and sometimes deliberately in the case of actors—as devoid of "emotional" content. The same is true of some kinds of aggressive behavior, in the loving and attachment behaviors exhibited by psychopaths in pursuit of some other end, and even in the case of sexual behavior. It can therefore be argued that there is a missing component in all of these instances and, as a bridge to the second adaptive aspect of emotional behavior, we can suggest that the missing component is the activation of the autonomic nervous system. The argument is that in the natural state, and particularly in subhuman species, the aggression, attachment, and sexual patterns are usually accompanied by discharge of the autonomic nervous system.

The importance of the addition of ANS discharge in order to qualify a behavior pattern as emotional becomes obvious when we consider a recent attempt to argue for an evolutionary basis for prototypic emotions. Plutchik (1962, also 1970) argues for eight prototypic dimensions of emotions: incorporation, rejection, destruction, protection, reproduction, deprivation, orientation, and exploration. He derives these eight types from J. P. Scott's (1958) listing of nine general types of adaptive behavior. Pruning these nine types to five and with three additions, Plutchik arrives at his list of eight prototypical emotions. Apart from the puzzling insistence that these eight dimensions apply to *all organismic levels,* the list is so inclusive (particularly considering its parentage) that essentially all behavior is classified as falling into one or another emotional dimension. There may be good reason for such an argument, but not based on Plutchik's insistence that there are eight prototypic dimensions of emotion.

The insistence on the fact that the emotional dimensions must apply to all organisms seems to be spurious and unnecessary. It is unnecessary because in the development of species, new patterns of behavior clearly emerge, and there is no reason why some of those patterns may not be new "emotional" patterns. It is spurious if one takes just a few examples as, for example, the definition of deprivation as a "pattern of reaction to the loss of something possessed or enjoyed" or the definition of protection which "occurs basically under conditions of pain." To apply the former definition to the amoeba or to accept the latter definition for the case of humans who are pain-insensitive and yet quite capable of protection (Kessen and Mandler, 1961) illustrates briefly the difficulty with that position.

I assume that it is autonomic nervous system activity that turns many of the evolutionary-derived response patterns into "emotions" in either my or the ordinary language sense of the word. The ANS arousal system may modify and potentiate any behavior, *including* aggressive and sexual behavior.

The activation of the autonomic nervous system in combination with innate behavior patterns is important because both the ANS activation and the release of the behavior pattern occur "automatically" to the identical stimulus situation. In other words, the same functional stimuli activate the behavior pattern and the autonomic nervous system arousal. These internal and external conditions act as releasers for situation specific behavior, which has adaptive significance for the population, but they also generate physiological responses that put the organism in a state of physiological readiness for the behavior pattern that it accompanies. Among these responses are release of adrenalin and other sympathetic and parasympathetic responses. Furthermore, it appears that it is only in the case where the behavior is accompanied by ANS arousal that we usually think of it as "emotional." But what is the adaptive function of this "emotional" addition?

An evolutionary analysis may first consider the functions of the autonomic nervous system without regard to any action patterns that it accompanies. Essentially, the action of the ANS can be seen as a signal system (and, if the term had not been preempted, I would call it the second signal system). In general the ANS acts as a secondary support system for initiating an evaluation of situations that require a meaning analysis. A particular environmental input might require a very extensive meaning analysis for an appropriate cognitive appraisal but, under some circumstances, a more direct although less informative analysis would be more adaptive. If some event is coded quickly to provide an independent input to the activation of the autonomic nervous system while meaning analysis is proceeding then, regardless of the outcome of the meaning analysis, a signal (ANS arousal) will be available to the psychological system that says "Something is going on, something needs to be done." As a secondary system, the ANS has the paradoxical advantage that it is relatively slow, and it may not respond until 1 to 2 seconds after stimulus onset. During that period there is extensive opportunity for the meaning analysis to occur and for appropriate action to be initiated. However, if such action has not been initiated, then the input from the ANS (i.e., the perception of ANS activity) provides a secondary system that alerts the organism and demands additional meaning analysis. In many cases the action of the secondary system is superfluous because meaning analysis has taken place and appropriate action initiated long before (i.e., half a second or more before) the secondary ANS signal arrives in the perceptual system. The best example, known to most drivers, is the response to an impending accident on the road that will frequently provide an appropriate action such as stepping on the brakes within a few hundred milliseconds, but the ANS still reacts, and the well-known postemergency autonomic response will occur.

The interaction between ANS arousal and emotional reaction on the one hand and cognitive factors on the other becomes both more complicated and, at the same time, consistent with this approach if we consider the temporal parameters in neural conduction. As Melzack

(1973) has pointed out, sensory information classically associated with painful stimuli is mainly carried by the relatively slow spinothalamic tract while, at the same time, information is also carried by the much faster dorsal columns. The pathways that eventually lead to sympathetic arousal are effective even later than either of these two systems. Thus even before some sensory evaluation and most of the ANS arousal information is available, signals that may determine the cognitive evaluations of the situation and of the subsequent "painful" and "emotional" effects arrive at the cortex. In other words, the cognitive interpretation of the situation and of the ANS feedback may, under some circumstances, be ready before these visceral signals arrive for their own evaluation in the central nervous system.

One of the most important aspects of the signaling functions of the autonomic nervous system is in the case of interruption. In Chapter 7 I shall discuss extensively interruption of plans and actions, which produces an immediate ANS reaction. The adaptive significance of that response is that it signals—by input to the perceptual system—that an ongoing system has been interrupted. If that interruption has not been immediately perceived it now requires meaning analysis for an appropriate response.

The signaling action of the autonomic nervous system may also be construed as a mediating system. In cases where meaning analysis is often not possible—because of the organism's inability to attend to the situation due to other organismic or environmental events—structures may develop in which particular action is tied to the appearance of the ANS response. The sequence of stimulus event $\longrightarrow$ ANS response $\longrightarrow$ action will occur. This is the pattern that Mowrer and others have used to explain avoidance behavior in lower mammals. The two-factor theory of avoidance behavior, in which an autonomic nervous system response is first "conditioned" to the experimental situation in which the animal is shocked and then serves as a mediating stimulus between the experimental situation and subsequent avoidance prior to the onset of the noxious stimulus, is of particular interest in the case of organisms that cannot engage in an extensive meaning analysis. In man, elaborate sequences that use the ANS system as a mediating signal are not necessary. The analysis that a particular situation may have noxious consequences need not await the mediation of the ANS system, and avoidance can be learned relatively quickly. However, lower animals, as well as small children, do not have the elaborate cognitive apparatus available for analysis and, in that case, the two-factor "theory" applies. Thus the two-factor "theory" is more a description of the uses of the ANS system by certain species under certain conditions rather than a general theory of avoidance behavior.

Avoidance in humans can often, although clearly not always, be carried out without such an elaborate apparatus.

I can summarize my argument about the adaptive basis of "emotional" behavior by focusing on the evolutionary significance of the activation of the autonomic nervous system (and, of course, the adaptive significance of having an autonomic nervous system at all).

First, the ANS functions both as an accompaniment and possible activator of certain action patterns. Second, activation of the ANS serves as a signal for action and colors the particular behavior it accompanies or mediates. Thus much of the behavior that is considered emotional is seen as such only because it has ANS accompaniments. As I have indicated earlier, there are some evolutionary significant behavior patterns that may occur without the ANS accompaniment and are then seen as "cold." Similarly the prototypical dimensions discussed by Plutchik are characterized by behavior that is often not perceived as emotional at all. It is only when it is accompanied by ANS discharge that it becomes "emotional." For example, orientation and exploration can frequently be seen in a nonemotional context, that is, when not accompanied by ANS discharge. Conversely, as I have argued throughout, practically any behavior pattern may be accompanied, because of the secondary support characteristics of the ANS system, by sympathetic or parasympathetic discharge and may have "emotional" characteristics. Thus to survey, even from my point of view, the varieties of emotional behavior is equivalent to a survey of all experiences and behavior under conditions when they are accompanied by ANS discharge. Under those conditions they become more intense, are accompanied by physiological indices and, because of the constriction of attention by the demands of the ANS system, will often seem to be narrow, monolithic, and "irrational."

I have described here some general adaptive "cognitive" uses of the autonomic nervous system. In the next sections I shall discuss in detail how ANS activity may affect attentional mechanisms and how these relations, in turn, affect behavioral efficiency and general perceptual processes.

Adaptive Attentional Consequences of Arousal

The dominant notion about the function and evolution of the sympathetic nervous system is the concept of homeostasis, primarily linked with W. B. Cannon's name. He described that concept unequivocally in 1930: "In order that the constancy of the internal environment may be assured, therefore, every considerable change in the outer world and every considerable move in relation to the outer world, must be attended by a rectifying process in the hidden world of the organism. The chief agency of this rectifying process ... is the sympathetic division of the autonomic system." Cannon, in order to remove terms with "psychological implications" from physiology, suggests that the distinction between voluntary and involuntary systems be replaced by the terms exterofective system (for the somatic, striped muscles and skeletal functions) and interofective system, which acts on the heart, smooth muscles, and glands. The latter keeps "the internal environment constant and fit for continued exterofective action."

However, throughout Cannon's description of this homeostatic function of the sympathetic nervous system (SNS), we are left with the uncomfortable impression of a passive organism adjusting its internal environment to external events, just as a physical thermostat, for example. What is more likely is that the organism may react to the requirement for internal adjustment by action on the environment. These actions may change external stimulation to the point where the internal environment is restored to its previous "normal" level. We assume therefore that homeostatic action by the SNS also mobilizes action systems (of the "exterofective" system) to act on the environment. And the first step toward such action is the analysis of the environment, a cognitive-interpretive evaluation of the outer world and the possible actions available.

There are three suggestive developments in the literature that point to the direction of possible adaptive consequences of ANS activity and its correlates. The first of these is purely attentional.

We assume that any environmental set of events that produces ANS activity also is the occasion for attentional activity (or, as we might call it, focused consciousness). Research by the Laceys and their associates has shown that attentional activity is accompanied by a parasympatheticlike ANS response, specifically, cardiac deceleration (Lacey and Lacey, 1974; Lacey et al., 1963). We might conjecture that this deceleration in part attenuates one of the internal attention-demanding stimuli: cardiac acceleration. The less internal noise there is, the better attention is paid to external demands. However, the Laceys also found that cardiac deceleration is correlated with fast reaction times; the organism reacts more effectively to environmental demands. Higgins (1971), in similar context, has suggested that the cardiac deceleration anticipates the *perception* of the stimuli that direct behavior. Similarly, Graham and Clifton (1966) have demonstrated a correlation between cardiac deceleration and the orienting response, a focusing and readiness response originally explored at length by Sokolov (1963). In terms of Pick's arguments about the evolutionary history of the ANS, it seems reasonable to suggest that a primitive response of the ANS to demanding situations is a parasympathetic one that, while energy conserving, also increases the capability of the organism to respond to coping demands of the environmental situation (be it threat or not). This particular response may proceed at the same time that an energy expending sympathetic activity is going on (similar to the fractionation of ANS activity reported by the Laceys, 1959, 1967).

In addition to this initial correlation of ANS activity with attention, there is a secondary mechanism of cardiac deceleration, which is in response to cardiac acceleration. Since the sympathetic response to stimulation has a relatively long latency of the order of 1 to 1.5 seconds, this particular reaction sets in "long" after the initial attention-directing mechanism, which can occur in a few hundred milliseconds. While the Laceys do not differentiate between the earlier mechanism and what I would call the secondary response, a case can be made that the cardiac deceleration in response to afferent visceral events is a later and different response. It occurs in response to increases in blood pressure, which are picked up by receptor mechanisms (baroreceptors) in the carotid sinus and other vessels. The Laceys have shown that this afferently induced deceleration has the same consequences as the earlier response to attention-directing mechanisms. Here, then, is a direct parasympatheticlike response *to* sympathetic arousal that produces the kind of mechanism conducive to survival and coping that I described earlier.

The third mechanism that might produce adaptive responses guided by ANS activity is a long-range effect that suggests more effective longterm adaptive action under conditions of ANS arousal. Like the others, it also has the effect of making it more likely that the organism will, once ANS activity has set in, respond more quickly, scan the environment more effectively, and eventually respond adaptively. Most of the work in this particular direction has been done by Frankenhaeuser (1971a, 1971b, 1975). The major evidence in this area uses another measurement of ANS activity: the peripheral appearance of adrenalin and noradrenalin (the catecholamines). This usually involves measurement of catecholamine levels in the urine. Another approach involves the infusion of catecholamines and observation of their effect on behavior and experience. The Marañon and Schachter experiments are two prime examples of this technique. As far as the infusion technique and the present problem of the adaptive functions of ANS activity are concerned, Rothballer (1967) has shown that EEG is activated in drowsy and sleepy animals when adrenalin is given intravenously. However, such activation is not present in awake and aroused animals. This finding suggests that adrenalin produces ANS arousal which, in turn, leads to environmental scanning, but does not do so when the organism is already "in contact" with the environment.

Concerning the level of peripheral catecholamines, Frankenhaeuser (1975) has argued that the traditional view of ANS and catecholamine activity as "primitive" and obsolete may be mistaken, and that the catecholamines, even in the modern world, play an adaptive role "by facilitating adjustment to cognitive and emotional pressures." Frankenhaeuser (1971a) has reviewed the evidence that normal individuals with relatively higher catecholamine excretion levels perform better "in terms of speed, accuracy, and endurance" than those with lower levels. In addition a study by Johansson and Frankenhaeuser (1973) indicates that good adjustment is accompanied by rapid decreases to base levels of adrenalin output after heavy mental loads have been imposed. Thus high adrenalin output and rapid return to base levels characterize good adjustment and low neuroticism. If it is the case that the increased ANS activity produces automatic scanning of the environment, we might speculate that attention to environmental events not only is adaptive when events take place that automatically produce a rise in ANS activity and catecholamine levels, but also that this signal from the ANS system needs to be discriminable. A constant low or high level, returning only slowly to base levels, would produce few such discriminable ANS signals to the attentive, scanning mechanisms. The quicker the return to baselines is, the more likely it is that the next event that produces catecholamine activity will be scanned and, on the average, adequately responded to with effective coping activities. Absence of "appropriate" stress responses to situations that demand attention for adequate coping would produce, in the long term, ineffectual adjustment to environmental demands. For example, cognitive gating of threat in the environment ("denial") might reduce the adrenalin response and the appropriate scanning. Johansson and Frankenhaeuser (1973) comment on the "paradoxical" response, which shows decreased secretion during stress *and* poor adjustment to these cognitive and emotional stressors. I conclude that there is at least suggestive evidence that a third, long-range system involves ANS activity (or adreno-medullar response) that is adaptive in making it possible for the organism to cope more adequately with environmental tasks by increasing attentive scanning activity.

Arousal, Efficiency, and Attention

There is another line of thought that relates degree of arousal (defined autonomically) and human cognitive efficiency. The notion that there is an inverted U-shaped relation between arousal and efficiency has existed at least since Freeman's description of the phenomenon (1940). Since the concept of arousal has received varied interpretation, ranging from muscle tension to activities of the reticular formation, we can just as easily relate SNS activity to efficiency. The notion to be advanced suggests that as SNS activity increases, the information-seeking activity of the organism similarly increases and thus produces more task-relevant information. As SNS arousal becomes very intense, it floods attentional mechanisms and decreases the amount of information that the organism can recruit effectively either from the environment or from its own memory store. One can also relate this effect to some of Berlyne's (1960) suggestions about the relation between collative variables (novelty, surprise, complexity, and incongruity), arousal, and effective thought. Berlyne's suggestion that conflict is an essential aspect behind the operation of these variables is, of course, consonant with the interruption of existing cognitive structures. Novel, surprising, complex, and incongruous input or structures interrupt the execution of ongoing structures—which could be interpreted as conflict. Berlyne (1960, 1965) notes that these stimuli produce arousal (seen theoretically), while the accrual of new information (which brings new operative structures into play) brings arousal down again. Arousal increases with interruption and decreases as the organism finds means of coping with the new interrupting information.

The finding that the interesting aspects of a situation may be mediated by its complexity is also derived from Berlyne's extensive research on collative variables. The more complex a stimulus, the more interesting it is, and the higher is the level of activation and attention (e.g., Berlyne et al., 1963). Another more recent attempt to relate attentional variables to stimulus properties is the claim that pupillary dilation is related to the pleasantness of a stimulus (e.g., Hess, 1965). In an extensive study of these and other variables Libby, Lacey, and Lacey (1973) found, in the first instance, support for the Laceys' hypothesis of autonomic fractionation: that parasympatheticlike (e.g., heart rate deceleration) and sympatheticlike (e.g., pupillary dilation) responses may coexist under specifiable conditions (Lacey, 1967). In general the data suggested that attentive observation of environmental events produces pupillary dilatation and cardiac deceleration, consistent with Laceys' hypotheses discussed earlier. However, unpleasantness did not produce cardiac acceleration, as some global theories of arousal, activation and "stress" might predict. As Libby, et al. note, " . . . subjects indeed can intend 'to note and detect' even when stimuli are noxious and unpleasant." In general, we can, of course, agree with their conclusion that physiological responses are not "isolated stimulus-attributes," but that autonomic activity is important in dealing with environmental demands. Thus sociocentric notions about a world filled with objectively pleasant and unpleasant stimuli seems biologically indefensible; instead, autonomic activity responds to informational demands of situations, with reactions dependent on coping activities rather than "stimuli." Attention to the hedonically attractive object is supplemented by attention to potentially threatening stimuli (cf. also Hastings and Obrist, 1967).

With respect to Berlyne's conjectures about complexity, Libby, et al. found that the correlation between autonomic activity and interest is not mediated by complexity or activation. Instead, an "attention-getting stimulus, whether simple or complex, whether conveying a sense of activity . . . or passivity . . . evokes an autonomic response-pattern characterized by pupillary dilatation [sympathetic-like] and cardiac deceleration [parasympathetic-like]."

In general, these various studies support the position that "automatic" reactions of the autonomic nervous system are, in the first instance, dependent on some general mechanisms such as cognitive or behavioral interruption, and that these may lead to cognitive and autonomic adaptations that involve attention and coping behavior. At the same time, attentional mechanisms independently may be tied to some highly specific autonomic responses. Whether in the long run commonsense ideas such as novelty and interest are demonstrably related to interruption phenomena, in the sense that what is interesting or novel is a deviation from ongoing cognitive "baselines," is a matter for future conjecture.

Another aspect of the relation between cognitive efficiency and arousal has been summarized and theoretically codified by Easterbrook (1959) in the cue-utilization hypothesis. After reviewing a large and divergent set of data, Easterbrook suggests that "the number of cues utilized in any situation tends to become smaller with increase in emotion." While Easterbrook tends to equate emotional drive and emotion, his definition of a dimension of emotional arousal or general covert excitement" is compatible with our more restricted use of the arousal concept. In 1959 Easterbrook related the restriction of cue-utilization to problems of attention, an emphasis consistent with our discussion up to this point. However, in light of our current view of the adaptive effects of ANS activity and the more restricted definition of arousal, it is possible to extend the Easterbrook hypothesis. In the first instance, Easterbrook does not claim to provide us with a mechanism that mediates the relation between arousal and restricted cue-utilization. I have already indicated that such a mechanism could be found in the attention-demanding characteristics of ANS arousal. Given the limited capacity of attention-consciousness and the presence of additional events that make demands on that limited capacity, it is not surprising that with increasing arousal the number of other events (cues) that can share conscious attention will be decreased. Thus arousal necessarily limits cue-utilization, or at least the sheer number of events that can share in focused attention. Easterbrook noted that in some cases restrictions in cue-utilization may be beneficial rather than detrimental to behavioral and cognitive efficiency. When the narrowing of attention excludes irrelevant cues, performance may be improved, but when effective action demands attention to a wide range of events, arousal will be deleterious to efficiency (cf. also Mandler and Sarason, 1952, for a related version of this effect).

Earlier in this chapter I suggested several ways whereby arousal may produce increased attention. The present discussion seems to point in the opposite direction—arousal decreases effective attention. The two processes are not conceptually contradictory, even though they may produce behavioral and cognitive interference. Specifically, we may be faced with a dialectic process whereby arousal generates scanning and then limits the effectively scanned material by, so to speak, drawing attention to its own occurrence. First, we note that the attention-directing processes are automatic, nonconscious processes, while the attention-narrowing processes take place within the conscious world of the individual. Second, the attention-directing mechanisms may, among other things, direct attention to the perceived arousal. When they do, the consequences, as described above, are more likely to be attention narrowing. When attention is directed to environmental events, on the other hand, the effect is likely to be a broadening of cue-utilization. In the actual case, there is probably an interplay among these various combinations. The literature on cue-utilization is, at the present time, both confusing and sparse. The present hypotheses suggest that one way out of the present impasse may be a more detailed cognitive analysis of the various experimental situations, which might predict different results depending on the predominance of attention-increasing or attention-narrowing processes. I shall return to a variant of this problem under conditions of extreme danger in Chapter 9.

One of the implications of our position on arousal and attention is that arousal competes with other events for the limited capacity available to the immediate conscious field. Bacon (1974), in an extensive study of the Easterbrook hypothesis, noted that arousal does not improve attention to stimuli that are central, but decreases attention to peripheral cues. Processing of peripheral cues is impaired by arousal, but the loss is generally a function of the degree of attention that the stimuli attract initially. In addition, Bacon noted that the impairment is a function of loss in sensitivity and not due to any changes in criteria imposed by the subject. In general Bacon's data support the notion that for cognitive tasks, arousal impairs attention because it competes for limited capacity but does not have any direct or automatic effects on attentive processes. The automatic effects discovered by the Laceys take place primarily during the initial task orientation.

The Functional Physiological Stimulus

It is useful to make a psychological distinction among types of physiological variables (Mandler 1962b, 1967). The important distinction is the one between peripheral physiological variables in general and psychologically functional peripheral physiological variables as such. The present enterprise is primarily concerned with the inputs to the mental organization that produce emotional behavior and experience. Thus psychologically functional physiological variables are those that can be shown to have inputs to the mental system and to have a controlling effect over the behavior and experience in question. In particular, I am interested in those physiological variables for which it can be shown that the presence of one or more of them is necessary or sufficient for variation in some behavior to occur. Physiological variables, in contrast to psychological variables that, by definition, have known effects on behavior and experience, may be divided into four classes—restricting ourselves, of course, to autonomic and endocrine events.

1. Psychologically functional physiological variables. This class of variables is of primary interest if we want to know what it is that determines emotional behavior. As I shall show later, there is relatively little evidence about the differentiated action of specific variables, but it is the effect of autonomic nervous system activity in general that is of primary concern in this chapter.

2. Psychologically nonfunctional physiological variables. This class is frequently developed before group 1 has been adequately distinguished. For example, much is known about complex responses such as skin resistance or conductance to a variety of different stimuli. At the present time, there is no evidence that variations in skin resistance are controlling variables for psychological events or, even more generally, that skin resistance can be discriminated by the organism. Many of the autonomic responses that have been measured in emotional situations belong in this category. They are important physiological variables in that they tell us something about the body's response to certain emotional situations, but they do not, as far as is known, significantly influence emotional behavior or experience. These physiological events are correlated with behavior and experience and, very frequently, they may be used as an index function, but they are not psychologically functional.

3. Physiologically functional psychological variables. Certain physiological events are, of course, determined by experiential and behavioral events. To the extent, for example, that a physiological event is an index function for behavior that preceeds it, this is an important category for the investigation of behavioral-physiological interactions. In a sense, much of the physiological work on emotion falls into this category. Many of the physiological responses measured by psychophysiologists may be the result of the emotional behavior as well as of the environmental stimuli that give rise to it.

4. Physiologically nonfunctional psychological variables. These events have no theoretically or practically important physiological effects and are of no particular interest in the present context.

In summary, I shall be primarily concerned with the psychologically functional physiological variables, that is, the variables that determine behavioral and experimental events.

It must be emphasized that there are a host of physiological events that are correlated with behavioral events, but about which we are inadequately informed to make any causal, directive inferences. For example, subjects who find sexual stimuli disturbing show an increase in their body temperature when exposed to these stimuli, while subjects who are particularly reactive and disturbed by aggressive stimuli show a decrease in body temperature (Mandler et al., 1961). In these studies we are unable to make any causal statement except to say that these variables are shown to covary, and that further investigations are necessary to find an explanation for this covariation.

The attempt to show that different patterns of physiological responses are the determining variables for different emotional reactions and experiences has existed in psychology at least since William James' statement that the emotion *is* the physiological response. Thus Ax (1953) showed that under conditions that were designed differentially to produce anger in one group of subjects and fear in another, some slightly different patterns of physiological reactions could be found in these two groups. However, none of this implies that the different physiological patterns are psychologically functional. It is highly unlikely that humans can discriminate slight differences in patterns of autonomic response. More important, it would have to be shown that, given the different patterns of arousal, different emotions will result. At the present time, all I can say about the different physiological patterns in different emotional situations, particularly since they are measured after the onset of the emotional response, is that they are either a response to the environmental conditions that produce differential emotions or they are a response to differential behavior. Nothing in these data shows that the emotional behavior or experience is a function of the physiological pattern.

The study by Ax is typical of the present state of knowledge about physiological variables that may control emotional behavior. Schachter (1970) has summarized these various points of view, and I shall only indicate here the current state of the evidence. Apart from the fact that it seems to be difficult to replicate the kind of patterns that Ax has produced (see, for example, Kahn, 1966) other studies fail to find large variations in physiological responses even merely correlated with emotional behavior. For example, Wolf and Wolff (1943) were able to study a patient whose stomach walls were exposed by a fistula. However, extensive study showed only two different patterns of visceral response, one associated with anger and the other one with fear. There are other studies that have shown that some physiological differentiation could be associated with emotions such as disgust (Brunswick, 1924) and with general response syndromes such as startle (Landis and Hunt, 1939), but none of these claim or show that emotional behavior is determined by patterns of physiological response.

Given that there is no evidence that patterns of physiological response or autonomic discharge determine different kinds of emotions, what is the most likely psychologically functional input from the arousal system that controls emotional behavior and experience?

Autonomic Perception

I indicated earlier that human beings apparently have difficulty in discriminating slight changes in physiological patterns. There is currently very little evidence about the discriminability of autonomic nervous system reactions. Since we do know that there is a paucity of receptors that can pick up changes in autonomic functioning, the most likely candidate for a functional autonomic stimulus is general autonomic arousal, which can, of course, vary in degree but not in discriminable pattern. I shall next examine the question whether it is likely that general autonomic arousal, varying in degree, is a psychologically functional stimulus for emotional behavior and experience.

One demonstration of the physiological changes that can be discriminated by man would be to make some other behavior, some external response for example, contingent on changes in physiological states. We made one such attempt where subjects were required to make a discrimination that was contingent on a change in heart rate (Mandler and Kahn, 1960). The subject was simply asked to say "fast" or "slow" whenever his heart rate changed perceptibly. The experimenter was able to provide the appropriate feedback by inspection of a cardiotachometer. Under these conditions, where the subject presumably only had changes in heart rate available as a discriminative stimulus, there was an improvement in discrimination, whether the subject determined the response onset or whether he was asked to give a response on a signal from the experimenter. Within a few hundred trials the subject was able to make 100% correct judgments of his heart rate. However, it turned out that what actually controlled the discrimination was not the heart rate but changes in the respiratory cycle. The more even, well spaced, and deeper the breathing cycle is, the more pronounced are the distinctions between accelerative and decelerative phases of heart action. Thus the subject was learning to breathe deeply and evenly and to make his fast and slow judgment on the basis of the movements of his chest cavity. In another experiment in which a subject was not told that he was to monitor his heart rate, the sequence with which two lights went on was determined respectively by increases and decreases in the heart rate of two beats per minute or more. A subject was required to predict which of the two lights would go on. If heart rate could be discriminated it should have acquired control over the predictions. The subject was run for a total of 4675 trials, and his performance never deviated significantly from chance. Our conclusion at this time was that "discrete changes in heart rate do not easily develop into discriminated stimuli," and that the "private" stimulus conditions that control "emotional" behavior are likely to be grosser visceral changes (Mandler and Kahn, 1960). Nor have any other studies, to my knowledge, that have attempted to bring behavior under the control of relatively small changes in visceral patterns, been able to show such a relationship. None of this denies the validity of recent research by N. E. Miller and others that has demonstrated the control of variations in autonomic response by appropriate environmental conditions and reinforcement procedures (e.g., Kimmel, 1974).

If minor changes in visceral patterning cannot be discriminated and if no evidence is available that the physiological patterns sometimes observed with emotional behavior in fact *precede* such emotional behavior, we may then embrace the general assumption that the adequate stimulus for emotional behavior is general gross autonomic nervous system discharge.

The assumption that the perceptual system that receives input from the arousal system is insensitive may also be tested indirectly by investigating the output from that perceptual system to consciousness. The test is indirect because it involves *two* theoretical systems— perceptual and conscious—and relates output from the arousal system to output from consciousness through the language system.

One approach to this question investigates what people are able to say about their perceived state of autonomic arousal in relation to the actual level of arousal. We obtained ratings from individuals indicating the extent to which they habitually notice or discriminate internal (autonomic) events. After they had been given a questionnaire that showed rather large individual differences in awareness of internal states, they were given three complex stressful tasks. At the same time, five different measures of visceral response were obtained. In this first study (Mandler, Mandler, and Uviller, 1958) only extremes were tested, and it was found that people who had a high degree of awareness of internal events were significantly more reactive as far as the autonomic measures were concerned. In a subsequent correlational study (Mandler and Kremen, 1958) it was found that reported habitual autonomic activity was slightly correlated with a summary measure of the five individual autonomic indicators. However, a measure of situational awareness of ANS activity, measured by a postexperimental interview, was more strongly and significantly related to actual ANS activity. In this particular study subjects were also required to perform an intellectual task, and it was expected that there would be some interference between autonomic activity and performance. In fact it was shown that performance varied inversely with degree of *reported* visceral activity but was not correlated significantly with any single autonomic measure or with a measure of total activity. We had assumed that there would be interference due to divided attention between the autonomic input and the requirements of the task, but we concluded that it "appears that while this interference may in fact occur, autonomic activity is not a necessary antecedent to preoccupation with autonomic events. What might be the case ... is that the autonomic feedback phenomenon is originally a function of autonomic activity," but that eventually perceptions of autonomic events become independent of the actual events. In other words, what evokes the perception of autonomic upheaval or visceral activity need not be the actual event, as in the past, but some antecedent environmental condition that has, in the past, been the occasion for autonomic arousal. In terms of our current conceptualization the structure that involves the perception of autonomic activity may be under the control of autonomic arousal on the one hand and of certain environmental events on the other.

In a final study (Mandler, Mandler, Kremen, and Sholiton, 1961) a more detailed analysis of the relationship between visceral perception and physiological response was undertaken. Here we found, essentially in substantiation of the earlier studies, that an overall summary measure of autonomic reactivity best predicts people's situational reports of awareness of autonomic arousal. None of the evidence suggested that different kinds of emotional responses were associated with different patterns of visceral response.

Similar findings have been reported by Thayer (1967, 1970). In these studies physiological indices (including skin conductance, heart rate, and blood volume) were measured under different situations and related to a self-report measure of activation (the Activation-Deactivation Adjective Checklist). While a measure of activation may be somewhat removed from ANS activity, many of the adjectives included in the checklist make reference to internal bodily (autonomic) processes. For my purposes the major finding of interest is that in both of the studies reported by Thayer, correlations between the self-report and physiological indices were consistently higher whenever combinations of physiological variables were used in contrast to single physiological indices. In summary, it is noted that " . . . self report may be an integrative variable more representative of general states of bodily activation than any single physiological variable" (Thayer, 1970). Or, to turn the argument toward the present orientation, bodily awareness is in response to general gross bodily activity.

We have seen that the relationship between autonomic perception and actual autonomic discharge, while positive, is relatively weak. In addition, the available evidence suggests that the human organism is rather ineffective in discriminating autonomic events. I have also suggested that the perception of arousal and its occurrence are not necessarily correlated and may even be disparate events. In the extreme case of autonomic imagery, perception may occur without actual stimulation, just as in visual or any other kind of imagery. Equally important is the distinction between people's reports of habitual and of situational reactions, a distinction that was subsequently codified as the difference between trait and state variables (cf. Chapter 8).

The degree of arousal that an individual believes to be operating at a particular time thus may be a function of actual arousal or of other factors. These other factors can be purely cognitive in that the general system produces inputs to the perceptual system that indicate that a state of arousal exists when it does not. ANS arousal is not an all-or-none stimulus system. Small degrees of arousal may be perceived as more extreme or may draw increasing attention under some conditions. However, suggestive data do exist that people can be led to believe that arousal has occurred when it actually has not. The relevant inputs may be based on transformations of information from the environment, or they may be misinformation available in the environment. Valins (1966, 1970) has tested this proposition in a different context. He presented subjects with purported feedback of their heart rate. These heart rates were actually prerecorded and, under various conditions, the heart rate was either at a normal level or was accelerated. Valins showed that when subjects believed that they were experiencing an accelerated heart rate in response to certain stimuli, their valuation of those stimuli differed significantly from stimuli (pictures) that were not correlated with the increased heart rate feedback. Valins noted that the actual heart rates of the subjects did not differ as a function of this false feedback, but that it was the cognitive evaluation of their arousal that affected their judgmental behavior.

In related work, Valins and Ray (1967) showed that similar simulated heart rate feedback changed subjects' reactions to feared stimuli. Subjects were presented with pictures of feared snakes and with slides consisting of the word "shock," which was followed by actual shock. They were "shown" that their heart rates only changed in response to the shock but not to the snakes and subsequently exhibited significantly more approach reactions to snakes than did control subjects who were given no information about any differential heart rate responses to the two kinds of stimuli. Valins suggests that desensitization methods may be effective because "they allow subjects to believe that a previously frightening stimulus is no longer having a physiological effect." This demonstration is relevant to my discussion of therapy in Chapter 9. Methods of desensitization and muscle relaxation (e.g., Wolpe, 1958) are effective in changing individuals' perceptions of their bodily reactions and, presumably, when one has learned to relax in the presence of previously frightening stimuli, these stimuli become less frightening because the accompanying arousal is not present. In the case of relaxation the perception of arousal is absent because actual arousal has been decreased. However, Valins has shown that the change in perception and decreased fear need not be directly dependent on actual changes in autonomic responses.

There is one difficulty with the Valins experiments and subsequent extensions and replications (e.g., Wilkins, 1971; Barefoot and Straub, 1971) that show that simulated heart rate feedback changes the "emotional" evaluation of stimuli. The presentation of changes in presumed heart rate also suggests an alternative attentive mechanism; that is, when a subject hears the increase in his "heart rate," he presumably believes that something is different about the particular stimulus with which it is correlated. That "something" need not, of course, be an interpretation of the feedback as an increase in arousal. Consider the possibility that a pure tone changed in pitch when some of the stimuli were presented. Might we not also expect some changes in ratings of the particular stimuli, which certainly would not be due to "cognitive arousal? There is an obvious difference between somebody *believing* that a particular stimulus has emotional significance for himself or for others and *experiencing* a different emotional response to that stimulus.

More information is clearly needed on this topic. Some additional data have been provided by Goldstein, Fink, and Mettee (1972). They followed a suggestion from Frankenhaeuser's (1967) research, which showed that injections of a placebo produced either arousing or depressing effects, depending on whether subjects had been told that they had been injected with a stimulant or a depressant. In a replication of the Valins study, in which nudes were rated, they not only provided subjects with false heart rate of feedback, but also measured their actual heart rate. The Valins data were agian replicated, but the feedback also increased actual heart rate. While there was no relationship between individual subjects' *changes* in heart rate and their rating of the stimuli, it was clear that increased heart rate feedback produced increased heart rate, and one or both of these two variables affected the rating of the stimuli. That this relationship does not hold for subjects' *changes* in heart rate is not surprising, since it may be weak and undetectable, and also because change measures of autonomic responses are notoriously difficult to interpret (cf. also Mandler, 1959). In any case, these data do not resolve the question whether Valins' findings are a "cognitive" arousal effect, a direct arousal effect, or an attentional effect unrelated to arousal.

In a subsequent experiment Goldstein, Fink, and Mettee showed that in an emotionally more salient situation (the presentation of male nudes to male subjects), individual ratings of "offensiveness" were clearly related to actual heart rate changes but unrelated to artificial feedback. Since the second experiment did not involve any stimulus ratings, subjects were not likely to interpret the feedback as an attentional cue. The absence of the artificial feedback effect suggests that the results may have been attentional in the first experiment and arousing-emotional in the second. In conclusion, the Valins experiments *in toto* still suggest some possible effects of simulated autonomic feedback, but a final judgment must await more evidence.

Some Evidence for Autonomic Generality

The point about the generality of visceral arousal as the starting point for emotional behavior must be underlined. Until now I have discussed evidence that the discriminated aspects of visceral arousal probably involve a general degree of arousal, and that the studies that have shown different patterns have failed to show that these patterns control emotinoal behavior. It is, however, also the case that widely different emotions show relatively little differences in physiological patterns. Here we need not go into the question of whether or not these patterns are antecedent to the emotional expression. If, with very different emotions, the patterns are similar, the argument can be made that it is highly unlikely the different emotions depend on different patterns. The autonomic patterns are unlikely, in this case, to have been different antecedents to the emotional response. If the subsequent patterns show great similarity it is unlikely that there were large differences between them prior to the onset of the emotional behavior and experience. I have already noted that most studies that claim differential patterning have demonstrated both slight and unreliable patterns of visceral response.

Another investigation of emotional differences in patterns of visceral response was presented by Averill (1969), who showed that both sadness and mirth produce measurable visceral responses and that both of them seem to involve primarily sympathetic nervous system patterns. Averill found slight differences between sadness and mirth, which is not surprising; these states are also marked by different kinds of experiences and actions, but the data give us no clues as to any visceral differentiating states that *produce* sadness and mirth. It is more important to note that in a single experiment such as Averill's it has been shown that two such divergent emotional states, that have not typically been investigated by psychologists, both produce similar sympathetic states of arousal.

Another study suggests, from the point of psychophysiological research, the ubiquity of general sympathetic nervous system discharge. Pátkai (1971) started with the Funkenstein (1956) hypothesis, partially related to Ax's (1953) position, that habitual reaction patterns in anxious and aggressive states may be differentiated by the selective release of adrenalin and noradrenalin, respectively. Although there had been previous evidence that the Funkenstein generalization might not hold (e.g., Frankenhaeuser and Pátkai, 1965), Pátkai tested the notion, consonant with the position taken here, that the magnitude of adrenalin release may be an "indicator of general activation rather than being related to a specific emotional reaction." In her study, Pátkai exposed subjects to situations with different emotional content and found that adrenalin excretion increased in pleasant and unpleasant situations when compared with a neutral situation. The highest value of adrenalin excretion was found for the situation described by the subjects as most positive. Pátkai concludes that her results "support the hypothesis that adrenaline release is related to the level of general activation rather than being associated with a specific emotional reaction. The quality of emotions elicited is probably determined by the characteristics of the experimental situation as well as by the past experiences of the individual subject."

Frankenhaeuser's laboratory (e.g., 1975) has produced additional evidence, again negative, on the question whether adrenalin and noradrenalin energize different emotional responses. Frankenhaeuser summarizes both of the problems addressed here when she says: ". . . [The] results indicate that adrenalin is secreted in a variety of emotional states, including both anger and fear. Similarly, a rise in noradrenaline secretion may occur in different emotional states, but the threshhold for noradrenaline release in response to psychosocial stimulation is generally much higher than for adrenaline secretion" (1975). Both Frankenhaeuser's laboratory (e.g., 1971a and 1971b) and Levi's laboratory (1972) have shown, in systematic studies, that conjectures such as Funkenstein's (1956) that adrenalin is associated with inward-directed aggression while noradrenalin secretion occurs with outward directed aggression are untenable. In general, just as studies cited above show that different emotions are not characterized by different physiological states, neither are they characterized by differential excretion of catecholamines (e.g., Levi, 1965).

There is probably another reason why highly specific and discrete peripheral visceral patterning cannot serve as an adequate signal for specific emotion. If we agree that at least part of the emotional complex resides in the conscious field, then the limited capacity aspects of consciousness severely limit the kinds of patterns and certainly their discreteness, which could serve as adequate stimuli for the perception of emotion. Given the limitation to some five dimensions with single values on each dimension, or some five values on any one dimension, then it is unlikely that the kind of discrete, multifaceted patterning that would be necessary to represent the different shadings of emotions can be consciously perceived and evaluated. Furthermore, if the conscious process is preoccupied with attention to visceral activity, then it would severely restrict other cognitive factors from interacting with the production of conscious emotional states. Conversely, any nonvisceral attention would restrict visceral awareness to some few attentional chunks. Since such cognitive and environmental activity is highly likely, it is also reasonable to assume that only a limited part of the limited capacity of consciousness is devoted to visceral attention. If that is the case, then the most likely candidate as the adequate perceptual input would be some form of a single dimension of gross visceral output.

The physiological evidence suggests that the difference between essentially similar, "negative" emotions such as fear and anger is relatively slight, but that the differences between contrasting emotions, whether they are arrayed on a positive to negative continuum or whether we contrast grief and mirth, are not any greater. This is additional supportive evidence for the notion that visceral patterns are unlikely to be the basis of differentiation of emotional behaviors and responses.

The Conditions for Autonomic Arousal

I now turn to the question of what the environmental conditions are that produce autonomic arousal, either innately or as a result of individual experience.

I shall make the distinction between releasing stimuli and functional releasers. For example, it is highly likely that a loud noise or sudden loss of support is a releasing stimulus for ANS discharge in the young infant, whereas the particular stimulus configuration that characterizes someone's boss is surely an acquired functional releasing stimulus and is unlikely to be an innate releasing stimulus for ANS discharge.

One of the difficulties in trying to arrive at phylogenetic generalizations is that most external events and stimuli are filtered extensively through the cognitive-interpretive system. In lower animals fewer such transformations into functional stimuli take place; therefore the functional stimulus often can be adequately described in terms of events external to the organism. However, particularly in the human, such environmental stimuli can be and are variously transformed into functionally active or nonactive stimlui; conversely, phylogenetically neutral stimuli may be transformed into functional releasers. Thus an advantage of doing research with lower animals is that the stimulus and the constancy of its effects may be known to the observer across both situations. For man, however, we must ask what the mechanisms m ght be whereby external stimuli become functional releasers. In the history of psychophysiology the central concern with autonomic nervous system arousal has been within the context of classical conditioning theory. It has been the conditionability of sympathetic nervous system responses that have provided some of the mainstays for the demonstration of classical conditioning. Russian research over the past 20 years (cf., for example, for the early attempts, Bykov, 1957) has shown that many physiological reactions, ranging from kidney secretions to the production of insulin, can be brought under the control of conditional stimuli. The mechanics of bringing visceral responses under the control of environmental stimuli are now fairly well known, but from our point of view what still needs to be specified—and still awaits a theory—is the mechanism whereby a previously innocuous stimulus becomes a stimulus for ANS response. Furtheremore, many investigators, foremost among them N. E. Miller (1969) and his associates, have shown that autonomic responses can be brought under stimulus control by reinforcement (i.e., by instrumental conditioning) just as well as by classical conditioning methods.

In light of our previous discussion about the functional physiological characteristics of arousal, it is unlikely that the conditioning, whether classical or operant, of single physiological responses or organs is going to be of central interest to a psychology of emotion. It is not likely that any single conditioned visceral effector controls a particular kind of emotion or general emotional arousal. We still know very little how the conditioning of one system within the autonomic nervous system might spread to an arousal of the whole system or how we might go about controlling more extensive blocks of responses in the autonomic nervous system.

There are a series of stimuli that have been identified as innate releasers of autonomic nervous system activity. In most cases the interest has been in identifying stimuli that are also releasers of other observable behavioral systems, but it frequently can be assumed that ANS arousal functions go together with such systems. For example, the species-specific responses to stress and pain (e.g. Bolles, 1970) presumably are accompanied by ANS response. In early infancy, loss of support and high levels of stimulation also tend to be ANS releasers. Bowlby (1973) follows Hebb (1946) and Schneirla (1959) in suggesting that strangeness is a source of fear and, we can assume, also a source of ANS arousal. I shall return to the notion of strangeness and problems of fear in Chapters 7 and 8.

The question of how a previously innocuous stimulus becomes transformed into a functional releasing stimulus is, of course, central to many areas of psychological investigation, not just the psychology of emotion. The traditional paradigm is the psychology of classical or respondent conditioning. Clearly, one of the *conditions* under which a previously innocuous stimulus (i.e., a stimulus that has no control over any behavior in a particular organism) becomes a functional stimulus for a response system previously under the control of an unconditioned or innate stimulus is the pairing of the two (i.e., the methodology of classical conditioning). In the most traditional example, the sound of a bell comes to elicit salivation, which previously had been under the control of meat powder. We then describe the conditions under which substitutions may take place. However, as in most associative theories, this describes the *conditions* under which a certain effect can be obtained; it does not provide any explanatory power or mechanism. Even the elaboration of a so-called "theory" of classical conditioning, which describes all the conditions under which this substitution of conditioned for the unconditioned stimulus takes place, is short of what we would like to see in terms of a theoretical model, and it becomes quite clearly inadequate when we think about the situation that confronts us in the current context.

If we were to ask how a particular individual comes to be in a state of autonomic arousal when presented with the sight of a child being nearly run over by an automobile, then it is difficult (though some learning theorists sometimes make the attempt) to describe the variety of prior conditionings that must have occurred in order that this particular set of events should produce a release of autonomic discharge. It is highly unlikely that the intricate concatenations of previous experiences have always been favorable in just such a way as to produce the "conditioned emotional response" that occurs. It is, in

fact, the very fine-grained analyses of classical conditioning and the
precise relationships among unconditioned stimuli, conditioned stimuli,
and unconditioned responses that these studies have shown to be
necessary for the substitution paradigm to work, that argue for the
implausibility that those conditions are met in the "conditioning" of
visceral responses in everyday life. A similar argument, with respect to
instrumental or operant conditioning, has been made in relation to
language learning: that the conditions of language acquisition in the
child are unlikely to fullfil the precise timing and topographical
requirements for the optimal establishment of operant behavior
(Chomsky, 1959). None of this argues that the descriptions of classical
and instrumental or respondent and operant conditioning are erroneous.
The critique of classical learning theories cannot be based on a denial
of their research contributions. It must be directed at the unwarranted
assumption that if a particular condition produces a certain behavior,
then that behavior is usually produced by identical or similar
conditions.

Laboratory experiments, particularly with lower animals, provide a
possible set of conditions under which the acquisition of new behavior
and the substitution of new stimuli can take place. These experiments
may even provide the optimal conditions under which these
phenomena occur, and they demonstrate the process for exercising
optimal control, not just over the behavior, but also over the
cognitive-interpretive system of the organism in question. Similarly,
the control of behavior by the precise control of environmental events
and the consequences contingent on certain behaviors, which has been
so convincingly demonstrated by Skinner and his students, is valuable
becuase it provides precisely the advantage of knowing what the
organism is exposed to, what it is permitted to do, and what the
consequences of such behaviors are likely to be. Control of behavior is
a control over the instructions we give to an organism. The only
instructions we can give to a nonverbal organism is through the strict
control of the contingencies of reinforcement. Instructions
(programming of cognitions and of plans) can be equally effective by
direct communication or by the appropriate control over the
input-output contingencies. The advantages of operant methods with
organisms who cannot hear, may not wish to hear, or deny hearing our
instructions is that they bypass some cognitive-interpretive inputs, but
deal directly with the operations of the cognitive-interpretive system.
The control of the behavior of animals, or of physiologically or
psychologically impaired human beings, is equivalent to the proper use
of instructions. Behavior therapy instructs the impaired organism in
new ways of behaving, just as other individuals may be instructed by
cognitive manipulation in classical psychotherapy. However, the

advocates of operant methods of control neither claim, nor should they be assigned the claim, that they can describe the mechanism whereby these changes take place.

Cognitive Transformations

I now return to the question of how innocuous stimuli, emotionally neutral events, may be translated into functional releasing stimuli for ANS arousal.

If we assume that some innate or functional releasing stimulus is always necessary for the triggering of autonomic nervous system response, then one of the central problems for an understanding of human emotional behavior concerns the nature of these functional releasing stimuli. For lower animals, particularly those that have relatively simple cognitive interpretive systems, it is relatively easy to specify the releasing stimuli. In general this same argument applies to psychological research with lower animals where the stimulus, or its constancy, or its effect, may be known to the observer in that he may adequately describe it, across both situations and individuals. Thus we can describe the releasing stimuli for sexual behavior for lower species, but less and less so as we ascend the phylogenetic scale (cf. Ford and Beach, 1952). When we come to the primates and man, it is generally conceded that so-called cognitive factors become more and more important in determining the onset and offset of sexual behavior. The congitive system becomes more and more effective in modifying the external stimulus. We may assume that the initiating events, or stimuli, may be practically of any character or variety, but that the cognitive system converts them into functional releasing stimuli. Thus the products of an elaborate and complex cognitive-interpretive system are the same as the initial stimuli for lower animals where the system provides relatively few transformations.

It does not matter what particular set of emotional behaviors we wish to subsume under the prewired, or innate, or genetically determined category (cf. Bruell, 1970). For example, we could start with J. B. Watson's crude distinction among rage, fear, and love (although he presumably meant lust), and translate his fear-rage distinction into the more popular contemporary flight-fight distinction. But the events that will produce fear or rage in a human are often considered to be surprising or irrational. The person who fears and flees from events and objects that others do not fear, as in common phobias, clearly has no prewired or genetically determined fear of such objects. For example, agoraphobia, or the fear of open places, must be related to the fact that such stimuli are functionally interpreted as fear releasers. Similarly, the man who flies into a towering rage because somebody took his place in a queue is interpreting the situation in a way that produces rage release. In the area of sexual arousal it is highly unlikely that handlebar mustaches have been genetically selected as releasing stimuli for female sexual arousal; instead, they may be *interpreted* as sexually arousing, just as an otherwise sexually arousing stimulus (such as a receptive cross-sex partner) may fail to arouse sexual behavior in some cases.

In terms of our notions of emotional arousal and behavior, two asymmetric interpretations of the effect or lack of effect of external stimuli need to be explored. In the case of the apparently neutral stimulus that gives rise to emotional behavior, two interpretations of this transformation are possible. One is that the arousal system may be in the state of activation because of some other set of events that are extrinsic to the specific situation. For example, the man who has just been fired from his job and is in a state of autonomic arousal may react violently to being supplanted in the queue for his bus, whereas he may not have done so had there not been any prior arousal. In other words, he is using the immediate situation to "explain" his state of arousal. The other possibility, the one favored by classical psychotherapists, is that the eliciting situation is reinterpreted as a threat. The question is then usually posed, "What are you really afraid of?" This is particularly posed in cases of irrational aggression and irrational fear. In our example, we would ask about the meaning of being pushed out of one's place in the bus line. I will deal elsewhere with the locus of effect of different kinds of therapies; for now I am only concerned with the two possible explanations why neutral stimuli may become functional releasing stimuli.

In contrast to socially "neutral" stimuli, when a species-specific stimulus fails to arouse the "appropriate" emotional behavior, we assume that only one factor is operative: reinterpretation by the cognitive-interpretive system. For example, the loss of support that occurs on a roller coaster is reinterpreted by the adult to function as an innocuous or even "positive" stimulus. The possibility exists, of course, that the system is not reinterpreting the stimulus but that it in fact fails to trigger the autonomic response. However, such a possibility would require that the autonomic nervous system can be turned on and off despite the existence of potent releasing stimuli. Such evidence exists in the case of yoga, but it does not seem to be understood well enough to be of major explanatory value.

"Instinctual" Behavior Patterns

Aggression

It is unfortunate that some of the most insightful writers on problems of innate or instinctual behavior patterns have very little to say about the functional releasing stimuli for these structures. For example, Lorenz (1963), in a volume much troubled by ethnocentric conceptions, talks about aggressive drives in man and some of their possible origins, but says little about research into the situations that are sufficient and necessary for the release of these aggressive patterns. It is obvious to the psychologist and to the anthropologist—although often not to the ethologist—that many similar patterns may not be expressive of a particular drive or drive condition but may be related to different drive systems or to different cognitive structures. Thus, from an ethological point of view, hitting an object with one's fist may be interpreted as the displacement of aggressive drive, but it also may be the only way of opening a walnut, which has very little to do with aggression. The conceptual problem involved in looking at complexly determined behavior should interest ethologists, psychologists, anthropologists, and others in some joint effort at both definition and specification.

Some of the speculations that Lorenz indulges may be interesting, but they are not particularly useful. To say the fact that man does not have much opportunity to discharge his aggressive drive in interspecies competition does not help to understand specifically the social or personal conditions to which the aggressive drive is tied when it *is* expressed, nor does it help understand the cognitive transformations that are necessary for the expression of that aggressive drive at a particular time. Psychologists as well as more popular writers have speculated about threat, encroachment, and many other "causes" to explain the occurrence of aggression and, although we have come a long way from postulating a unique link between frustration and aggression, we have not come very far toward an analysis of the instinctual elicitation of aggressive behavior. On the other hand, we know much about the cultural and personal conditions, and they are legion, that may under various conditions produce aggressive behavior. Thus past research at least suggests that cognitive-experiential causes of aggression (as well as other "instinctual" patterns) are easier to find than innate releasers or prewired patterns.

While the same behavior may have different sources, we also know that the same sources may lead to different kinds and very often quite antagonistic and disparate behavior patterns. Whether we learn to channel certain cognitive structures or drives into socially acceptable patterns because of our early development or because of the operation of fear and dread, and whether we call these redirections sublimations as Freud did or redirected activity as Tinbergen and Lorenz do is not relevant; what is important is that we should be aware of the multiplicity of causes and outcomes that are operating on so-called innate behavior patterns. We know very little about the mechanisms that would lead to an adequate conceptualization of behavior that may easily be *called* instinctual, but much less easy to explain.

One interesting by-product, which should be treated at least parenthetically, is an attempt to understand the behavior pattern known as *laughter*. Lorenz makes the argument that laughter is "derived from aggressive behavior and still retains some of its primal motivation" (Lorenz, 1963). He sees it as the "ritualization of a redirected threatening movement" that also produces strong fellow feeling among participants and "joint aggressiveness against outsiders." Whatever the function of laughter and the origin of its releasing mechanisms, we still know very little, despite efforts from all directions of psychological thought, about the conditions under which laughter and humor will appear. Laughter is one of those cases where many conditions other than the primitive ones that Lorenz talks about produce the same kind of behavior. One of the origins of laughter can be found in discrepancy, which produces arousal and therefore emotional response. However, what the conditions are under which this particular kind of discrepancy leads to the experience of humor instead of some other emotional content is still unclear. Olympian statements about the salutary redirection of aggression into laughter tend to obscure the search for understanding.

If stimuli other than innately programmed ones can release so-called instinctual behavior, it is equally obvious that in complexly cognitive animals such as human beings the response to "innate" releasers is not inevitable. Human beings can and do control unacceptable behavior (whether it is aggressive, sexual, or whatever), although the history of evil often obscures the ethical achievements that go counter to some of our evolutionary history. We might even speculate that evolutionary pressures may have eliminated some of the aggressive patterns in some human subgroups. We need not speculate, but we can assert, that in many individuals the instinctual stimuli have been cognitively redirected.

The social, economic, and cultural substrate of our mental organization redefines these ancient and primitive signals. Given the dependence of the cognitive system on the social environment, many such redefinitions appear as cultural *givens* for practically all members of a particular society. The variety of aggressive outlets that can be found to be "natural" in different societies attests to this interpretation, which is common knowledge to social anthropologists but is often ignored by many modern and popular ethologists of man.

Harlow and his co-workers (e.g., Deets, Harlow, and Harlow, 1971) have shown how early experiences can fundamentally redirect aggression, fear, and love in the monkey. The immensely greater complexity of human mental organization suggests that problems of redirection and reinterpretation may be more important in understanding ourselves than simple analogies with primitive animals or societies.

To understand innate and functional releasing mechanisms may require us to understand how we *think* about our world as often as we understand how we *act* in it. The stimulus that led our ancestors to aggress physically may often play only a minor role today in determining the contents of emotional experiences.

Human aggression (at least as viewed by its protectors) takes a variety of different forms; it is not—as in lower animals, who are usually posited as the prototype—either stimulus or response pattern specific. There are no fixed action patterns in human aggression. As behaviorists would say, human aggressive responses vary widely in their topography. If, then, there is no fixed action pattern of human aggression, what is it that is innate? One popular alternative is that it is some idea or motive or drive of aggression, a position that again reduces the position to some eighteenth-century notion of prior ideas divorced from the realities of life and behavior. And certainly the notion of an evolutionary motive that energizes practically all aspects of human action would be difficult to defend on the very genetic grounds that its defenders espouse.

The instinctivist position states that humans have an innate drive toward aggression that serves the survival of individual and species. In many of its forms the position also invokes the idea that when aggression cannot be expressed, it is dammed up, and as a consequence, often inappropriately released. The latter, hydraulic model can be found in Lorenz, Freud, and many others.

An examination of the use of this notion of an innate drive suggests that it has been used for purposes other than objective explanation. Consider that the instinctivist position implies that the innate drive must be seen in *all* aspects of human aggression. However, they prefer to restrict the aggressive act to a physical attack on another human being, when any action or plan that harms another human should fall under their rubric. It is somewhat revealing of the *Weltanschauung* that motivates the instinctivist point of view that it prefers the aggression typical of the poor and deprived classes, but glosses over the aggression exercised by the powerful classes of society. Causing people to starve or denying them the right to join their loved ones should be aggressive actions by the definition of innate aggressive drives, although they are rarely enumerated in the instinctivist literature. Physical aggression is seen as a phenomenon of all people but, curiously, it is found to be more likely among the poor and powerless. Indirect aggression by the powerful is rarely put into the same rubric. The intelligent and wealthy are somehow genetically exempt from the ravages of our aggressive "instincts." However, if their acts are also seen as aggressive, what is it that is passed on from generation to generation among all members of the species? Would the instinctivists still endorse a genetic motive if that drive was expressed in lower-class physical aggression on the one hand and in refined laws that keep the poor in poverty and the exiles away from their homes on the other?

Once we ask about the world view that motivates the invocation of such a useful innate motive, we are tempted to concur with the editor of a collection of papers on the analysis of aggression that the promotion of an aggressive instinct also inevitably promotes the defense of a society directed unilaterally toward competition. Competition is a close relative of aggression, and if we cannot defend the latter, maybe it would be more difficult to defend the former (Selg, 1971).

A similar critique of the instinctivist and hydraulic models of aggression has been presented by Bandura (1973). He notes the self-serving aspects of these explanations and the absence of any evidence for the various energy models of aggressive behavior (cf. also Hinde, 1956). More important, Bandura's social learning theory of aggression is, in many aspects, similar and consistent with the view advanced in these pages. Bandura assumes that "aversive experiences produce emotional arousal that can elicit a variety of behaviors, depending on the types of reactions people have learned for coping with stressful conditions." Among these reactions are dependency, achievement, withdrawal, constructive problem solving, and aggression. But aggression is seen as only one possible reaction to the concatenation of aversion and arousal. I would only add that aversive experiences are not a necessary antecedent for the emotional arousal that precedes aggression. There is no necessary stimulus for arousal that produces aggression among its consequences; only arousal and the opposite cognitive evaluations are required. By way of example, we need only consider pathological or commonplace sadistic behavior, which is aggressive, but which is not necessarily preceded by aversive conditions; on the contrary, these may be typically absent. Fromm (1973) has described in great detail the conditions that produce this kind of destructiveness.

It is beyond the scope of this chapter to deal in great detail with the various attempts that have been made by writers such as Lorenz to defend and justify not only some unalterable destructive human urge, but also the forms of societies that are congruent with such a view. Fortunately, a brilliant attack on these views has been mounted *in extenso* by Erich Fromm in *The Anatomy of Human Destructiveness.* His work is more than an attack; it is a wise and insightful defense of what human character might and can be. Fromm dissects the instinctivist view from physiological, behavioral, paleontological, and anthropological vistas, and he lays bare its often shoddy thinking and some of the motives that might underlie such a view of mankind. Fromm notes that flight is as "natural" a human reaction as is fight, a point of view sensitively depicted by the playwright Robert Bolt in his portrait of Sir Thomas Moore in *A Man for All Seasons.* Bolt has Moore saying at one point that "our natural part is in escaping." The notion that moral courage and physical flight are compatible is unfortunately alien to an aggressive, competitive society.

Fromm does posit one kind of biologically adaptive aggressive response: defensive aggression. Flight or fight actions are mobilized when "vital interests of the animal are threatened, such as food, space, the young, access to females. Basically the aim is to remove the danger; this can be done . . . by flight, or if flight is not possible, by fighting or assuming effective threatening postures. The aim of defensive aggression is not lust for destruction, but the preservation of life." In terms of our view, to be detailed in the next chapter, such threats would be interpreted as interruptions of dominant and well-integrated action patterns. Given the ensuing arousal—which is likely to be intense—the emotional quality at these intensities may well bring into play innate systems such as flight or attack. But once the interruption has been removed, there is no remaining destructive urge, nor are the flight or fight patterns in the service of some higher destructiveness; they are, as Fromm would say, in the service of protection of life.

The Facial "Expression" of Emotion

The title of this section is at variance with the general theme of this book. To say that facial expressions "express" emotion implies some prior emotional quale, hooked to some facial movements that are elicited whenever the prior "emotion" is activated. Having rejected the idea of undefined emotional qualities, ideas, or feelings, we must deal in some detail with the unavoidable fact that a variety of facial "expressions" seem inevitably tied to emotional experience and behavior. The question then becomes whether these expressions express anything at all, or whether they are an important set of acts that contribute to rather than express the emotional complex.

Any discussion of facial expression must start with Darwin's painstaking investigation of the generality of emotional expression across and within species. Darwin's thesis was that just as these expressions directly externalize the lower animal's emotions, so do they express human emotional states. He developed three general principles to explain their occurrence and particularly to address their persistence in nonadaptive contexts. After discussing Darwin's contribution, I shall return to the role of these "expressions," which seem to occur not only in direct response to "emotional" situations, but also are generated in other contexts and even frequently and easily inhibited by humans.

Darwin's (1872) three major principles opened up major lines of thought for succeeding scientists. His principle of serviceable associated habits postulates complex actions that are "of direct or indirect" service, given certain states of mind. These habits will also occur when they "may not then be of the least use" but simply because some "state of mind" similar to the originator is present. That is, expressive movements may be indices of internal states even though they may have no adaptive significance whatsoever at the time. This principle justifies the study of expressive movements *per se* rather than their functional significance.

Darwin's second *principle of antithesis* asserts that certain actions will be induced by opposing states of the mind and that these actions (or movements) may be "of no use" but will be "directly opposite in nature" to the actions and movements induced by the original state of mind. Darwin here asserts the bipolarity of certain expressive movements (reflecting the bipolarity of mind states), an assertion that has led to the respectable tradition of seeing emotions as dimensional on such bipolar axes as pleasant-unpleasant, active-quiescent, and attending-rejecting.

Finally, the third *principle of the direct action of the nervous system* states that certain expressive results are dependent solely on "excess nerve-force," independent of other factors. The lack of knowledge of the nervous system at mid-nineteenth century prevents any unequivocal interpretation of Darwin's statement. My own reading, particularly of his examples, convinces me that in the majority of cases Darwin refers to the inevitable effects of intense autonomic nervous system reactions—again a theme that is still with us today.

There are undoubtedly some few universal, unlearned, cross-cultural "emotional" expressions, primarily facial in nature. But to show the universality of facial expressions is a long way from claiming that what is universal is the expression of emotion. The misleading cue resides in the idealistic notions that the facial expressions express something "behind" them, some emotional *quale,* feeling, or idea. We can dispense with such a naive nineteenth-century psychology but still assume that there are situation-specific evolutionary remnants shown in facial expression. These facial expressions, just as other innate actions, including many approach and withdrawal sequences, define the situation-action complex. Our reactions to the environment in turn give rise to some emotional evaluation. We must remain with William James' insight that the emotional *quale* follows the bodily response. For example, laughter following tickling is presumably innate, but tickling does not generate a "good" emotion followed by laughter; the sequence is actually the reverse. Action patterns may be inherited to specific stimuli, and these action patterns may then be transferred to new situations. With time and experience we learn more about the evaluation and meaning analysis of the situation in which these innate action patterns occur. We can also disengage the action, the facial expression from its releaser, and emit it in its absence, but again we must learn to do that. Thus, while the blind show the "proper" facial "emotional" expression, Dumas (1932) has shown that they cannot act out these expressions when given the name of the emotion. There is no innate connection between an idea of "hate" and baring one's teeth. Teeth are bared to specific stimuli.

The preoccupation with facial expression is not surprising, since we find so few cross-cultural constancies, particularly ones that we encounter, one way or another, in everyday experience. But this delight with finding universals should not hide the fact that we are dealing, as Darwin knew, with evolutionary *remnants.* The evidence for the universality of facial expressions is good, although not as good as some investigators (e.g., Ekman, 1973; Izard, 1971) would like. There are strong situational and contextual determinants as to who will recognize what emotion under what circumstances. Certainly the consistency between Western stereotypes and non-Western nonliterate isolated cultures evaluation of these stereotypes suggests that there is some cross-cultural constancy, and the case against those who insist on no such constancy (e.g., La Barre, 1947) is quite solid. But what is it that is general to all members of the species?

In the first instance it should be noted that what is general are certain facial expressions, best expressed in terms of certain muscular action consistencies. Our facial muscles have preprogrammed consistencies just as our leg muscles do when they make it possible for all members of the species to walk. But do they "mean" the same thing, regardless of context or situation? The interesting aspect of most of the research with facial expressions is that it usually classifies expression into some very few categories, such as anger, happiness, sadness, disgust, fear, and surprise (e.g., Ekman, 1973). These broad semantic categories suggest, in contrast, that the fine muscular patterns with which we are dealing are probably remnants of communicative acts, not expressions of some underlying palpaple emotion. Given our evolutionary history, it is not unreasonable that some broad categories of events are classified by these semantic categories and that they may, in part, have a common history with some facial expressions. In other words, some situations that are "happy" ones are also situations that tend to elicit a smiling facial expression; some unexpected aversive events are classified as fearful and some facial expressions are also associated with those situations. Although we should note that Ekman and his associates found that a nonliterate culture in New Guinea could not distinguish surprise and fear, which suggests cultural differences in adding the aversive to the surprising aspect of events.

In other words, there are certain archaic situational events that have a high probability of producing specific muscular facial events and also have a high probability of being cognitively classified by certain "emotional" values. But it is surely the case that human plasticity prevents us from saying that a particular releasing stimulus will *always* produce a certain expression or a certain valuation. Even for nonhuman primates, the best available summary of the evidence notes that "the functional context-dependency of emotional expression is an extremely important concept, for it is only in conjunction with context that affect expressions can coordinate social interaction" (Chevalier-Skolnikoff, 1973).

The remnants of these "expressive" characteristics occur occasionally to specific stimuli. Not only did they probably evolve as communicative acts, but they may also be acquired as communicative signs. In nonhuman primates "the appropriate contextual use of and reaction to facial behavior and its role in coordination of social interactions are highly dependent upon a normal socialization experience" (Chevalier-Skolnikoff, 1973). The development of both the use and recognition of facial expression over early childhood and the difficulty the blind have in acting out the "appropriate" expression both speak to this point in humans. In other words, humans may use facial expressions as communication devices, but they must learn how and when to do so. This is a far cry from the unsupported speculation that our common experience suggests that "signs of anger act like the stickleback's red belly as a sign-stimulus for fear . . ." (Gray, 1971b). Any viewer of television or of small children can deny this "common experience."

Laird (1974) has shown that if people are induced to "smile" or "frown" without being aware of the specific character of their expression, they will report the appropriate feelings in response to relatively innocuous pictures or cartoons. Laird concludes that "expressive behavior mediates the quality of . . . emotional experience." Again, expressive behavior does not follow some emotional quality; instead the emotional quality is derived from the "expressive" behavior.

We are then with the expression of emotional experience where we were with the notion of "innate" aggression. It is an overgeneralized notion based on an inadequate analysis and an uncritical acceptance of idealistic notions of thoughts and feelings preceding all decisions and actions. Facial expressions do not "express" anything in the usual sense of the word. They are correlated with situations that often lead to particular "emotional" experience. More important, and once again with William James, they are often the precursor of the "emotion." Self-observation of one's expressions may often be one of the determinants of the emotional complex. In addition we acquire cognitive structures that tell us how to interpret other people's expressions and with what events they are often correlated. By induction we assume that the cooccurrence signifies the expression of an underlying "emotion." As a communicative act, they frequently, but not always, tell us something about the actor's evaluation of the situation. Just as words tell us about such evaluations, facial movements can communicate to others in a social context. The fact that these two avenues of reaction are not *always* correlated provides grist for the mill of the perceptive observer, be he therapist or not.

The Cognition of Emotion

Much of the discussion of the functional stimulus for ANS arousal could be translated into a discussion of the sufficient conditions for the cognitive emotional interpretation of an environmental event. Some theories of emotions have failed to make the distinction between stimuli that are ANS arousers and those that are signals for a cognitive emotional interpretation. Bowlby (1973), in discussing so-called fearful stimuli, talked about the general complex of fear without making the arousal-interpretation distinction. That is perfectly appropriate when a stimulus, such as strangeness of a situation, clearly has a similar and simultaneously effective signal function both to the arousal system and to the cognitive-interpretive system. On the one hand it activates the ANS because it is novel (cf. Chapter 7); on the other hand it is evaluated by the meaning analysis as strange and therefore to be responded to appropriately with fear. But in many cases the stimulus that gives rise to ANS arousal and the event that is interpreted at the same time not only may be two different events but may have different effects. For example, a stimulus that originally provided both ANS arousal and interpretation as an aversive negative emotional stimulus may be reinterpreted in one respect and not the other; thus it may lose its effectiveness as an ANS arouser and still be interpreted as aversive but produce essentially little if any emotional reaction. The habituation to loud noises may provide one instance of this kind of change. On the other hand it may still produce ANS arousal but may be cognitively reinterpreted on the basis of past experience so that it now produces a positive emotional reaction, as in the roller coaster effect.

The way in which an individual deals with a situation that is emotionally relevant (i.e., where arousal may take place and meaning analysis may be required) often depends on his past experience with that situation. For example, he will approach a situation if in the past the cognitive consequences—and thus the emotion—have been positive and pleasant. On the other hand, a situation that terminates in a negative unpleasant emotional response may be avoided or even reinterpreted.

Lazarus, whose work on coping I shall discuss presently, deals primarily with the evaluation of the external social and material world. Another important aspect of cognitive response to a situation consists of the evaluation of our own behavior and in particular of our ability to control a particular situation. An event may be differently appreciated depending on whether we believe that the outcome of one's transactions with it are going to be positive or negative. In particular the sense of control, whether or not the onset and offset of a particular event is under the individual's control, may be of particular importance. This variable presumably controls our positive response to the roller coaster (and the negative response to the loss of support), the control of masochistic behavior (and the fear of pain), and generally the child's developing sense of mastery. Mastery is a generalized concept saying that events may be controlled, and the sense of mastery will color the way in which a particular emotional situation may be interpreted. Thus what may be frightening at one point may become amusing, not because there has been an objective change in the situation, but because a sense of mastery has drastically changed the cognitive interpretation of the same situation.

However, sense of control is only the anticipatory part of self-observation; it says that the individual will be able to control a situation. Sometimes the cognitive consequences of ongoing mastery are more important without necessarily having anticipated it. In a new situation we frequently find that we may not expect to be able to avert bad consequences but cannot escape being in the situation. As the events unfold and actual mastery (i.e., control over the events) is observed, the experience of changing emotional tone, merely as a result of changing self-observation, is often dramatic. The euphoria of the underdog as he overcomes the favorite in sports, the soldier's joy at surviving a battle, and the child's delight at mastering a new task are all relevant examples. Similarly, socially defined negative stimuli—our disgust with the mores of a society or the behavior of a group—may be decoded and recoded as a result of personal experiences.

The discussion of mastery raises a related issue of baseline levels of ANS activity. I have assumed that the intensity of emotional experience is a function of the degree of ANS activity. However, some degree of ANS arousal is present in all living human beings at all times. It is necessary therefore, to assume a species-wide or individual threshhold before arousal becomes "emotionally" functional. Some related issues will be discussed in connection with psychopathy in Chapter 9. The issue of mastery is relevant because, in a different sense than that used above, mastery is also related to the ability of managing or tolerating high degrees of arousal. Thus individual differences in the functional threshhold of ANS activity may be related to such mastery. By not reacting "emotionally" to even high levels of arousal, individuals may differ in their ability to manage (master) different situations.

I shall now turn to Lazarus' discussion of some of the complexities of this cognitive response of coping.

The notion that emotion is best seen as a response syndrome has been brought out by many different writers and probably in the most explicit and useful way by Lazarus (1968). Noting that emotions are related to other reactions to the environment, to ways of coping with environmental demands, Lazarus reviews first some alternative formulations and, in particular, the positions that equate emotion with other motivational constructs. His excellent review and rejection of the "emotion as motivation" position need not be rehearsed here. What is important for our present purposes is his concept of appraisal, which refers to the restructuring of environmental inputs into functional stimuli and deals with the functioning of cognitive structures. Lazarus divides the consequences of appraisal into two categories: benign appraisal and threat appraisal. This dichotomous division is a little unwieldly, since it is highly likely that appraisal is continuous from extreme threat to extreme positive or benign evaluations. More important, however, is the fact that judgments of whether a particular situation is benign or threatening are complex and require further evaluations of individual actions and experiences. These judgments and their development need some theoretical basis, not an intuitive appreciation, of what is benign or threatening, or good or bad.

At the same time, and these minor misgivings notwithstanding, Lazarus does suggest some important variables to be considered in the outcome of appraisal. As far as benign appraisal is concerned, he first considers automatized coping, which is a handling of the situation that does not bring "emotion" into play. In our terms this means that a particular response occurs in a particular situation, but no part of the structure of that input has an arousal effect or an emotional consequence. The second outcome of benign appraisals is so-called reappraisals, which restructure the stimulus and make a potentially threatening, unpleasant, or unwanted situation more positive and produce essentially benign perceptions. The third class of benign appraisals is what Lazarus calls the positive emotions, such as elation, and he suggests that when these occur there is usually an implied mastery of danger. While it is likely that the mastery of danger is involved in some of the positive emotions, there are many positive emotions that do not involve the mastery of danger, and that we need not have escaped a threat in order to be joyful or elated. This notion that some of the positive emotions are necessarily tied up with the avoidance of noxious events is a recurring theme in psychological writing and somewhat puzzling, since it can be found all the way from psychoanalytic writings to that of behavior therapists. It seems to be a last remnant of the notion that anxiety and fear are the emotions of choice, the basic fundamental emotions, and that even when we want to talk about elation and joy, we somehow ought to relate them to the "fundamental" emotional states.

The consequences of threat appraisal are twofold in Lazarus' view. First, there is direct action and negative emotion, which presumably includes the typical flight-fight reaction and the appearance of aggression and anxiety. The second possibility is benign reappraisal, which changes the situation into a benign one and thus eliminates the negative emotional experience in action. It is this benign reappraisal of the threatening stimulus that may, under conditions of arousal, produce some of the positive emotions that involve the mastery of danger. Danger can be mastered both in the real world and in the mind.

Finally, Lazarus' discussion makes excellent use of some of the psychoanalytic notions of denial and repression as mechanisms of appraisal and reappraisal, and he has shown experimentally the importance of these reappraisals in objectively handling threatening situations.

In a similar approach I have shown (Mandler et al., 1961) that the degree to which people are able to cope with threatening material by recoding it also determines their degree of ANS arousal. Response modes such as recoding the threatening material, that is by changing its meaning to something innocuous, or rationalizing it (by making its implications innocuous), significantly decreased degree of visceral arousal. However, treating the content of a communication by making it personally relevant or by trying to avoid its implications, although acknowledging the meaning, tended to increase visceral arousal.

The discussion of arousal has led us from its definition to an appreciation of its adaptive significance and to an exploration of its causes and the means whereby we learn to cope with its effects. I turn now to a specific set of conditions—the occasions of interruption—that produce arousal as well as cognitive consequences.

Chapter VII
The Interruption of Plans and Behavior

In this chapter I shall deal in detail with the consequences of the interruption of plans and actions. The major emphasis will be on theory and evidence that relate interruption to arousal and emotional consequences.

The emphasis on interruption, already apparent in previous chapters, is motivated by three major arguments. First, interruption is a sufficient and possibly necessary condition for the occurrence of autonomic nervous system arousal. Second, interruption of ongoing cognitive or behavioral activity sets the stage for many of the changes that occur in cognitive and action systems. Third, and in extension of the previous two points, interruption is important in that it signals important changes in the environment, which often lead to altered circumstances of living, adapting, and surviving.

The autonomic consequences of interruption are offered, at this point, as a hypothesis, albeit one with a high degree of credibility. Some of the positive evidence will be mentioned below, and there is no available evidence against the hypothesis that the interruption of highly organized activities generates autonomic arousal. If it is kept in mind that the unexpected is, by definition, interruptive of ongoing cognitive activity, the general agreement that novel and unusual events generate states of arousal is relevant to this proposition. In addition, the general class of aversive events also falls, usually although not always, into the category of disruptive (*ergo* interruptive) and unexpected occasions.

Regardless of the autonomic consequences of interruption, one of the main avenues for change in existing cognitive and action systems is undoubtedly a consequence of the failure of existing structures. An

[1]Some of the following material is an updated version of Mandler (1964a).

interruption occurs when a current structure fails in handling available input or action requirements. Thus the adaptation to the requirements of the world, "learning" in traditional terminology, occurs subsequent to interruption. Any satisfactory theory of cognitive structures must contain means whereby structures are changed whenever any ongoing cognitive or behavioral activity fails or is interrupted.

The adaptive consequences of interruption become obvious from the foregoing. The organism responds both with physiological preparedness and potential cognitive and behavioral restructuring whenever interruption occurs. Or, to turn the argument around, it seems reasonable for organisms to have evolved such that whenever well-organized actions or plans cannot be completed (i.e., fail), two major adaptive mechanisms come into play—one physiological, the other cognitive.

Of particular interest for present purposes is the arousal function of interruption. From an evolutionary point of view the fact that arousal comes into play whenever current activity is maladaptive can be seen to have important survival values. These can be considered from two points of view. First, arousal has preparatory flight and fight functions. These functions are of primary value whenever the organism is engaged in activities essential to species survival, such as food seeking, and the protective organization of the group. Preparation for flight or fight is important when usual (well-organized) activities in these areas cannot be carried to completion. Second, the autonomic response is relevant to the role of the autonomic nervous system as an additional signal system, which I discussed in the previous chapter. Increased attention and information seeking when ongoing activity is interrupted is evidently adaptive.

In the pages that follow, I shall deal first with the interruption of behavior, primarily because most of the evidence and conjecture in the psychological literature has dealt with this aspect of the phenomenon. I shall then extend these ideas to the interruption of plans and cognitive structures in general.

The term interruption, because of its neutral connotation and greater generality, is preferable to other terms such as frustration or blocking. All that is implied by the notion of interruption is that an organized response is "interrupted" whenever its completion is physically blocked or temporarily delayed—for whatever reason. Examples come readily to mind: a key sticking in a lock, a pellet not found in a foodcup, or a brake failing in a car; all of these are instances of interruption. We must assume in all of these cases that the response sequence involved actually has been organized (i.e., previously used and practiced—smoothly and frequently) and that a well-defined structure can be described to represent the action.

The Consequences of Interruption

We can distinguish between general "motivational" and very specific behavioral consequences of interruption. The distinction is related to Gallistel's (1974) use of the term "motivation" for higher-order nodes that organize action. In the same sense we might call all the consequences that represent a wide variety of different possible behaviors "motivational." "Motivational" effects of interruption are those that may produce a variety of different subsequent responses—depending on the stimulus stiuation at the time of interruption, the prior experience of the organism, and the hierarchy of action and behavioral structure that is being interrupted. Interruption may, on the other hand, produce one or more very specific responses, previously acquired and specific to the activity or sequence that has been interrupted.

We can postulate a continuum of action systems and stimulus conditions. Such a continuum ranges from conditions that elicit one and only one response to conditions that may elicit one or more of a family of responses or actions. Interruption, in turn, will have consequences ranging along this continuum.

In discussing the consequences of interruption I shall follow this continuum from those cases that have relatively little variance in the response patterns generated to those that seem to be motivational in the traditional sense; that is, the variance of possible responses is fairly large.

Persistence and Completion

In Chapter 2 I mentioned the inevitability of an organized response. Once initiated, it rushes to completion, and nothing external to the organism is necessary to insure the continuation of the sequence, even though external factors are crucial for its initiation.

Once an organized response has been interrupted, it is assumed that a tendency to completion persists as long as the situation remains essentially unchanged. There might at first be persisting attempts to complete the sequence despite the interruption and, obviously, in many cases such second attempts will be quite successful and run off smoothly. The key may turn on the second try; ink may appear at the tip of a fountain pen. In passing we might speculate, as others have done before, that the tendency for aggression to follow interruption may be due to previous successful attempts to remove the blocking agent through force.

The tendency to complete or to persist is a tricky and challenging problem. We shall encounter it again later on, when I shall also present two suggestions for the origin of the tendency to complete—one cognitive, the other "emotional." For the time being, and generally until the problem has been further explored empirically and we know the conditions that affect this tendency, I suggest that the phenomenon might be accepted without necessarily understanding it completely.

Organized sequences tend to follow the dictum: "If at first you don't succeed, try again." The failure to complete a telephone connection because of faulty or interrupted dialing simply produces a return to the beginning and a second run through the sequence. Cigarette lighters often work on the second try. Thus, in the first instance, interruption of many organized sequences produces repetition.

My reluctance to ascribe energetic aspects to the problem of completion and repetition echoes Miller, Galanter, and Pribram's "renunciation of the dynamic properties of Plans." They state that "as long as it stays alive, the psychobiological machine must continue to execute the successive steps in some Plan" (1960).

However, even a second try may not lead to completion of the response sequence. In that case—instead of or in addition to repetition —we might find increased vigor in the completion responses.

When a key won't open a lock, sometimes the application of a little pressure produces the desired end result. The same method might work when a tackle attempts to block the completion of a drive for the goal line. Repeated and more vigorous striking of a cigarette lighter may produce a flame. The same method might produce results with a recalcitrant horse. Thus both increased force and repetition of some part of the organized sequence might produce the end state. In none of these cases is the organized sequence appreciably altered.

It is tempting to speculate at this point that the increased vigor of response following interruption is a motivational, energizing phenomenon (cf. Amsel and Roussel, 1952). However, the application of increased vigor may also be a well-learned response from previous experiences with interruption (cf. Marx, 1956). I shall return to the problem of so-called motivational factors involved in completion at a later point.

Response Substitution

By substitution I mean sequence completion by other organized sequences that are more or less specific to the interrupted sequence. In this area the major contributions have been made by Lewin (e.g., 1935) and his colleagues and by Lissner (1933) in particular. The various factors that influence substitutability have been summarized by Deutsch (1954). In brief, they are: (1) similarity between original and substitute actions; (2) contiguity of the substitute and the original goal; (3) the nature of the original goal activity; and (4) active rather than passive participation in completion. In terms of Gallistel's organization of action systems, we might assume that under specified conditions, actions and behaviors subsumed under a single superordinate node are substitutable one for another.

Miller, Galanter, and Pribram (1960) have discussed the problem of interruption in terms of memory storage and the load put on storage when an ongoing organized activity is interrupted. Thus they explain the recall of interrupted tasks in terms of the storage of the uncompleted portion in the working memory. In many ways—as they point out—their position is similar to Lewin's, but they make one important addition for our purposes. They suggest that whenever an organized sequence has interchangeable parts—as in writing several letters to friends—the sequence in which the parts are executed is immaterial. However, we should add that interruption between the parts of the sequence (e.g., between letters) should produce a problem of completion, just as interruption within a part (e.g., while writing a letter) should. Clearly, two organized action sequences are being interrupted: writing letters and writing a particular letter. The effect in the case of the interrupted letter should be more pronounced, but it should not be absent when only the larger, higher-order sequence is interrupted between parts. I suggest that the lower in the hierarchy of action systems the interruption occurs, the more marked is the effect.

Up to now I have discussed only specific substitution. The problem of substitution may, however, be posed differently. It may be that substitution involves much more than the specific consequences of a particular organized response. Lewin's theory did, of course, specify such a general principle by suggesting that substitution follows a general state of tension.

I would like to assume that whenever the organism is prevented from completing any one organized sequence he will then tend to complete the sequence by substituting any other even minimally relevant organized sequence.

A word needs to be said first about stop rules. Recently, it has been recognized in psychological theorizing that some mechanism needs to be invented that explains the cessation of ongoing activity. I have discussed this problem in passing in previous chapters and elsewhere (Mandler, 1962b). N. E. Miller (1963), among others, also has speculated about the existence of a stop mechanism. The completion of an organized response is obviously one stop rule; it may be the only one. The stop rule is important here because the substituted organized action—in the case of interruption—produces a new stop rule for the organism. In other words, the flow of action may be shortened or extended.

It is assumed that interruption—in the absence of situationally relevant substitutes—will result in the production of some other organized action available to the organism. Such substitution will presumably depend on two factors: the availability of organized responses in general and their relative accessibility as a function of immediately preceding events and experiences.

The Problem of Completion

Up to now I have discussed only problems involved in the completion of interrupted response sequences. I now return to the question whether interruption produces some sort of state of tension that is dissipated by completion (*vide* Lewin) or whether there is a completion need, or whether we can, as I believe, get along without an energy concept. It might be appealing to think of completion as the result of a frustrated need or drive or stored up tension. I do not believe that this is necessarily the easy way out. For now, I want to entertain the notion that an organism will complete an interrupted sequence—whether directly or through substitution—without invoking extraneous energy states. As I indicated earlier, I would prefer to believe that the phenomena that seem to indicate greater vigor or energy are derivable from previous experiences that have produced completion by the application of force or—as I show below—from certain emotional, although not energetic, states.

Completion can be derived from the continued functioning of some cognitive parallel of the overt organized response. If, at the time of interruption, the sequential order of the organized sequence has been laid down centrally, then the uncompleted part of the sequence will persist at the cognitive level as a plan (cf. Miller, Galanter, and Pribram, 1960), even though interruption may disrupt the overt sequence. Then, as soon as the blocking agent has been removed, the original overt sequence can be picked up where it left off, and the overt sequence will follow the isomorphic plan that represents the original action system.

Such a sequence is, of course, an integral part of the theory of plans, and it can easily handle the problem of substitution. A variety of substitute plans may be interchangeable within sets of such structures.

The cognitive plan existing parallel to the overt, organized response generates completion or at least attempts at completion. We thus avoid the postulation of an independent and superfluous completion need. Having avoided a drive model so far, we can also move on to the more immediate problems of emotional arousal.

Emotional Consequences of Interruption

The central postulate of our interruption hypothesis is that interruption leads to a state of arousal that is followed by emotional behavior. As noted earlier, I treat visceral arousal here entirely as a stimulus of varying intensity, not as a drive.

I suggest that the interruption of an organized response produces a state of arousal that, in the absence of completion or substitution, then develops into one or another emotional expression, depending on the occasion of the interruption. Thus interruption may lead to expressions of fear, anger, surprise, humor, or euphoria, depending entirely on factors *other than the interruption itself.*

There have been several theoretical suggestions about the motivational or emotional effects of interruption, all of which imply to some degree that these consequences are noxious and aversive in character. I shall return to these shortly, but first I shall indicate my preference for the more general statement.

In the first place it is more parsimonious to fit the emotional consequences of interruption into a general treatment of emotion instead of letting it stand by itself and occupy a unique position.

Second, it seems reasonable to conclude from the observation of everyday behavior that interruption in some cases does lead to nonaversive, pleasurable states of emotion. The prime example can be found in play behavior, particularly in that of children. Given the proper attitude or situational definition, children may be safely interrupted in the midst of organized sequences and find that such interruptions are pleasant, even delightful. A toddler laboriously climbing stairs may cry when suddenly snatched off them; however, he may also cry in delight when the snatching is done by a smiling parent in the spirit of play.

It should be emphasized that the conditions of interruption that lead to positive, or any other, emotional expression must be the previously acquired evaluations appropriate for these emotions. Frequently, of course, the laughing parent *per se* presents a cue for an organized sequence that is pleasurable. Maybe more applicable to the present argument is the response to a practical joke in the adult. When the context in which a chair is pulled out from under someone is clearly playful, the response will be one of humor; but when the event occurs without such preparation, the practical joke usually is found to be not at all funny by its target.

In general, conditions where interruption leads to pleasurable emotions are somewhat difficult to find. Interruptions are, on the whole, disruptive, because they usually block the activity that is most appropriate to the situation.

More important, we find different aversive emotional states in the adult who, depending on the occasion, may react to interruption with annoyance, aggression, or withdrawal. If interruption had specific emotional consequences such diversity would be difficult to explain.

Finally, even in the adult, the same interruption may result in noxious emotional states or in pleasant ones. A telephone call in the midst of dinner from a pestiferous salesman results in annoyance; a call from a friend one has not heard from in a long time may result in delight.

Contact should also be made with a discussion of the inhibition of distress (see Chapter 8), which Kessen and I presented a few years ago and where we first suggested the generality of the emotional sequelae of interruption (Kessen and Mandler, 1961). We argued there that distress or anxiety sometimes seems to be inhibited or controlled by behavioral or situational inhibitors. In that connection we speculated that the removal or withdrawal of an inhibitor of distress may lead to distress. Thus the child discovers early that the interruption of inhibitors, which *are* organized sequences, leads to distress. This process suggests one mechanism for the appearance of distress: at the interruption of some organized response. It is interesting to speculate that all organized responses may act as inhibitors and that visceral arousal is a necessary consequence of the withdrawal of an inhibitor— and thus the antecedent for emotional behavior.

At this point it is appropriate to review some of the theoretical statements and empirical explorations that have investigated the "emotional" properties of interruption.

Interruption: Theory and Experiment

The single major proponent of motivational properties of interruption has been Kurt Lewin. There is neither space nor reason to review in detail the work that he and his collaborators have done in this area. Most of their work has concentrated on the interruption of cognitive rather than behavioral sequences, although the work of Zeigarnik and others could easily be translated into the behavioral arena (cf. Butterfield, 1964, for a summary of research and theory on this problem). The major theoretical proposition advanced by Lewin (cf. 1935, and 1940 for a summary) is that any intention to reach a goal produces a tension system, which is released when the goal is reached and which, conversely, is preserved if the goal is blocked. It is the postulation of such an undischarged tension system that led Lewin and Zeigarnik to predict superior recall for interrupted activities. The major difference between the Lewinian and the present position is that we distinguish between two effects, the tendency to complete, which is present prior to the interruption; but more important, we add an emotional response that does not emerge unless the organized response has been interrupted. I do not intend in the present sketch to go into any more detailed comparison of Lewin's system and the present one except to say that to the extent that the Lewinian postulates apply to overt response sequences, the findings of his group seem to be congruent with my present position.

A more specific statement about the relation between interruption and emotional discharge was made by Freud in both his early and his later theories of anxiety. In the former he postulated that anxiety was directly derivable from the damming up of libidinal energy, with particular reference to unsuccessful attempts at the completion of the sexual act—an interruption of an organized response par excellence. This "motor" theory—akin to Lewin—was later replaced by statements such as: "Anxiety . . . seems to be a reaction to the perception of the absence of the object" (Freud, 1936), which is clearly closer to the present thesis.

The first important nonmotivational statement on the emotional consequences of interruption was made in 1946 by Hebb (see also Chapter 5). The hypothesis developed by Hebb is that "fear originated in the disruption of temporally and spatially organized cerebral activities" (Hebb, 1946). Here again we are dealing primarily with the interruption of a cognitive event; Hebb demonstrates his thesis in the field of perception; he buttresses it with a neurophysiological argument. I would not want to restrict myself to the former, nor do I see any need to embrace the latter. Furthermore, his argument seems to restrict the emotional consequences of interruption to fear. Against these previous views on the general properties of interruption, I shall maintain the major thesis that interruption has as its most important consequences the innate arousal of the ANS—that it is the prime preprogrammed releaser of the autonomic nervous system.

I have argued from an evolutionary point of view that some special consequences of interruption are likely to be highly adaptive. When an organism is engaged in well-practiced, habitual, and adaptive (i.e., well-organized) behavior, then any change in his condition or the conditions of his surrounds that make these organized structures maladaptive or in need of change should be signaled intensely and uniquely. In addition, the signaling function of the ANS system would also be highly useful to indicate that new behavior is required, that the situation needs to be further explored, and that a variety of new and old behavior patterns may be appropriately brought into play. Sudden changes might be important for survival and therefore immediately attended and responded to.

There is very little empirical evidence on the effects of interruption on the ANS. I have shown that the interruption of verbal material shows the expected effects. The more highly organized the material was, the stronger the ANS effect—the bigger the autonomic response, regardless of whether organization was newly learned or previously acquired (Mandler, 1964). Sher (1971) pointed out that these studies might have confounded interruption with the novelty value of interruption. While I would argue that novelty is intricately related to the notion of interruption, it is gratifying that Sher's experiments significantly extended the generality of previous studies. Using pupillary dilation as a measure of arousal, Sher (1971) showed that whereas arousal was *lower during* the recall of familiar (versus unfamiliar) sets of words and digits, *following* interruption the degree of arousal was *greater* for the familiar sequences. Fry and Ogston (1971) used the interruption of a well-organized cognitive pattern to produce arousal. At the same time, they introduced a confederate who exhibited emotional behavior. Their results showed the expected coaction of interruption and environmental-cognitive cues; "aroused [interrupted] subjects were generally more susceptible to the confederate's expressed mood."

Probably the best set of evidence concerning the adequate conditions for ANS arousal and their relation to our concept of interruption comes from the work of Frankenhaeuser and her associates (e.g., 1971, 1975). I have already noted her work in connection with the relation between catecholamine secretion and environmental coping. I now turn to the conditions that produce catecholamine secretion. Frankenhaeuser (1975) notes that conditions characterized by novelty, anticipation, unpredictability, and change usually result in a rise in adrenalin secretion. More important, repeated exposure shows a decrease in adrenalin output "provided that the subject gains better control over the situation." In other words, when ongoing organized cognition or behavior is interrupted, adrenalin output increases. Adaptation only occurs when a new and adequate sequence has been found, that is, when control over the situation has been achieved (e.g., Frankenhaeuser and Rissler, 1970). Similarly, any change from a "normal" level of stimulation produces increases in adrenalin output, whether the situation involves under- or overstimulation (Frankenhaeuser, Nordheden, Myrsten, and Post, 1971). Once again, the prevailing cognitive organization defines interruption; whether the level of stimulation is reduced or increased is unimportant, as long as it goes counter to the operating level of cognitive planning.

In summary, I suggest the following general principles relating interruption and arousal.

1. Degree of organization (i.e., tightness and invariance of structure) will be reflected in degree of ANS arousal when the structure is interrupted.

2. Degree of arousal will vary with the discrepancy between the interrupting event and the interrupted structure. Discrepancy is partly a function of the degree to which structures are available that can integrate the interrupted structure and the new event or behavior. Thus substitute behaviors available at the time of interruption may decrease arousal effects.

3. The more highly organized behavior and plans will also more likely be the ones that are resumed if the situation permits it. Thus, while the degree of arousal may be high, it is also more likely to be short lived under conditions of high degrees of organization and noncontinuing interruption.

Interruption of Consummatory Behavior

So much for the hypothesis that interruption, in general, has emotional consequences. I shall now turn to a line of inquiry restricted to the interruption of a particular set of organized responses: consummatory behavior.

The notion that the absence of an expected reward or reinforcement may have emotional consequences has been bruited about in contemporary reinforcement theories at least since 1938 (Skinner, 1938). After a variety of attempts to develop a satisfactory theory of extinction, the notion finally became respectable in Hullian circles in the early 1950s, with the most popular relevant concept being Amsel's frustration effect. Amsel (1962) has reviewed this history and has also given us the best documented series of hypotheses dealing with the motivational properties of nonreward. Parenthetically, it might be said that at the same time Amsel suggested a specific emotional response consequent on nonreward, Brown and Farber (1951) developed a theoretical statement of emotion and frustration that was more general in intent, although far less influential. Their hypothesis derived emotional consequences not only from interruption or nonreward, but also from competition between excitatory tendencies or between excitatory and inhibitory tendencies—far too general a statement and somewhat removed from the mainstream of the *Zeitgeist.*

Because of the large amount of empirical evidence relevant to the Amsel hypothesis, which deals with the interruption of behavior and not of cognitive or perceptual structures, a brief description of its relevance to the present position is desirable. The hypothesis and the data suggest that the withdrawal of reward has motivational or emotional consequences only after a particular sequence leading to consummatory behavior has been well learned, or, as I would say, after it has been organized. The data generally show that behavior following the interruption is enhanced (i.e., it exhibits increased vigor). In addition, data by Wagner (1963) and others have shown that the emotional consequences of nonreward (interruption) can be classically conditioned. In short, I see very little in the studies cited in Amsel's reviews (1958, 1962) that is inconsistent with the position advocated here, despite the obvious gulf separating our theoretical predilections. The major differences that I would stress are as follows. First, I believe that the initial emotional consequences of interruption are visceral arousal, directly observable and measurable autonomic events that need not be reduced to the states of theoretical variables. Second, I believe that anticipatory goal reactions are not necessary or relevant in the case of well-organized response sequences. Third, I particularly emphasize the opportunities and behaviors available to the organism immediately following nonreward as determinants of its effects. Apart from these not unimportant differences, I would call on the frustration effect as important evidence for the general hypothesis about the arousing consequences of interruption. Not just consummatory behavior, but the interruption of any well-organized sequence should produce effects very similar to those demonstrated by the introduction of nonreward.

Once again, we are faced by the suggestion in these studies that the effect of interruption is noxious. Thus Amsel states that fractional anticipatory frustration "operates in many respects like fear . . ." (Amsel, 1962), and Mowrer (1960) talks in this connection about frustration, disappointment, and anger. It may well be that the emotional effect of nonreward is usually aversive.

Turning from consummatory acts to aggression, Berkowitz (1964) has suggested that aggressive acts are evoked by appropriate cues in the environment and supported by visceral arousal, a position consistent with my notions about the conditions for emotional behavior. More important, he noted that "if the aggressive sequence is set into operation, but completion is prevented, internal tension is induced which is channelled into whatever response happens to be under way at the time." This statement suggests that the additional visceral arousal following interruption of an aggressive sequence acts as an additional stimulus for the support of ongoing (aggressive) behavior.

In Chapter 8 I shall discuss at length the emotional effects of interruption when no other relevant behavior is available. Briefly, I shall suggest that since onset of interruption is, by definition, unexpected, and since the organism frequently has few other situationally relevant responses available or high in his repertory at the moment of interruption, it is this lack of environmental control, this "helplessness" in the face of interruption, that is responsible for the high frequency of negative affect in response to interruption. While fear is not a necessary consequence of interruption, it is, under the conditions that we observe it in and out of the laboratory, a highly likely one. In other words, it should be possible to manipulate the degree of negative affect by varying the responses available to the organism immediately following the interruption.

Completion and Arousal

One other possibility should be considered regarding the emotional consequences of interruption. This hypothesis concerns a possible interaction between the completion tendency and arousal and is generally akin to Lewin's drive theory without, however, invoking a hypothetical drive state.

It is possible that whenever the organism is interrupted prior to the completion of an organized sequence, the resulting state of arousal is maintained until completion, or completion by substitution, has been achieved. If we assume (as I do not) that interruption leads typically to an aversive state of distress, then this state will presumably persist until completion has been achieved. However, by definition, this state is one that the organism will, whenever possible, terminate and, if completion—by whatever means—terminates that state, then the emotional effects of interruption may provide an adequate explanation for the occurrence of completion tendencies. Completion of an organized sequence removes the state of distress that is usually produced by the interruption.

While this is a reasonable account that reduces the two factors to a single mechanism, I would prefer to entertain both possibilities for the time being, if for no other reason than that completion tendencies seem quite compelling when seen in the raw. There is, of course, no reason why cognitive completion tendencies, emotional consequences, and completion driven by distress cannot coexist side by side.

Disruption as a Consequence of Interruption

Whenever an organized sequence is interrupted we expect the occurrence of some emotional responses. If, as is often the case, this emotional eruption is incompatible with completion or continuation of the sequence, we would expect some further disruption of organized behavior to occur. If, on the other hand, the organism learns that completion is possible despite the interruption, the emotional consequences will be outweighed by the completion tendency, and recovery will, of course, be more rapid the better organized the action. Common evidence for the disruptive effects of interruption is abundant.

At the cognitive level, the disruptive effects of interruption are commonplace. The inability of the writer or student to return to his train of thought or assignment following an interruption needs no documentation. The anxiety—or helplessness—in the absence of organized continuation in any intellectual task is well known to writers, artists, and scientists. Equally apparent are the disruptive and interfering consequences when a motor skill sequence repeatedly fails of completion. Even a householder skilled in fixing the vacuum cleaner will show emotional disruptive effects when repeated attempts at going through the motions that "worked the last time" fail on a particular occasion.

Of particular interest to the experimental psychologist is the disruption found during extinction of previously learned responses. I have previously discussed (1962a) the problem of extinction as a cognitive phenomenon in the special case of discrimination reversal. In that case alternate responses (i.e., to the previously nonreinforced stimulus) immediately become available to the organism and, in that context, I have stressed the importance of cognitive representations of organized response systems. The disruptive aspects of interruption apply more clearly to simple extinction, where no alternative responses are available to the organism. This is not to say that the former case does not involve emotional consequences or the latter cognitive ones; rather, it is a matter of emphasis.

Extinction of an unorganized response sequence is the typical case in most studies where the organism is exposed to extinction procedures immediately following the acquisition of the response. We may assume that in these cases, where the organization of the full sequence has not yet been adequately developed, the interruption of the consummatory response produces emotional consequences in the goal box and may make the goal region aversive. Since the pregoal sequence has not yet been organized, there is no automatic running off of the sequence up to the goal box, and the behavior should soon fail to appear.

Extinction in the case of organized sequences is more complicated—again leaving aside the cognitive aspects. Not only is the consummatory sequence interrupted in the goal region, but the established organization of the behavior in the goal path inevitably brings the organism back to that goal, where he is interrupted time and again. The organism thus keeps running to a region that is becoming more and more noxious.

Theios and Brelsford (1964) have presented data that support the notion of two competing factors in extinction. They suggested that resistance to extinction increases as a function of number of trials and decreases as a function of the number of rewards in the goal. The former factor presumably describes the growth of organization, which brings the animal to the goal, while the number (and amount) of rewards determines the intensity of the noxious emotional reaction when the consummatory response is interrupted. The aversiveness of the interruption may work backward along the goal path, but it is pitted against the inexorable pull of the organized sequence. Thus the organism is repeatedly brought into contact with interruption. The consequence will, in the first instance, be an active search for substitutable responses, coupled with increasing helplessness and ensuing distress as these search behaviors turn up no way to complete the sequence. Eventually—and actually fairly early in the extinction series because of the incorporation of aversiveness in the cognitive representation of the goal path—the sequence will be abandoned. Some available data support this notion that overlearned animals—compared with animals trained to mastery—do show a tendency for a more consistent approach to the goal during early extinction trials, followed by a steeper extinction slope (North and Stimmel, 1960, Experiment II; Birch, Ison, and Sperling, 1960). There should also be more searching for substitutable responses, possibly exploratory behavior, during the extinction of an organized sequence than during the extinction of a barely learned sequence.

The Organization of Emotional Behavior

The notion that emotional arousal—and its sequelae—may disrupt behavior should not mislead us into thinking that the emotional consequences of interruption are necessarily unorganized or disruptive. In the first place, well-learned (i.e., organized) emotional behavior will have the same characteristics of unity and organization as any other response system. A fine rage is as well organized and may even be as productive of desired consequences as the most banal and unemotional organized sequence. Well-practiced aggressive responses to well-learned objects in well-defined situations may be just another organized consequence of interruption. We must recall that the apparent lack of a "goal" does not deny the presence of organization. Organized emotions need have no "goal"; they must be freely available and have well-trodden paths.

Another possibility is that emotional arousal may become integrated into an already existing organized sequence. The best example—and I follow here Amsel's reasoning (1958)—is found in the effects of partial reinforcement. If an organism has learned a goal path well and is interrupted (i.e., nonreinforced) on some proportion of subsequent trials, final extinction will be substantially slowed; the animal will show the partial reinforcement effect. If we assume that during partial training the emotional consequences of interruption become part of the organized sequence, then the early extinction trials will not be different from the partial reinforcement trials. By that time, the organized sequence will consist not only of sequences that include emotional arousal as well as terminal reinforcement, but also sequences that include emotional arousal without terminal reinforcement. These latter will—at least as a start—run off just as smoothly as the reinforced ones; the persistence found after partial reinforcement will be apparent. Since, however, the organism is hungry (i.e., organized consummatory responses are likely to occur), more and more attempts at executing these responses will be interrupted, no subsequent substitute behavior will be encountered and arousal will become more and more apparent, disorganized emotional consequences will appear, anxiety and helplessness will eventually be encountered, and the sequence will be disrupted. Disruption and extinction will follow.

It is interesting to speculate that prolonged partial reinforcement might lead to a preference for a partial over a continuous sequence. It is possible that after extended partial training—well beyond asymptotic levels—the pairing of arousal with reinforcement (on the reinforced trials) will produce a positive emotional response and ensuing preference. If this turns out to be the case it would also explain the emotional appeal of gambling, just as the partial reinforcement effect explains its persistence.

In summary, whenever emotional behavior is controlled within specific, situational limits, it may well be organized or integrated into another sequence. When no relevant behavior—emotional or otherwise —is available to the organism, the emotional consequences of interruption will be disruptive.

An Example of Interruption

The consequences of interruption, as enumerated here, can be shown as part of a single syndrome in the case of a child's response to the loss of his mother figure or of his familiar environment.

Bowlby (1969) has summarized the phenomenon, based largely on the work of James Robertson, who observed the behavior of two- and three-year-old children in residential nurseries or hospital wards.[2]

> *In the setting described a child of fifteen to thirty months who has had a reasonably secure relationship with his mother and has not previously been parted from her will commonly show a predictable sequence of behavior. This can be broken into three phases according to what attitude to his mother is dominant. We describe these phases as those of Protest, Despair, and Detachment. Though in presenting them it is convenient to differentiate them sharply, it is to be understood that in reality each merges into the next, so that a child may be for days or weeks in a state of transition from one phase to another, or of alternation between two phases.*
>
> *The initial phase, that of protest, may begin immediately or may be delayed; it lasts from a few hours to a week or more. During it the young child appears acutely distressed at having lost his mother and seeks to recapture her by the full exercise of his limited resources. He will often cry loudly, shake his cot, throw himself about, and look eagerly towards any sight or sound which might prove to be his missing mother. All his behavior suggests strong expectation that she will return. Meantime he is apt to reject all*

[2]The following section is reprinted by kind permission of Dr. J. Bowlby.

alternative figures who offer to do things for him, though some children will cling desperately to a nurse.

During the phase of despair, which succeeds protest, the child's preoccupation with his missing mother is still evident, though his behavior suggests increasing hopelessness. The active physical movements diminish or come to an end, and he may cry monotonously or intermittently. He is withdrawn and inactive, makes no demands on people in the environment, and appears to be in a state of deep mourning. This is a quiet stage, and sometimes, clearly erroneously, is presumed to indicate a diminution of distress.

Because the child shows more interest in his surroundings, the phase of detachment which sooner or later succeeds protest and despair is often welcomed as a sign of recovery. The child no longer rejects the nurses; he accepts their care and the food and toys they bring, and may even smile and be sociable. To some this change seems satisfactory. While his mother visits, however, it can be seen that all is not well, for there is a striking absence of the behavior characteristic of the strong attachment normal at this age. So far from greeting his mother he may seem hardly to know her; so far from clinging to her he may remain remote and apathetic; instead of tears there is a listless turning away. He seems to have lost all interest in her.

Should his stay in hospital or residential nursery be prolonged and should he, as is usual, have the experience of becoming transiently attached to a series of nurses each of whom leaves and so repeats for him the experience of the original loss of his mother, he will in time act as if neither mothering nor contact with humans had much significance for him. After a series of upsets . . . he will gradually commit himself less and less to succeeding figures and in time will stop altogether attaching himself to anyone. He will become increasingly self-centered and, instead of directing his desires and feelings towards people, will become preoccupied with material things such as sweets, toys, and food (Bowlby, 1969, pp. 27–28).

Perceptual and Cognitive Interruption

We assume that essentially the same arguments that apply to the interruption of organized behavior or action sequences also apply to the interruption of mental structures. Given that a particular environmental input activates a specific organization, we assume that that structure determines the individual's perception and evaluation of the environment. A new input that activates a new structure may be interrupting, if the new structure is incompatible with the old, or if it contradicts the operation of the old structure or, more generally, if it provides inputs that are not manageable (i.e., cannot be assimilated) by the existing structures.

In the first instance we are dealing with the general notion that the operation of an existing structure defines the expectation of certain events in the environment and their sequence. Turning a switch is part of the structure that includes the perception of a light going on—if it doesn't, the structure is interrupted. The running off of cognitive structures based on past experience fills our daily life and its so-called expectations. Answering the telephone, driving a car, and talking to people, all have well-established structures and serial organizations that act as "expectations" and are easily interrupted. The use of ordinary terms such as "sudden, unexpected, unlikely, and surprising" usually implies that an existing structure that predicted some event other than the one taking place was in operation. Even the contemplation of a dull, even environment is interrupted when there is a sudden and intense change in stimulation, whether it is a sudden shape, a sudden noise, or a drastic change in illumination.

I indicated earlier that statements about environmental stimuli that are fear inducing because they are "strange" are best subsumed under the notion of interruption. I would thus interpret Bowlby's and Hebb's discussion of the fearful properties of strange stimuli. In addition, stranger anxiety in infants does not emerge until schemas for faces have been developed. Strangeness depends on the prior establishment of familiarity. Strange events are fearful because (1) they are arousing; they interrupt the ongoing familiar structures, and (2) they are interpreted as fearful, because they cannot be assimilated and no relevant action is available—a topic to which I shall return in Chapter 8.

I indicated earlier that structures may be interrupted by their own consequences as well as by external events. Consider any planning activity that is not executed but is only contemplated and examined within consciousness. At one time or another some consequence of the planned series of acts may be incompatible with the overall plan, in which case it would be interrupted. For example, we may plan to visit a friend and thus generally explore the actions to be set in motion when, in sorting through relevant memory structures, we discover an appointment, unbreakable and at the same time as the envisaged visit. Or we find that a particular plan would involve an interaction that is unpleasant or that for one or another physical or social reason cannot be executed. In all these cases, ongoing cognitive activities and their structures may lead to interruption within the mental organization without an additional input from the environment. I shall discuss this topic further in my exploration of guilt and anxiety.

In general, the interruption of either organized behavior or cognitive plans is a phenomenon that has been inadequately analyzed, both empirically and theoretically. Such analyses should go hand in hand with a better understanding of the organization of plans. Miller, Galanter, and Pribram (1960) have plotted out the hierarchical structure of plans. Particular structures and particular cognitive plans form subparts of other more general and often, in the lifetime of the individual, more important and more extensive cognitive structures. Thus the interruption of a low-level plan may not produce much in the way of arousal because the executive plan in existence at the time is a much "higher" one and, because alternatives are available, there is nothing in interruption of the low-level plan that necessarily interrupts the higher one. For example, sitting in front of a table laden with different kinds of foods, the removal of one of the dishes, even though one was in the midst of partaking from it, may not be an interruption at all of the more dominant plan of having a full meal, since we can immediately switch to another dish and continue the overriding plan in existence at the time. The major point is to note that interruption at any one point must be analyzed closely in terms of a hierarchy or levels of plans in order to ask which, if any of them, have been interrupted. We can assume that when all the plans, including the high-level ones, are interrupted, the degree of arousal will be intense and will produce an intense emotional reaction.

At the beginning of this chapter I noted that most cognitive change involves some kind of interruption. These are essentially of two types: first, the new event that is not "expected"—that does not fit into the ongoing cognitive interpretation of the environment; and second, the "expected" event that does not happen. While distinguishable, these two types have the same kind of interruptive structural consequences; the new event is disruptive because it occurs instead of the "expected" event, and the absence of the "expected" event implies the presence of something else "unexpected." In either case the ongoing cognitive activity is interrupted. At this point, coping, problem solving, and "learning" activities take place. It is apparently also at this point that the focus of consciousness is centered on the interruption.

In Chapter 3 I noted that consciousness has "troubleshooting" as one of its functions. Unconscious structures often enter consciousness when they fail (i.e., when they are interrupted). This phenomenon has long been known as Claparède's law of awareness; actors become aware of automatic actions when these are disrupted or fail (e.g., Claparède, 1934). We assume, therefore, that one of the cognitive functions of interruption is to bring some adaptive problem into consciousness where extensive repair work and coping activities can take place. It appears that this sometimes happens without any emotional sequelae.

Thus interruption may, under some circumstances, simply focus a problem into consciousness and, as the problem is quickly solved, no emotional consequences follow. Only when the repair operation is not immediately successful is the situation evaluated "emotionally" and some emotional *quale* also enters consciousness. We have already seen in Chapter 5 how this additional emotional awareness restricts attentiveness (consciousness) and may further interfere with adequate coping. In addition, however, planning for "troubleshooting" may avoid arousal altogether, since the interruption and conscious problem solving become part of a higher-order plan. When working on a difficult problem we expect to find one or another cognitive structure inadequate, and the ensuing "troubleshooting" becomes part of the organized sequence; no arousal occurs and no emotional consequences ensue. Once again we are reminded that it is the operative executive plan that is potentially interruptible and not just any action that occurs as part of it.

The importance of currently available structures leads us to a brief discussion of interruption in the very young child. The newborn infant presumably has few cognitive and action structures available, although we have come to reject fairly universally the *tabula rasa* view of the newborn. Both cognitive and action structures exist in the newborn in rudimentary ways. This view is represented in the corpus of Piaget's contribution (see also Kessen, 1965, for a historical view).

However, given the primitive form of these infantile structures, we would expect a more labile organism, subject to influences other than the immediate interruption. Sroufe and his co-workers (Sroufe and Wunsch, 1972; Sroufe, Matas, and Waters, 1974) have demonstrated this point in their studies of emotional development in infants. In general, they assume that novel, incongruous stimuli will, within a positive context such as the home, produce positive, smiling, and reaching actions, while negative contexts will produce crying and avoidance. Sroufe et al. (1974) note that the amount of discrepancy will not predict the nature of the affect by itself (e.g., Berlyne, 1960; Kagan, 1971). Instead, and completely consistent with the theme of my discussion, discrepancy determines amount of attention and "tension" and the magnitude of the affect, while direction of the affect is largely a function of context. Novelty, such as approach of a stranger, and different contexts are relatively ineffective for the younger (six-month old) infant, but with the development of familiar schemas and "cognitive sophistication," contexts become more and more important. The novel situation will then elicit both approach and avoidance tendencies, and the effect generated will be determined by contextual features such as setting, sequence of environmental events, familiarization, and the duration of the event. Sroufe et al. conclude that the next important step in determining the development of emotional expression in response to interruption (discrepancy or novelty) must be in the study of the development of "sensitivity to contextual factors." In a similar vein, Rothbart (1973) has reviewed the evidence on the determinants and development of laughter in children. Shw showed that the available data are consistent with the view that laughter follows first from arousal contingent on the experience of unexpected stimuli and second, an evaluation that the stimulus is safe or inconsequential. Clearly, such an evaluation is easier for a cognitively sophisticated organism than for a newborn.

But what is the definition of safe or inconsequential or aversive for the adult organism? Consider what happens when an attention-demanding event not only interrupts ongoing cognitive activity but, in addition, cannot be handled by any of the available mechanisms that adapt to such events. All of these fall into the general class of either accommodation or assimilation (Piaget, 1970b). In the case of accommodation the structures are changed so that the new events become part of the evaluative structure; our view of the world is changed by including the new event as a legitimate part of some new conceptual or perceptual structure or by adapting some action structure to accommodate the new demands of the situation. Alternately, assimilation changes the interpretation of the event or the required action such that existing structures may deal adequately with the problem at hand. What about the situation where some kind of event, whether perceptual, conceptual or action-demanding, is of such a nature that it cannot be handled by accommodation or assimilation? This discussion uses Piaget's concepts quite broadly. I want to speak about the assimilation and accommodation of complex event and action structures rather than of perceptual structures. Events that cannot be assimilated or accommodated are in principle not registered. However, information may be processed by some parts of perceptual structures, without the system being able to integrate the new event into existing structures or adapt existing structures to the new event. The identification of a vague shadow, an unfamiliar noise, or an unidentifiable taste or smell occurs, but it does so at a very general and relatively unstructured level. Similarly, when a particular structure has been activated, then the occurrence of a nonfit or interruption is usually not immediately handled by either assimilation or accommodation. Any wide discrepancy between existing structures and new events may produce such a condition of nonfit. A good example of the perceptual case is the panic exhibited by primates when presented with a truncated head. The perceptual structure of the "whole" animal and the separate head are too divergent to be easily accommodated. I suggest, and the case will be made strongly in the case of helplessness, that the inability to accommodate or to assimilate such an event produces the phenomenal experience of aversion. On the other hand, novel events and actions that are easily assimilated are "attractive"—they produce approach tendencies. Or, more directly, the phenomenal experience of "good" and "bad" may derive directly from cognitive structures that are actively and successively processing new information in contrast to the stymied cognitive structures that are incapable of adapting to the new input. This proposal is also related to the general notions of ego-syntonic and ego-alien material. The former is considered to be desirable and consistent with the individuals cognitive system, while the latter is considered to be unpleasant because it is inconsistent with existing structures. As a working hypothesis, this discussion is offered as an addendum to the puzzle of the origins of phenomenal experiences of "good" and "bad."

Chapter VIII
Anxiety—Theories, Complexities, and Resolutions

Introduction

The reasons for a special chapter on anxiety are diverse and idiosyncratic. No other single topic within the domain of emotion has received as much attention or argument during the past century. Poets have decried and celebrated anxiety's pervasive effects on the human condition. Theorists have made anxiety the central concept of their attempts at understanding the human mind, or they have felt unfulfilled if their theory did not adequately handle "the problem of anxiety." Philosophers have argued about the meaning and structure of anxiety. Experimentalists have attacked and defended dozens of attempts to measure, produce, and avoid it. A book about emotion should at least illustrate some of the theoretical sallies in the direction of anxiety and show how its particular approach is apposite.

At a more personal level, I have been preoccupied with the problem of anxiety for a quarter of a century. Since it was that problem that has led me to the more general considerations of problems of emotion, I find it necessary to include here the salient aspects of some thoughts on anxiety that have preoccupied my colleagues and me over the years. I shall start with a review of three major positions on anxiety and some recent excursions into the problem of measurement. That review is followed by a critique of received opinion about the sources of anxiety, coupled with a new look at its possible elicitors and inhibitors. William Kessen and I developed these ideas some years ago in a break with traditional concepts. My collaboration with Kessen generated my further thoughts about interruption and helplessness. In the final sections of this chapter, I bring these developments forward and place them in the context of the present volume.

175

Historical Background[1]

There is no single problem of anxiety. Different theorists and different experimental investigators have tackled various aspects of a broad complex of phenomena, all of them summarized under the conceptual category of anxiety. Anxiety has variously been considered as a phenomenal state of the human organism, as a physiological syndrome, and as a theoretical construct invoked to account for defensive behavior, the avoidance of noxious stimuli, and neurotic symptoms.

The role of anxiety in the study of personality has been peculiarly a child of the past century. The eighteenth- and nineteenth-century precursors of modern psychology were first of all concerned with the rational aspects of human personality development, and it was not until the work of Alexander Bain (1859) that motivational concepts became important in speculations about complex human behavior. Thus, with the exception of such forerunners of modern existential philosophy and psychology as Kierkegaard (1844), historically little attention was paid to the problem of anxiety.

However, negative, aversive, and unpleasant emotions have preoccupied many modern thinkers. Anxiety has not only been considered as the negative emotion par excellence in the theoretical writings of psychological theorists but, even apart from its prototypical status as a negative emotion, it became generally the central emotional concept of many theoretical treatments in psychology. Anxiety *was* emotion.

On the whole, anxiety has remained the child of the psychologist and the problem of the individual. While philosophers, anthropologists, and sociologists have at various times taken the psychologist's notion of anxiety and speculated about its social and cultural antecedents, the major contributions in the area of anxiety have been those of psychologists.

The following schema briefly recapitulates the various theoretical and empirical topics that have collectively come to be known as the problem of anxiety.

The Three Faces of Anxiety

Three general rubrics describe various emphases within the problem of anxiety: antecedent, organismic-hypothetical, and consequent conditions. While this triad can be conceptually delimited, there are, as will be obvious, borderline problems that defy any simple categorization.

[1]The section on pp. 176-188 is reprinted in part with some changes from Mandler (1968).

Antecedent Conditions

In the first instance, there has been a continuing interest in the conditions that give rise to the anxiety phenomenon. Practically all workers in the field have, at one time or another, been concerned with the stimulus that elicits anxiety. What is it in the environment that gives rise to the experience of anxiety or to the behavior that is symptomatic of anxiety? With the notable exception of the existentialists and some psychoanalytic writers, considerations of these conditions have usually viewed anxiety as an acquired emotion, rarely found until the organism has gone through some learning experiences. As an acquired emotion, it is often distinguished from the fear aroused by a threatening or noxious event, and it is usually reserved for those learned conditions that signal or cue the impending occurrence of some threat to the integrity of the organism.

Organismic Conditions

The second set of conditions that is subsumed under the problem of anxiety is the hypothesized or observable state of the organism. While a theoretical purist can easily postulate the anxiety state as a hypothetical theoretical device with explanatory functions only, most notions about the phenomenon have assumed some physiological or specifically autonomic arousal state. Those who have taken a position in this regard have usually assumed that the experience of anxiety is accompanied by some measurable level of sympathetic nervous system discharge. While there has been some speculation about whether this discharge shows a specific pattern for the emotion of anxiety, it has generally been assumed that while the discharge may be specific to the individual, it is likely not to be specific to the emotion. Unfortunately, the specific autonomic processes involved have been frequently ignored and, while some state of the organism has been postulated, its specific empirical referents have not necessarily been investigated. This position is particularly true of the concept of anxiety used by learning theorists in the United States. Even they, however, have at times spoken about the internal cues associated with the anxiety state.

Consequent Conditions

The consequential, experiential, or behavioral aspects of anxiety have been given the widest variety of definition and emphasis. The subjective experience of anxiety is accessible primarily through the report of the experiencing individual, and one major group of anxiety theorists, the existentialists, has concerned itself primarily with the experiential correlates. In addition to what the anxious human being says about himself, the problem of anxiety deals with the effect of the various antecedent and physiological states on practically all aspects of his behavior. Apart from the effect of anxiety on neurotic or other pathological behavior, anxiety has been studied as it affects early learning, child rearing, adult acquisition of normal aversions and apprehensions, motor behavior, complex problem solving, and so forth (cf. Cofer and Appley, 1964). Anxiety has also been defined in terms of expressive behavior, general level of activity, and a whole class of diagnostic behavioral and physiological symptoms.

While these three general classes of variables—antecedent, organismic, and consequent—provide a general overview of the extent of the problem of anxiety, they are hardly mutually exclusive. Various conditions may at various times shift from an organismic to a consequent state, or even from a consequent to an antecedent as, for example, when anxious behavior becomes the cue for further anxiety. Quite understandably, several writers on the problem have stressed the importance of different aspects of this triad. When the learning theorist is dealing with anxiety, he is dealing primarily with antecedent-consequent relations; when the existentialist speaks of anxiety, he is concerned primarily with the experience of anxiety, whereas he has relatively little concern with antecedent conditions of learning.

With these general considerations in mind, I move to a brief exposition of three major theoretical positions.

Theoretical Positions

Psychoanalytic Theory

Whereas much has been written about the development of and changes in the psychoanalytic concept of anxiety, the major position, even after several decades, remains Freud's own set of statements. Nothing better attests to the complexity of the problem of anxiety than Freud's struggle to build an adequate theory of anxiety. In no other area did he change his point of view as dramatically as he did toward the origins and mechanisms of anxiety, in fact presenting two theories on the topic.

Freud's early theory of anxiety (1952), generally stated in 1917, was relatively straightforward and part of the general energy system of psychoanalytic theory. Anxiety was defined as transformed libido. The transformation occurs as a result of repression, which distorts, displaces, or generally dams up the libido associated with instinctual impulses. This transformation-of-libido or "damming-up" theory of anxiety suggests that whenever the organism is prevented from carrying out an instinctually motivated act, whether through repression or through some prevention of gratification, anxiety will ensue. Such anxiety may then serve as a motive for a symptom that in turn functions to terminate or prevent the subsequent occurrence of anxiety. This theory was amended in 1926 when Freud published *Inhibitions, Symptoms and Anxiety.* The new position was restated in the *New Introductory Lectures on Psychoanalysis* in 1933 and remained his final statement on anxiety.

The second theory reversed the relationship between repression and anxiety. Although Freud tended to maintain the possibility of both kinds of relationships, the second theory added the possibility that repression occurs *because* of the experience of anxiety. To Freud, this was the more important possibility. In this context, anxiety becomes a signal from the ego. Whenever real or potential danger is detected by the ego, this perception gives rise to anxiety and mobilizes the defensive apparatus, including, of course, repression. Thus, because of the impending danger from unacceptable or dangerous impulses, the unpleasantness of anxiety produces repression, which leads the organism out of danger.

Avoidance of Overstimulation

A central concept in both of Freud's theories of anxiety is the notion of the avoidance of overstimulation. Whether libido is dammed up by not executing some instinctual act, or whether the ego signals impending stimulation that cannot be adequately handled, in both cases anxiety anticipates an impending situation for which no adequate coping mechanism is available to the organism. The ultimate unpleasantness is overstimulation, including pain and, in both theories, anxiety signals or anticipates this prototypical state. Thus Freud derives the origin of anxiety from the prototype of overstimulation. Such a derivation is necessary at least for the second theory, which presupposes cognitive, perceptual actions on the part of the ego. Here anxiety is learned; it is acquired as a function of past experience. It is in this sense that the psychoanalytic theory of anxiety, including its several revisions, has never abandoned the first theory, which describes the development of "automatic" anxiety. In the second theory, anxiety is derived from "automatic" anxiety; in the first theory, all anxiety is "automatic."

Antecedent and Organismic Conditions

The origin of "automatic" anxiety is traced by Freud to the very earliest period of life: the birth trauma and the immediate period thereafter. Emphasis on the helpless infant and on the birth trauma as the origin of the anxiety state places him apart from Rank (1924), who relies solely on the birth trauma as the source of anxiety.

For Freud (1936), the experience of anxiety—as distinct from its antecedents or consequences or as a theoretical state—has three aspects: (1) a specific feeling of unpleasantness; (2) efferent or discharge phenomena; and (3) the organism's perception of these discharge phenomena. In other words, the perception of autonomic arousal is associated with a specific feeling of unpleasantness. As to the primitive occasions for this anxiety experience, Freud is frequently hazy. While on the one hand he considers the predisposition toward anxiety as a genetic mechanism, at other times he considers anxiety as arising from separation from the mother, castration fears, and other early experiences. He considers the specific unpleasant experience of the anxiety state as derived from the first experience of overstimulation at the time of birth. The birth experience "involves just such a concatenation of painful feelings, of discharges and excitation, and of bodily sensations, as to have become a prototype for all occasions on which life is endangered, ever after to be reproduced again in us as the dread or 'anxiety' condition" (Freud, 1952).

It is possible that some of the discussions that have arisen out of several interpretations of Freud's theory of anxiety have confused the specific experience of anxiety derived from the physiological makeup of the organism and the birth trauma with the conditions that produce or threaten unmanageable discharge. The conditions that produce such an anxiety state are, in addition to the birth trauma, separation or loss of the mother, with the attendant threat of overstimulation caused by uncontrollable impulses and threats, and castration fears with similar consequences. Thus, where Rank places both the affect and the prototypic antecedent conditions at the period of birth, Freud lets the organism inherit or learn the affect at birth, but also adds other specific conditions that elicit it later on in early life. On this basis it is reasonable to claim, as Kubie (1941) does, "that all anxiety has as its core what Freud has called 'free floating anxiety'." In other words, given the initial affect of anxiety that a child either genetically or experientially brings into the world, specific anxieties and fears are then situationally developed out of this basic predisposition.

In this context, the various types of fears or anxieties that Freud discusses are not different in their initial source of the affect but, instead, differ in the specific conditions that give rise to them. They are fear, where anxiety is directly related to a specific object; objective anxiety *(Realangst)*, which is the reaction to an external danger and which is considered to be not only a useful but also a necessary function of the system; and neurotic anxiety, in which the anxiety is out of proportion to the real danger and frequently is related to unacceptable instinctual impulses and unconscious conflicts. I shall consider Bowlby's critique of this distinction later.

Freud's notion that anxiety is brought about when the ego receives those external or internal cues that signal helplessness or inability to cope with environmental or intrapsychic threats is mirrored in Karen Horney's position that basic anxiety is "the feeling a child has of being isolated and helpless in a potentially hostile world" (Horney, 1945). For Horney, primary anxiety is related eventually to disturbances of interpersonal relations, initially those between the child and significant adults. A similar position is taken by Harry Stack Sullivan, who relates both parental disapproval and the inadequacies, irrationalities, and confusions of cultural patterns and requirements to the development of anxiety.

In summary, the psychoanalytic position not only treats anxiety as an important tool for the adequate handling of a realistically threatening environment, but it also relates anxiety to the development of neurotic behavior. The "cultural" psychoanalysts then go on to stress the social environment at large, while Freud sees the basic anxiety mechanisms in early separation and castration fears. In all cases, however, anxiety is related to the inability of the organism to cope with a situation that threatens to overwhelm him and to the absence of adequate acts to deal with environmental or intrapsychic events. As Freud phrased it in one of his later formulations, "anxiety . . . seems to be a reaction to the perception of the absence of the object (e.g., goal)" (Freud, 1936). With the object absent, no action is possible and helplessness (i.e., anxiety) ensues.

Learning Theory

The theoretical position taken by most representatives of modern learning or behavior theory is generally derived from the work of I. P. Pavlov and J. B. Watson. The two major positions are those of C. L. Hull and B. F. Skinner, although neither of them have worked extensively on the problem of anxiety. Most of the work on anxiety within the framework of learning theory has been carried out by representatives of the Hullian school. While most of their experimental work has involved lower animals, the "conditioning" concept of anxiety has been extensively applied to complex human behavior (cf. Dollard and Miller, 1950).

As Mowrer (1960) has shown, the role of anxiety for learning theory is derived mainly from the attempts to explain the nature and consequences of punishment. In the case of punishment, the application of a painful or noxious event following the performance of a response inhibits or interferes with the performance of that response on subsequent occasions. Similarly, when an organism avoids a situation, it is, through the operation of some mediating mechanism, precluding the occurrence of a noxious or painful event. The nature of this mediating mechanism, learning theorists contend, is what is commonly called fear or anxiety.

Anxiety as an Acquired Drive

The conditioning model states that a previously neutral event or stimulus (the conditioned stimulus, or CS), when paired with an unconditioned stimulus (US), which produces a noxious state such as pain, will elicit a conditioned response (CR) after a suitable number of pairings. This conditioned response is commonly called fear. In a typical experimental situation, an animal might be placed in a white box with a door leading to a black box. The floor of the white box is electrified, and the animal receives a shock (US) that becomes associated with the white box (CS). If the animal is then permitted to escape from the shock through the door to the black box, he will eventually run from the white box to the black box prior to the application of shock. Learning theorists assert that the fear (CR) conditioned to the white box (CS) motivates subsequent activity. The reduction of the fear—by escape from the CS—produces avoidance of the original noxious unconditioned stimulus. Fear—or anxiety—is viewed as a secondary or acquired drive established by classical conditioning.

The Skinnerian point of view has been described by Schoenfeld (1950), who argues against the notion that the organism "avoids" the unconditioned stimulus. He suggests that the organism escapes from a stimulus array that consists of the conditioned stimulus *as well as* the proprioceptive and tactile stimuli, which precede the unconditioned stimulus. However, this description is not basically divergent from the more general statement that the proprioceptive and tactile stimuli are a conditioned response functioning as a drive.

Antecedent Conditions

Whether avoidance learning is achieved by the mediating effect of the conditioned fear or ascribed to conditioned aversive stimuli, the question still remains open as to the necessary characteristics of the original, unconditioned, noxious, or aversive stimulus. In one of the early statements on conditioned fear, Mowrer (1939) suggested that fear was the conditioned form of the pain response. However, we shall see shortly that pain cannot be a necessary condition for the establishment of anxiety. In a more general statement about the nature of acquired drives such as fear, Miller (1951) has extended the class of unconditioned stimuli adequate for fear conditioning to essentially all noxious stimuli, and Mowrer (1960) comes close to a psychoanalytic position when he expresses essential agreement with the position that fear is a psychological warning of impending discomfort. However, work with experimental animals usually centered on painful stimuli has failed to establish unequivocally that fear can be conditioned on the onset of other discomforting primary drives or USs. This failure hampers the generality of the conditioning model.

Organismic Conditions

The above evidence becomes important when we consider not only the antecedent conditions for the establishment of fear, which the learning theorists relate to the conditioning paradigm, but also the nature of the mediating response (the CR). A variety of data (e.g., Wynne and Solomon, 1955) has shown that the development of the anxiety or fear state in animals depends on an adequately functioning autonomic nervous system. Within the confines of the conditioning model, the writers who have speculated on the nature of the mediating fear or anxiety state have suggested that it presupposes some sympathetic arousal. It follows from this that fear or anxiety can be conditioned only if the unconditional stimulus also is one that produces such sympathetic or general autonomic effects. To the extent that a learning theory position assumes emotional, autonomic responses correlated with the fear state, it also suggests that fear necessarily derives only from those primary conditions that are autonomically arousing. At least as far as writers such as Mowrer are concerned, the threat of discomfort, rise in primary drives, or overstimulation in general can be prototypes for anxiety only if these conditions have autonomic components. However, this does not seem to be the case for divergent states such as hunger and thirst.

Consequent Conditions

As far as the consequences of conditioned fear are concerned, there seems to be general agreement, both theoretical and empirical, that they fall into two general classes. In the first class, fear and anxiety operate as secondary drives and exhibit all the usual properties of drives, serving as motives for the establishment of new behavior. When fear acts as a drive, new responses are reinforced by the reduction of that drive. This response-produced drive is the major emphasis that learning theory has placed on fear or anxiety. In the second class, the conditioned fear response or the CER (conditioned emotional response) may, in a variety of situations, interfere with or suppress ongoing behavior. In this sense, it is no different from the general anxiety concept of the psychoanalysts in that behavioral anxiety or preoccupation with anxiety may be incompatible with other behavior or thoughts required from the organism in a particular situation.

Existentialist Psychology

The emergence of existentialism from a purely philosophical school to an important influence on psychology has been a phenomenon of the mid-twentieth century. What existentialist thinking has done for psychology is not so much to present it with a new theory in the tradition of well-defined deductive positions that became popular in the early part of the century but, rather, to provide it with a wealth of ideas and challenges to conventional wisdom. While a variety of different positions and schools can be discerned within the movement, the existential exposition of anxiety has remained essentially unchanged from Kierkegaard's pathbreaking formulation, published more than 100 years ago (1844). For example, Jean-Paul Sartre's position on the problem of anxiety is, for present purposes, not noticeably at variance with it (1943). Kierkegaard's central concept of human development and human maturity was freedom. Freedom is related to man's ability to become aware of the wide range of possibility facing him in life; possibility in that sense is not statically present in his environment but is created and developed by man. Freedom implies the existence and awareness of possibility.

Anxiety is intimately tied up with this existence of possibility and potential freedom. The very consideration of possibility brings with it the experience of anxiety. Whenever man considers possibilities and potential courses of action, he is faced with anxiety. Whenever the individual attempts to carry any possibility into action, anxiety is a necessary accompaniment, and growth toward freedom means the ability to experience and tolerate the anxiety that necessarily comes with the consideration of possibility. In modern terms, any choice situation involves the experience of anxiety; therefore, for the existentialist, the antecedents of anxiety are, in a sense, the very existence of man in a world in which choice exists.

Kierkegaard endows even the newborn child with an unavoidable and necessary prototypical state of anxiety. However, since the child is originally in what Kierkegaard calls a "state of innocence," a state in which he is not yet aware of the specific possibilities facing him, his anxiety, too, is an anxiety that is general but without content. Possibility exists, but it is a possibility of action in general, not of specific choices. The peculiarly human problem of development faces the child as he becomes aware of both himself and his environment. Possibility and actualization become specific, and anxiety appears at each point where development and individuation of the child progresses; at each point a new choice of possibilities must be faced, and anxiety must be confronted anew.

The consequences of this notion of anxiety are that as the individual develops, he is continuously confronted with the unpleasant experience of anxiety and with the problem of mature development in the face of it. It is not only unavoidable as a condition of man; it is, Kierkegaard maintains, actually sought out. "Anxiety is an alien power which lays hold of an individual, and yet one cannot tear oneself away, nor has the will to do so; for one fears, but what one fears one desires. Anxiety then makes the individual impotent" (Kierkegaard, 1844). Since anxiety is unavoidable and must be encountered if we are to grow as human beings, all attempts at avoiding the experience of anxiety are either futile, or they result in a constricted, uncreative, and unrealistic mode of life. Only by facing the experience of anxiety can we truly become actualized human beings and face the reality of human existence.

Kierkegaard also makes a clear distinction between fear and anxiety. Fear involves a specific object that is feared and avoided, whereas anxiety is independent of the object and, furthermore, is a necessary attribute of all choice and possibility.

The importance of Kierkegaard, and of the existentialist development in general, is in the emphasis—found *inter alia* in some psychoanalytic writings—that anxiety is not primarily a learned experience derived from past encounters with painful environmental events, but is a naturally occurring initial state of the organism. Man may actually be born with anxiety instead of learning it through experience. While existentialism has not produced any clear definitions of anxiety apart from appealing to an assumed common phenomenology, it has raised important questions both about the general problem of anxiety and, in the field of psychotherapy, about the proper treatment for the conditions that show pathological effects of anxiety. Clearly a therapeutic attitude that considers anxiety as a normal state is radically different from an attitude that stresses the avoidance of primary and secondary traumata.

Human Anxiety—Empirical Generalizations

Since 1950, when May remarked on the absence of experimental work on human anxiety, literally hundreds of studies have been published, using a quantitative, experimental approach to the problem of human anxiety. Many investigations have used the concept of anxiety primarily as an explanatory concept. These studies fall more properly under rubrics such as conflict, stress, and frustration, and they will not be dealt with here. However, a large body of research has been devoted specifically to anxiety. This rash of experimental investigations was, in the first instance, instigated by the development of the so-called anxiety scales. The most widely used and influential of these is the Manifest Anxiety Scale, developed by Janet Taylor Spence (Taylor, 1953). The Test Anxiety Questionnaire developed by Mandler and Sarason (1952) has also been used extensively.

Anxiety Scales

The Manifest Anxiety Scales, consisting of 50 true-false items, was originally developed to test some of the implications of the anxiety or fear concept within the general system originated by Hull and by Spence (e.g., 1958). It was expected that individuals who had high anxiety scores would exhibit a more general drive level than individuals with less anxiety, since anxiety is—within this theoretical position—considered to be a secondary, or acquired, drive. In keeping with that theory, individuals scoring high on this scale acquire conditioned responses based on aversive (but not nonaversive) unconditioned stimuli much more rapidly than individuals scoring low on the scale.

A further prediction, which has been generally borne out, was that individuals with high anxiety should perform better on simple tasks than on complex ones, but that individuals with little anxiety should perform better on complex tasks (Taylor, 1956).

Whereas the Manifest Anxiety Scale concentrated on the drive aspects of anxiety, the Test Anxiety Questionnaire was concerned more specifically with interfering responses generated by the anxiety state. It consits of graphic scales specifically concerned with the experience of anxiety in test or examination situations. The hypothesis suggested that the more an individual tends to report the occurrence of anxietylike experiences on a questionnaire, the more likely it is that these will occur in any situation that involves examination or test pressures such as potential success or failure, time pressures, and so forth. In general, here, too, the predictions about the interfering nature of anxiety in complex situations have been borne out.

Correlational studies of two scales have shown a low positive relationship, but the Manifest Anxiety Scale seems to tap more general characteristics of the individual, while the Test Anxiety Questionnaire is more sensitive to situational cues, particularly those that indicate to the subject that he is being tested or examined.

After the initial introduction of anxiety scales, the questionnaire or objective test approach to anxiety continued in vigorous fashion. However, since it insists on measuring response characteristics and patterns, this approach has tended to be atheoretical. A typical example is Spielberger's work (e.g., 1972), which has stressed a distinction between an anxiety *trait* and an anxiety *state*. The state is defined in terms of physiological and subjective reactions to a situation that the individual sees as potentially "harmful, threatening, or dangerous." The trait is inferred from the frequency and intensity of occurrences of the anxiety states over time. Unfortunately, this typically American (behaviorist) preoccupation with the measurable, which then is related to whatever else might be relevant, preempts theory. The typical "theoretical" attempt is to summarize whatever has been or can be said about "anxiety" and to speculate how it might be related to these measured realities. For example, Spielberger (1972) emphasizes the necessity of including stress as a central theoretical concept and defines it by the measurement or enumeration of "objective" stressful stimuli. In contrast, this definition of stress is abandoned when threat is defined as the *subjective* evaluation of danger which, in turn, determines the anxiety state. Thus a situation may at the same time be "objectively stressful" and not, in fact, threatening to any given individual. We can only empathize with the reasoning, since it leads directly from the need to accept common language terms such as threat or stress and, finding them too vague, redefines them to the point where they lose the surplus meaning that brought them into the discourse in the first place.

A useful theory about an appropriate concept of "anxiety" would be under no such constraints. Much more, it would dictate what is to be measured. By trying the approach through response processes, we are invariably led, as is Spielberger, into the position of decoupling anxiety states from cognitive variables. Anxiety as a state then becomes nothing more than reported "feelings of tension and apprehensions with associated arousal of the autonomic nervous system" (Spielberger, 1972). But that apprehension must be contentless if it is not cognitive —and I shall return later to Bowlby's argument that contentless anxiety is, if not in fact useless as a concept, at least infrequent. More important, however, this definition of the state fails to distinguish it from guilt or grief or many other "emotions," all of which include tension, apprehension, and arousal. And, once again, the response-oriented psychologist has defined himself into a corner.

I shall argue in the following paragraphs that anxiety as a trait is generally a cognitive variable. Such a trait summarizes habitual interpretations and appraisals of the world. However, the disappointingly low correlations that personality measures generate with criterion variables (cf. Mischel, 1968) suggests that evaluations of individual consistencies in appraisal are best conducted at the individual and situational levels. Even habitual cognitions of the world should preferably be assessed in terms of individual reactions to specific situations, and not by normative evaluations of responses to lists of possible threats and worries.

What Do Anxiety Scales Measure?

Practically all the work on these scales has related subjects' self-reports to specific situations and tasks. I want to reconsider the anxiety-performance relationships within the context of an information-processing approach.

The first questions that need to be raised are: What are the effects of instructions on subjects? How do instructions work? To what extent do subjects instruct themselves about a task? Various aspects of this problem have been taken up in a variety of different contexts as, for example, in the important work on demand characteristics of tasks and experimenter bias. Furthermore, what is the interaction between what the experimenter tells subjects about a particular task or situation and what they tell themselves about that particular task? Instructions and self-instructions are a mode of selecting structures and programs, of selectively tuning the system as to what it will or will not do, and what particular strategies it will use to process the information given. Instructions are not always, and may not even be frequently contained in the verbal instructions to the subjects; they are communicated by the structure and form of the task. For example, if subjects in a memory task are given lists of words one at a time and in constant order, they will assume that the task requires serial reproduction (Mandler and Dean, 1969).

Let me now propose that anxiety scales may be an established, although undiscovered, method of measuring the self-instructional tendencies of our subjects. They tell us about subjects' habitual tendencies in response to the instructions they find implicit in a variety of performance-oriented tasks. I think we have here a method of looking at the interaction of what we tell a subject and what he tells himself about a situation. In other words, self-instructions may program one approach to the task, one particular way of handling it, while the experimenter's instructions may suggest another way or may reinforce or counteract the self-instructional tendency.

I am assuming that the high-anxious subject tells himself that the appropriate (not necessarily useful or adaptive) behavior in a testlike situation consists of observing his own behavior, examining his failures, ruminating about his responses and his emotional reactions, and thinking about standards set by himself or by the performance of others. The low-anxious subject, on the other hand, gives himself few such instructions—he does not even think about them as possibilities— and may, instead, orient his behavior and cognitions toward the specific requirements of the task, excluding extraneous ideations, analyzing appropriate task oriented behavior, and so forth.

Given the fact that high-anxiety subjects have self-instructions that are self-deprecating, interfering, and failure inducing, under what conditions are those instructions operative? I am, of course, returning to a variant of the position that Seymour Sarason and I took long ago: test anxiety scales measure task-irrelevant responses (Mandler and Sarason, 1952). What I am adding is that it tells us that high-test-anxious subjects give themselves instructions about the test situations that say: This is a task in which I will do badly, this is a task in which I will have difficulties, this is a task in which I am going to be upset. As soon as these subjects then find themselves in a test situation, these instructions are let loose and interfere with performance under certain conditions. But, under what conditions can we tell a subject to turn off these self-instructions?

As an example, let us look at the question of reassuring subjects. I believe that reassurance counteracts the self-deprecating, interfering self-instructions of the high-anxiety subjects. It provides instructions at variance with the self-instructions. Reassurance instructions have the opposite effect for the low-anxiety subjects. We assume that low-anxiety subjects do not generate and do not even think about making self-deprecating, interfering responses in the test situation. However, the reassurance instructions essentially suggest to them that it might be possible to think that way. I have suggested elsewhere, in an entirely different context, that it is difficult to tell subjects in cognitive experiments *not* to think about something (Mandler, 1967b). The effect is usually the opposite of the one desired; the instructions suggest specific cognitions. I believe this is also what happens with the low-anxiety subject. He is told: This is the place where you might consider worrying. The high-anxiety subject does not need to be told that; he is already worrying and he may, in fact, be reassured.

In other words, the instructions may tell the high-anxiety subject something he already knows: that he will do poorly in complex tasks. At the same time, these instructions tell the low-anxiety subject something he does *not* know: that he, too, is likely to do poorly.

We might consider test anxiety scales, for example, not as "measures of anxiety in testing situations," but as test-relevant self-instruction scales that measure individual differences in the manner in which people instruct themselves about their appraisal of and response to testing situations. This kind of notion also fits the two-factor theory of emotion: that the test situation is arousing in the first instance, but that the quality of that particular emotion will be determined primarily by cognitive factors, by the way the subject interprets the situation, and by what instructions he gives himself as to the appropriate behavior.

Such a perspective on paper and pencil "anxiety" scales in terms of task-relevant perceptions and actions generates no fundamentally new insights. Self-oriented, task-irrelevant reactions to "anxiety" are deleterious to performance (see also the discussion of Easterbrook's cue-utilization in Chapter 6). In 1971, Wine provided a more general and widely informed discussion of the relationship between anxiety and attention. Noting developments after 1952 and the original postulation of task relevance and irrelevance, Wine draws special attention to the aspects of anxiety scale measurement that are related to task efficiency and those that are not (see also Liebert and Morris' distinction between worry and emotionality, 1967). Wine concludes that "arousal appears to bear no *consistent* relationship to performance" (my italics), and that self-referential "worry" is attention demanding and detracts from available attention processes. Wine notes that an attentional emphasis focuses on how people use their available time, what they are thinking about, and concludes that "degree of arousal is irrelevant unless the subject is attending to his arousal." In conclusion, then, anxiety scales and, specifically, test anxiety scales, are indicators of the way people handle their interpretation of arousal, its initiators, and their current situation.

Anxiety, Pain, and Inhibition[2]

We have seen that theories of anxiety have been developed from evidence as diverse as the avoidance behavior of animals and the symptomatic behavior of human neurotics; the language of these theories ranges from existentialism to learning theory. For all the differences in detail, however, there is some similarity in the approach of different theorists to the problem of anxiety.

We shall examine the proposition that these theoretical communalities do not fully encompass available data about human and animal distress, and we shall then go on to present several theoretical propositions supplementary to current theories of anxiety.

Briefly and without extenuation, the following shared characteristics of contemporary theories of anxiety can be noted. First, an archetypical event or class of events exists that evokes anxiety primitively, innately, or congenitally. For Freud (1936) this original inciter was overstimulation; for Mowrer (1939) it is pain; for Miller (1951) it is the "innate fear reaction"; for Rank (1924) it is the birth trauma; for Selye (1956) it is stress; for the existentialists, it is the very fact of being human and alive. The second communality in theories about anxiety is the postulation that, somehow, the response to the archetypical event is transferred to previously innocuous events, events either in the external environment or in the action of the organism. The typical

[2]The section in pp. 190–199 is reprinted in part with minor changes from Kessen and Mandler (1961).

assumption has been that this association takes place with contiguous occurrence of trauma and neutral event, although the students of human learning have been more detailed than this in discussing the conditioning of fear (see, for example, Dollard and Miller, 1950). Finally, it is assumed that the events terminating or reducing anxiety are closely related to the events that evoke it. Thus the primitive danger of overstimulation is controlled by a reduction in level of stimulation; similarly, the "fear" of electric shock is reduced by moving away from events associated with shock, presumably in inverse analog to the model of hunger and thirst, where a deficit of some substance (deprivation) is repaired by its replacement (eating or drinking).

These common elements of present-day conceptions of anxiety—the archetypical evoker, the mechanism for association to previously neutral events, and the parallel state of the elicitation and the reduction of anxiety—have produced discernable biases in contemporary psychology. In theory, in research, and apparently in therapy, the problem of anxiety has come to be, on one hand, largely a problem of trauma (i.e., what events set off the anxiety) and on the other hand, largely a problem of flight (i.e., what responses will lead away from the inciting event). In what follows, we shall discuss the place of the "trauma" or "archetype" notion by examining in detail the best candidate for primary primitive evoker of anxiety—pain—and then go on to consider a position that is alternative to, but not necessarily incompatible with, the common elements of anxiety theory sketched out here.

Death of Pain

We shall defend the position—coming to be widely held in American psychology—that a theory of anxiety based solely on pain as an archetypical precondition is untenable. The evidence at hand suggests two conclusions: first, that pain is not a necessary condition for the development of anxiety and avoidance behavior; and second, that when pain is apparently a sufficient condition for the development of anxiety, there is a variety of factors at work rather than a single, innate link.

There are three areas of evidence that support the conclusion that anxiety can occur even when pain does not occur. First, there are external events other than pain that arouse—without prior experience of association with pain—behavior that bears the marks of distress or anxiety. Of particular interest to our argument in the next section are the startle and distress responses of the newborn human infant to loud noise or to loss of support (Peiper, 1956; Watson, 1919). Among animals, escape, avoidance, and species-appropriate signs of distress to nonpainful events have been reported in abundance by ethologists; the

mobbing of chaffinches at the appearance of an owl is an example
(Hinde, 1954). Unless a severe twist is given to the behavioral
interpretation of "anxiety," these cases, among others, stand against
the Original Pain principle.

More striking as a demonstration of the separability of pain and
anxiety is the behavior of human beings afflicted with congenital
analgesia. This apparently inherited syndrome consists typically of a
complete absence of pain sensitivity, despite otherwise normal
registration of the environment. A review of some 30 cases reported in
the literature (Fanconi and Ferrazzini, 1957) shows the severely
debilitating effects accompanying the absence of pain mechanisms. The
patients are usually discovered to be mutilated during childhood;
undiscovered fractures and scarred tongues and limbs are among the
injuries found. Despite the fact that these patients fail to develop
specific adaptive avoidance behavior in the face of many injuries and
noxious situations, anxiety toward other (nonpainful) events always
seems to develop normally. The conclusion applied to one such case by
West and Farber (1961) can be generalized to all observed cases of
congenital analgesia: "Anxiety plays a motivating role in determining
certain aspects of the patient's behavior." In brief, the development of
anxiety and avoidance behavior is not halted by the absence of pain
sensitivity, even though the avoidance of normally painful events is
absent.

The foregoing two points have shown that distress will develop in
the absence of pain. A third collection of evidence supports the
assertion of the disjunction without conclusively demonstrating the
absence of an association with pain, but the data, when seen all in a
row, strongly indict an exclusive commitment to a pain-traumatic
theory of anxiety. I refer here to the evidence in Chapter 7 that
anxiety or discomfort occur when highly practiced and well-organized
responses are interrupted. It is at least difficult to fit these cases to a
theory of anxiety that depends primitively on pain or any other
archetypical trauma.

If it can be agreed that pain is not a necessary condition for the
development of anxiety, another question arises. To what degree or in
what fashion is pain a sufficient antecedent condition for the
development of anxiety? The skeptical answer that appears to be
warranted by the evidence is that the relation between pain and
anxiety is rarely simple or obvious and, furthermore, that attention to
the distinction between pain as a sensory event and the distress
reaction that usually but does not always accompany pain may clarify
the complexity somewhat. The presentation of this line of discourse is
made easier by a review by Barber (1959) of problems associated with
pain and Melzack's (1973) theoretical contribution. We shall, therefore,
only summarize what seem to be legitimate supports for the

two-or-more-factor theory of pain and then move on to a more extended treatment of the nature of distress.

There is some, although admittedly very little, evidence that the appearance of discomfort with painful stimulation requires early experience of as yet unknown character. Puppies raised by Melzack and Scott (1957) in a restricted environment showed indifference to stimulation painful to normal dogs and great difficulty in learning to avoid objects associated with pain. These observations are of crucial importance to speculations about anxiety and warrant replication and extension. In human infants, there is a striking temporal difference between the first "defensive" response to painful stimulation (withdrawal or startle) and the second "distressful" response (crying, increased motility, and so on). Peiper (1956) reports that the first response has a latency of 0.2 seconds while the second response has a latency as high as 5 to 7 seconds.

A similar separability of what might be called cognitive pain and distress occurs in some cases of prefrontal surgical interference to deal with intractable pain. Barber (1959), in reviewing the evidence, concludes: "When prefrontal leucotomy alleviates intractable pain it does not necessarily elevate the pain threshold or alter 'the sensation of pain' . . . (Further,) with few, if any, exceptions, investigators report that the 'sensation' or 'perception' of pain is practically unaltered by any of these procedures."

Barber suggests that noxious painful stimulation has wide cortical effects and argues against a neurology of pain based exclusively on specific pain pathways or pain areas, a position developed in fine theoretical detail by Melzack (e.g., 1973). The discomfort-pain association seems to depend on extensive cortical organization—in the words of the present argument, on experience of pain and discomfort.

The death of pain as original in all anxiety does not rule out alternate formulations of the traumatic or archetypical variety. Solomon and Brush (1956), for example, have taken students of aversive behavior to task for neglecting the investigation of noxious stimuli other than electric shock. When they ask, "Are all aversive anticipatory states alike?", they point to one alternative suggested by the elimination of pain as the sole antecedent of anxiety. Another alternative, which will be explored here, is to examine a postulation of anxiety that is independent not only of pain, but of any archetypical traumatic event.

Nature of Fundamental Distress

It is our contention that a nontraumatic theory of the sources of anxiety can be defended and, furthermore, that anxiety may be reduced or terminated by devices other than escape from and avoidance of threat. These alternative formulations are proposed as supplements to, rather than as substitutes for, the archetypical theories of anxiety.

The schematic model suggested here for the occurrence of anxiety— in distinction from the classical model of the organism fleeing the associations of pain—is the cyclical distress of the human newborn. There may be antecedent events that could account for the crying and increased activity we recognize as distressful in the young infant (e.g., food privation and shifts in temperature), but *it is not necessary to specify or even to assume such a specific antecedent event.* It is a defensible proposition that the strong bent of the archetypical formulations to study those conditions of distress for which a specific evoker could be discerned seriously limits the range of proper investigation. The distress of the human newborn, as obviously "anxious" as a rat in a shuttle box, can be taken as an example of human anxiety and as a starting point for changes in speculations about human emotion, regardless of the absence of known or well-guessed "unconditioned" archetypical evokers. More than that, this modification suggests that there are cases in which the old and respected saw about anxiety as the conditioned form of the stimulus-specific fear reaction may be misleading; that is, there may be interesting cases in which a stimulus-specific fear (as indicated by flight or avoidance) may be better understood as a conditioned form of primitive anxiety or *fundamental distress* (cf. also Auersperg, 1958).

To see anxiety as fundamental distress raises the ghosts of the dispute between James and Cannon. Let us take a further theoretical step and suggest that the crucial event in fundamental distress is the perception or afferent effect of variable and intense autonomic, visceral activity. This is, of course, a rough restatement of James' position. Most of Cannon's counterarguments are not relevant to the postulation of such an effect during early infancy, since his position largely depends on the identification of external threatening stimuli—a feat beyond the powers of the newborn (Cannon, 1927). But Cannon's major argument that emotional reactions take place with a latency far shorter than the latency of autonomic reactions deserves particular attention here. To recapitulate some arguments from Chapter 5, the delayed emotional response of infants, as well as the variable, badly organized reactions of infants, suggests just such a delayed emotional mechanism as Cannon ascribes to James. If we assume further (cf. Mandler and Kremen, 1958) that these visceral reactions are eventually represented centrally as autonomic imagery, then ascription of a developmental shift from a Jamesian to a Cannonic mechanism becomes plausible. As I noted in Chapter 6, the argument that visceral discomfort may become centrally represented does not imply that the vicsceral response will not thereafter occur; the postulation of central representation is required to explain the quick and efficient reaction of the adult to threatening events. However, given rapid removal from the situation of threat, the "postthreat" visceral response may not occur. A closely related point has been made by Schneirla (1959): ". . .although the James-Lange type of theory provides a useful basis for studying the early ontogeny of mammals, . . . a Cannon-type theory of higher-center control is *indispensable* for later stages of perceptual and motivational development. If ontogeny progresses well, specialized patterns of [approach] and [withdrawal]. . ., or their combinations, perceptually controlled, often short-circuit or modify the early viscerally dominated versions."

One final comment on the nature of distress is warranted. It is not assumed that the distress reaction is usually terminated suddenly by the occurrence of an escape or of an avoidance response. Instead, we assume that, except for a few laboratory situations, the distress reaction is reverberatory in character. Particular events or responses do not terminate the anxiety immediately; moreover, the distress reaction will serve as a signal for further distress. Depending on partially understood environmental and organismic conditions, these reverberations will augment the initial anxiety (see Mednick, 1958) or gradually damp out and disappear.

In short, fundamental distress is held to be a state of discomfort, unease, or anxiety that bears no clear or necessary relation to a specific antecedent event (archetypical evoker). The model or "ideal case" of fundamental distress is held to be the recurrent distress of the human newborn. What remains for consideration is an examination of the occasions of reduction or termination of anxiety and the relation of such occasions to fundamental distress.

Inhibition of Anxiety

The second departure from conventional views of anxiety has to do with techniques for the reduction or termination of anxiety. It is proposed that, in addition to the classical mechanisms of escape and avoidance of danger, anxiety is brought under control (i.e., diminished or removed) by the operation of *specific inhibitors.* Before moving on to a discussion of the inhibitory mechanism, however, we must emphasize a point that is implicit in the foregoing treatment. The undifferentiated discomfort of the infant that we have taken as an example of fundamental distress may accompany particular conditions of need or drive; that is, the newborn may be hungry *and* distressed, thirsty *and* distressed, cold *and* distressed, and so on. With the removal of the privation or drive, the distress may disappear, but this reduction by the repair of a deficit—which is formally equivalent with escape from danger—is not of primary interest in the present discussion. Instead, our concern is with those responses of the organism and events in the environment that inhibit distress, *regardless of their relation to a specifiable need, drive, or privation.*

Anecdotal evidence of the operation of congenital inhibitors of anxiety in infants abounds, but there has been relatively little systematic exploration of these inhibitors in the newly born human or animal. However, two empirical studies illustrate the character of the inhibitory mechanisms; one is based on a response of the infant, the other on a particular pattern in the environment. Research by Kessen and his associates has shown that infant distress, as indicated by crying and hyperactivity, is dramatically reduced by the occurrence of empty (i.e., nonnutritive) sucking as early as the fourth day of life. The performance of the congenital sucking response on a rubber nipple stuffed with cloth brings the newborn to a condition of motor and vocal quiescence. Thus sucking appears to fit the pattern of the congenital inhibitor of distress or, more broadly, of anxiety. Also, the hungry infant, during the first days of life, with little or no experience of feeding, will quiet when given breast or bottle, even though it is unlikely that his hunger has been reduced during the first several sucking responses.

The second instance of distress-inhibition derives from Harlow's (1958) research with infant monkeys. These animals, when distressed, whether by a frightful artificial Monster Rhesus or in the routine cyclicity of discomfort, seek out a situation—the experimental "mother"—that inhibits the distress. Harlow has made some provocative assumptions about the characteristics of the model that reduce the infant monkey's distress, and he has established an empirical procedure for testing them. Beyond doubt, a complex environmental event terminates a condition of the animal that meets our usual criteria for the presence of anxiety; this event bears no obvious relation to physiological privation or deficit.

There are undoubtedly several congenital or early developed inhibitors of distress that have not received adequate empirical examination; the quieting effects of rocking and the response of the 2-month-old infant to the adult face come to mind. A strong presumptive case can be made for the operation of a class of such distress terminators that do not depend on escape from or avoidance of a specific evoker of distress for their effects. One group of inhibitors of distress appears to be characterized by rhythmic periodicity: regular sounds, rocking, the nodding of head of the adult, and so on. Investigation of the relation of this class of events to visceral rhythms would lead to increased precision in speculations about fundamental distress. It is interesting to speculate in this connection that distress may be related to inhibition as sympathetic is related to parasympathetic activation.

There is a further aspect of the problem of distress-inhibition that will illustrate the relation of fundamental distress and its inhibitors to anxiety of the archetypical variety. If distress is under control by the operation of an inhibitor, what is the effect of withdrawing the inhibitor? What, in other words, are the consequences of disinhibition of distress? For the occurrences of some inhibitors (e.g., rocking the hungry and distressful infant) it seems that disinhibition "releases" or "reinstates" the distress. For others (e.g., sucking on the hands until asleep) the withdrawal of the inhibitor does not result in the recurrence of distress.

The following proposals can be made to deal with this kind of disjunction. Archetypical evokers (e.g., pain, hunger) are accompanied by or lead to distress. This distress can usually be reduced in two distinct ways: by action of a specific inhibitor that reduces distress but does not necessarily affect the primitive evoker; or by changes acting directly on the level of the primitive evokers. The best example of mechanisms working together in nonlaboratory settings is nutritive sucking. The infant's *sucking* inhibits the fundamental distress accompanying hunger; at a slower rate, the ingestion of food "shuts off" the source of distress. It is maintained here that these two mechanisms for the reduction of distress or anxiety are profitably kept separate in psychological theory.

The separation of distress reduction by specific inhibition and distress reduction by changes in archetypical evokers can be defended on other grounds as well. As noted earlier, much infantile (and later) distress is of a periodic variety without obvious relation to specific environmental evokers. Specific inhibitors may tide the organism over the peaks of these distress cycles, whatever their source, until some other occurrence (e.g., the onset of sleep) results in a more stable reduction of the level of organismic disturbance.

It is reasonable to assume that the inhibitory mechanism under discussion is not limited to the operation of primitive inhibitors early in development. Instead, events associated with inhibitors may, under appropriate circumstances, acquire learned or secondary inhibitory properties. Under this proposal it can be maintained that the immediate "satisfying" effects of food may be ascribable to its association with the inhibition of distress by eating, rather than the other way around.

With the foregoing reservations in view, we would argue finally that among the earliest differentiations the child makes are those that have to do with the handling of distress. Whether in regard to what we have called fundamental distress or in regard to distress set off by specific environmental events, much of early infant behavior can be related to the management of discomfort or unease. Furthermore, it is probably in these connections that the infant first learns about the consequences of interruption of organized response sequences or expectations. Just as it has been assumed that secondary inhibitors of distress can be developed, so it is assumed that learned signals of disinhibition (i.e., the reinstatement of distress at the withdrawal of an inhibitor) can be developed over the course of infancy. Thus the phenomenon of separation anxiety seen in the young child can be understood as the interruption of well-established inhibitory sequences. The failure of the mother to appear (i.e., the omission of an important inhibitor) leads to the rearousal of distress. It is tempting to speculate that tendencies in the older organism to be active (Bühler's *Funktionslust,* 1930, or White's "competence motivation," 1959) may be related to the repeated arousal of distress as a consequence of the withdrawal or omission of a well-entrenched inhibitor of anxiety. In other words, and as I shall argue again later the interruption of well-established behavior sequences may lead to anxiety and their continuation may ward it off.

In short, anxiety is not only the trace of a trauma that must be fled, but it is also a condition of distress that can be met by the action of specific inhibitors. The model of fundamental distress and its inhibition that is proposed here may serve to provide a testable alternative to the metaphysics of anxiety (May, Angle, and Ellenberger, 1958). It is suggested that whereas, for the young child, there is only a limited repertory of events and behaviors available that will inhibit or control the basic state of distress, any organized activity in the older child and in an adult will do so, and that finally any organized activity serves to ward off the state of distress. Trusted companions and our relations with them are important inhibitors of anxiety in adults as well as children—separation anxiety can be with us throughout the life span (cf. Bowlby, 1973). Whenever the organism has no well-organized cognitions or behaviors available to him, he is in a state of distress. Thus, whenever the organism is not able to draw on some behavior, act, or companion that control his environment (e.g., whenever he is in a condition of helplessness, unable to control stimulation or environmental input in general), he will be in a state of anxiety.

This view is consistent with the psychoanalytic tenets on overstimulation and Freud's statement about anxiety being related to the loss of the object. When either overstimulation threatens, or no object (goal) is present, the organism has no behavior available to him and cannot act; therefore, he is anxious. As far as the existentialist position is concerned, the state of anxiety occurs, of course, whenever the individual has no way of coping with environmental demands, in other words, no way of confronting possibility, no way of overcoming the anxiety that goes with possibility and freedom. Finally, the noxious, painful unconditioned stimulus of learning theory typically is an event that is unmanageable, represents overstimulation, and disrupts ongoing behavior. When the organism does find a way of coping with this situation by escape, this escape behavior is the way of overcoming helplessness vis-à-vis the noxious stimulus, and it will appear on a signal (the conditioned stimulus) prior to the occurrence of the unconditioned stimulus.

Fundamental distress, from this position, involves a general and variable state of arousal in the absence of well-developed organized actions or plans—the state of infancy. However, unlearned organized actions do exist, such as sucking, and these can—at a very early stage —inhibit fundamental distress. Thus the very occurrence of organized behavior preempts the occurrence of distress. In the adult, organized action and thought is the norm, not the exception. I turn, therefore, to the relation between arousal and the specific conditions that generate phenomenal anxiety.

Anxiety and Interruption[3]

In Chapter 6 I discussed the arousing consequences of the interruption of plans or actions. What are the occasions that turn the arousal engendered by interruption into distress or anxiety? I hypothesize that the emotion of choice is anxiety when the onset or offset of visceral arousal is not under control of the organism. Thus, when no response is available whereby the arousal initiated by the interruption can be terminated, the emotion to be expected would be anxiety, distress, or fear. In other words, anxiety should appear when the organism, interrupted in the midst of well-organized action sequences or in the execution of a well-developed plan, has no alternate behavior available. The inability to complete a sequence and the unavailability of alternate completion sequences produce helplessness, a plan or action sequence that has been initiated but that cannot be completed; the organism does not "know" what to do. The lack of adequate sequences and the absence of what, in another language, might be called purposeful behavior, define the disorganized organism. Helplessness and disorganization *are* anxiety.

The major consequences of interruption and the absence of relevant or suitable strategies will be continuing visceral arousal and disruption of any other ongoing behavior sequences. One reason for the disorganized aspect of anxiety-dominated behavior is that with interruption and arousal a search for relevant substitutable behaviors is initiated. As long as such a search—seen often as inefficient attempts at

[3]The section on pp. 199–206 is reprinted in part from Mandler and Watson (1966).

initiating a variety of different actions—is unsuccessful, and as long as the sequence is incomplete, further arousal will continue, more disorganization will result, and the typical picture of interference caused by anxiety will emerge. I have already pointed out how the discovery of some apparently satisfactory substitute acts may control the arousal. Such acts, when nonadaptive, are usually called neurotic symptoms and are frequently illustrated by obsessive-compulsive behavior.

It is appropriate here to return to the distinction between fear and anxiety in order to appreciate two other related views on anxiety and helplessness. In a critique of the attempts to distinguish fear from anxiety, or real from neurotic anxiety, Bowlby (1970, cf. also 1973) has pointed out that fears usually do have a reasonable basis, both on theoretical and clinical grounds. He reminds us that "reality" is "never more than some schematic representation of the world that happens to be favored by a particular social group at a particular time in history" (1970). Similarly, the reality of fears and anxieties are socially and historically determined. It is, of course, this particular truism that often leads to the discovery of emotional "problems" among the poor—based on the definition of social reality by the powerful. Bowlby points out that the reality of dangers in the world is in the eye of the beholder. It is not in the definition by governments or established professional groups. Given that the personal environment defines the reality of dangers, Bowlby concludes that to confine the term anxiety to those conditions in which threat is "realistically" absent might define the term out of existence.

Bowlby notes that what is feared includes "not only the *presence,* actual or imminent, of certain sorts of situation but *absence,* actual or imminent, of certain other sorts of situation" (1970). His own work (1973) has stressed in an important way that a principal source of fear is "simply the strangeness of a situation" (cf. also Schneirla, 1959). Bowlby suggests that the term anxiety seems appropriate for the feeling tone that "accompanies impeded approach or threatened separation." The similarity between his formulation and the current one is obvious. I would add, however, that the term anxiety is probably most appropriate when the approach is impeded or the separation threatened *and* no readily apparent substitute is available, then interruption issues into helplessness and anxiety.

A similar view of anxiety dependent on cognitive interpretations has been proposed by Beck (1972). He notes that cognitive factors may outweigh "realistic external stresses." Again, the danger is real because the individual so interprets the situation. This interpretation of danger, together with an underestimation of one's coping capacity, produces "high levels of anxiety and autonomic arousal" (1972). Beck adds that the cognition of arousal is also read as danger by the cognitive system and thus produces a spiraling anxiety effect. Obviously, I disagree on the latter point, but only to the extent that the arousal must be interpreted in terms of the current cognitive status. With that addendum there is essential agreement with Beck's position. More important, however, Beck has noted that one's evaluation of coping ability (comparable to Lazarus' position) is an important contributor to anxiety. The evaluation of being able to produce situationally relevant actions will determine the degree to which one interprets a situation as being productive of helplessness. If no coping actions are in sight, the situation is necessarily interpreted as one in which no relevant actions are or even might be available, and helplessness results.

Environmental Determinants of Anxiety

Any situation that interrupts, or threatens the interruption of organized response sequences, and that does not offer alternate responses to the organism, will be anxiety producing. There is some evidence that some plans and cognitive structures may be temporally quite flexible, that is, that the organism plans for *what* will happen relatively independently of *when* it will occur (Elliott, 1966). Such flexibility applies particularly to real-life sources of interruption. In this section we discuss two such instances: guilt and social factors in anxiety production.

Anxious guilt may be seen as an instance of the effects of interruption. The guilty person is one who feels anxious about some past action, real or imagined. Usually, of course, he cannot undo what he has done. Attempts to begin a sequence leading to the undoing of the previously committed act are invariably interrupted by the situational fact that the consequences of the act are in the past. We can atone, but we cannot undo. The cognitive sequence that would lead to the undoing of some act is, in reality-oriented persons, inevitably interrupted by the knowledge that the act is in the past and cannot be undone.

We often teach our children that they should always be good and do no wrong. It follows that certain cognitive sequences, such as the plan to right the wrongs that we have committed, will be well organized. Furthermore, such sequences will be organized so that there are very few substitute sequences that can be performed if the original sequence is interrupted. The knowledge of having committed some wrong, therefore, should activate the sequence to right the wrong but, if the act is in the past and cannot be righted, then the cognitive sequence will be interrupted. Short of reversing time, the wrong act usually cannot be undone; there are no substitutes, and the consequences of the act are often unchangeable. Thus the guilty person is continually instigating a sequence to undo what cannot be undone and is therefore continually interrupted in this sequence, yet has no alternate response available following interruption. This is the prototypical situation for anxiety.

The only difference between the emotions of anxiety and guilt may be the situational variables that lead us to label the two situations differently (cf., Mandler, 1962b). Such an analysis would explain two of the aspects of guilt. The guilty person ruminates on his guilt, which we would describe as persistent attempts to complete a sequence of undoing. But the guilty person may feel better after confession or making amends, possible substitutes for undoing. There are social variables that determine the degree to which confession or amends are available and the degree of their accepted relevancy as alternate responses. A Catholic child, for example, is likely to be taught that confession is a socially acceptable substitute for the interrupted cognitive sequence leading to undoing. The point of confession is that it enables the guilty person to complete a substitute sequence.

The consequence of confession may seem paradoxical; while it enables guilty individuals to complete at least some cognitive sequences, it leads to punishment as often as it leads to forgiveness. The paradox does not persist, however, if we view the punishment that may follow confession as the completion of a sequence instead of as a peculiar or even masochistic goal. Confession feels good, whether it leads to punishment or forgiveness, because it leads somewhere: particularly it enables the human to complete organized sequences that have often been unsuccessfully initiated before. The assumption that people seek goals often leads us to posit situations in which the goals that are sought are distinctly unpleasant. By not making this assumption, but by postulating that we seek to complete organized sequences, the paradox is resolved.

The relation between guilt and social variables raises the general question of the relationship between social factors and anxiety or psychopathology. This issue has been of concern to social scientists and psychiatrists (cf., W. A. Scott, 1958). In considering the influence of social or cultural factors in psychopathology, a number of different problems have been noted. One of these is the question: How do social or cultural factors influence the production of anxiety or other symptoms? Symptom formation might occur when some objectively inappropriate response systems are used in the completion of an interrupted sequence. We shall discuss briefly the effects of social variables on the interruption of long-range plans as well as shorter organized sequences.

Social and cultural variables can influence the anxiety of the members of the society by (a) inculcating organized sequences or plans that have a high probability of interruption; (b) interrupting organized sequences for various reasons; (c) not providing alternate responses to follow such interruption; and (d) providing only inappropriate alternate sequences.

A society inculcates organized sequences with a high probability of interruption when, for example, it teaches a high degree of "achievement motivation" to a large number of the members of the society but offers only a limited number of social positions that are sufficient to gratify the achievement motive. In other words, a number of the members of the society develop well-organized plans leading to success, but the society does not provide a relatively equal number of social positions through which the organized sequence can be completed. Social pressures provide almost continuous interruption of organized sequences to success for all but the fortunate few.

Societies or groups often interrupt the organized sequences of their members for a number of reasons. For example, it may be efficient from the group's point of view for most of its members to possess organized sequences and plans leading to positions of social power in that it guarantees sufficient competition so that the most promising gain power. However, once any given group has arranged itself into some power structure and achieved its goals, the group may not allow its members to continue attempts at the exercise of power. Thus the group would interrupt the organized sequences leading to power that are attempted by group members who continue to strive for it after a "desired" condition has been achieved.

A group or society, then, can inculcate organized sequences and, at the same time, provide for their interruption. Furthermore, the society may not provide substitute behavior to follow the interruption. There may be, for example, no socially acceptable substitute for success, even though not all members of a society have an opportunity to achieve success. In our society, blacks are exposed to many communications that would lead to the development of organized sequences and plans leading to the achievement of social power. At the same time, they are denied access to social positions through which they could complete the necessary sequences and are provided with few socially acceptable substitute sequences.

Last, a society, group, or culture may provide substitute responses that are either inappropriate to whatever organized sequences are interrupted or serve to interrupt other organized sequences. Becoming the town's best garbage collector is probably at best only a partial substitute for an interrupted sequence leading to social recognition. Becoming a juvenile deliquent may enable a youngster to complete certain sequences, but it is likely to lead to the interruption of others.

Zander and Quinn (1962) have summarized a number of studies of social structure that also bear on the question we are discussing. For example, Raven and Rietsema (1957) demonstrated that membership in groups that had unclear goals, or unclear paths to attain the goals, produced unpleasant emotional states among the group members. Unclear communication procedures, inefficient work flow, and vague power channels produce a type of social disorganization maximally designed to interrupt response sequences and fail to offer alternate responses following the interruption.

Social or cultural variables can determine both the degree of control a person has over potential interruption and what he can do if interruption occurs. If an individual has a good deal of control over situations, he is much less likely to be interrupted. Furthermore, his "control" implies that he has relevant alternate responses available to him. We suggest that any social system can be analyzed in terms of (1) the degree to which it inculcates or presses for completion of sequences that are, in fact, often interrupted; (2) the degree of control that it allows over potential interruption; and (3) the range and availability of alternate responses that it offers.

It might be useful to engage in such an analysis of American society, its promises and failures to fulfill those promises, its egalitarian pretensions and failures to act on them, and its educational programs and their failure in order to understand the degree of emotional reaction that this society can engender, particularly among those who have been taught to take its social and political plans seriously, but find them sadly lacking when they meet the larger world. It should not be surprising that this kind of discrepancy may provide a conjunction of arousal and cultural cues toward violence that lead to anger, aggression and, too often, to hopelessness.

The Responses of the Individual to Interruption

We have been speaking of certain situational determinants of anxiety. Obviously, any dichotomy between situational and individual determinants of anxiety is a false one, but we may vary the emphasis. In this section we want to pay more attention to the individual. A number of theorists have spoken of the anxiety of schizophrenics and, among the several theories of schizophrenia, one seems particularly relevant to the notions that we have advanced here. That is the idea of the double-bind communication (Bateson, Jackson, Haley, and Weakland, 1956; Weakland, 1960) to which schizophrenics are supposedly subjected. Briefly, the idea is that the communications from important others, such as the mother, that are directed to schizophrenics are within themselves contradictory. If we view the intent of certain communications as setting the recipient into action, the communication can be seen as activating some organized sequence on the part of the recipient. A double-bind, however, would be one that, as soon as it has activated some organized sequence, interrupts it. Completion is not allowed, for example, when the child is told: "Love me, but don't touch me." To the degree that schizophrenics are subjected to such communications, it is not surprising that they develop a great deal of anxiety, since the organized sequences that they could execute are almost continuously being activated and then interrupted. Any conflictful situation, of course, can be seen as one that both activates and interrupts response sequences.

Given that socially induced acts, produced by the double-bind communications, are anxiety producing, it is also not surprising that the individual will develop idiosyncratic, often socially irrelevant, acts that can be completed. Schizophrenic behavior then becomes an admirable substitute for the acts demanded and interrupted by the social milieu.

Lazarus (1964) has spoken of the necessity of evaluating an individual's cognitive appraisal of a situation in order to determine the threatening or stressful aspects of the situation. Lazarus and his colleagues (Lazarus and Alfert, 1964; Lazarus, Speisman, Mordkoff, and Davison, 1962) have shown that by altering a subject's cognitive appraisal of a situation (e.g., viewing a disturbing movie of a subincision rite from the stance of anthropological detachment or as a simple spectator) it is possible to alter the subject's emotional responses to produce less anxiety. Lazarus is providing his subjects with an alternate response that they can execute when confronted with the anxiety-provoking movie. He has suggested that the subjects identify with the people in the film, and identification can be seen as a shared set of cognitions or plans. The subjects would like to escape from the potentially painful situation, but the sequence of escape is interrupted by the constraints of the psychological experiments. Lazarus has used various sets of sound tracks to provide the subject with alternate responses (i.e., psychological escape), and thus his anxiety is lowered.

Janis (1958), working with surgical patients, demonstrated the expectation of a future threatening event—postoperative pain—lowered anxiety-producing characteristics. The data of Janis' indicate that, at least at the cognitive level, it is possible for the human organism to incorporate the expectation of pain into a plan. In our terms, the patients who expected postsurgical pain were not interrupted, while those who did not expect pain were interrupted. The patients who expected pain were not rendered helpless, since any distress could be a cue for the thought, "Things are going as planned." Hence there would be no experience of interruption and no arousal.

Lazarus and his colleagues and Janis, it seems, are studying phenomena very similar to those we have discussed. In the studies by both Janis and Lazarus, certain subjects either had organized sequences that dealt with potential interruptions by incorporating them into the sequence, or they were explicitly provided with alternate responses. The point is that in these studies the subjects were provided with some control over interruption. From our point of view, defense mechanisms can also be construed as attempts to control interruption. They are either responses that avoid interruption or alternate responses that follow interruption.

The idea of control over interruption is somewhat similar to the idea of competence discussed by White (1959). Competence as a personality variable is, from our point of view, the degree of control an individual can exercise over the environment. This concept includes the notion of control over the interruption of organized sequences. A sense of competence is presumably generated by the individual's felt control in executing organized response sequences. White's term "competence" can be defined as the individual's ability to avoid interruption or, if he is interrupted, to provide alternate responses that aid in completion of the interrupted sequence. Related is the notion of frustration tolerance, which can be defined as the ability to delay responding following interruption until an appropriate substitute response can be found. It is quite obvious that individuals vary in their ability to delay, (cf. Mischel and Metzner, 1962) and also, because of either experiential or constitutional factors, in their ability to find or learn appropriate alternate responses.

One further variable that should be mentioned is the degree of control over the environment that the individual appraises himself to hold. Rotter, Seeman, and Liverant (1962) and their colleagues have developed a locus of control scale that differentiates individuals according to the degree to which they appraise themselves or the environment in control of the occurrence of reinforcement. In terms appropriate to interruption theory: the degree to which persons consider themselves to control reinforcing events should be highly correlated with their appraised degree of control over interruption. Since a high degree of appraised control over interruption is presumably based on the individuals' history of successful attempts to cope with interruption, they would presumably be rendered less anxious by any present interruption, since they would have a repertory of available alternate responses and would also be more likely to search for substitute responses when confronted with interruption.

The problem of personal control involves the establishment of cognitive plans that are consistent with the realities of the world—not an easy task. As the term "personal control" suggests, it is a highly individual phenomenon; we believe that we have personal control of the world around us when we plan for what is likely to happen, whether we "control" the events or not. Planning to encounter a traffic jam on the way home may give me an illusion that I am in control of the local traffic. In fact, its nonoccurrence may be disappointing—interrupting.

In an extensive review of the literature on personal control of aversive stimuli, Averill concludes that "the stress-inducing or stress-reducing properties of personal control depend upon the *meaning* of the control response for the individual; and what lends a response meaning is largely the context in which it is imbedded" (Averill, 1973). That the illusion of control can have powerful effects has been demonstrated, for example, by Bowers (1968), who showed that the perceived painfulness of shock varied with the perceived control over its occurrence. Equally interesting and consistent with the complexity of the problem was his finding that individuals who typically view themselves as in control over their environs showed differentially greater anxiety about the shock over which they had no control. Glass et al. (1973), in an extensive empirical investigation, also found that belief in control decreased the aversiveness of the situation. They conclude that ". . . magnitude or intensity of stimulation is less important than contextual variables such as the belief that one has little control over stimulus occurrence."

Anxiety, Helplessness, and Hopelessness[4]

I can now summarize the question of the ontogeny of anxiety. I have argued that the cyclical distress of the human newborn may be the basis for the original experience of anxiety. I suggested that fundamental distress is to be viewed as a state of discomfort, unease, or anxiety that bears no clear or necessary relation to a specific antecedent event. I further proposed that one of the mechanisms to bring such anxiety under control is the operation of specific inhibitors. These inhibitors control distress regardless of their relation to a specifiable need, drive, or privation. Among such possible inhibitors I suggested sucking, rocking, and others. Furthermore, I assumed that while the inhibitor operates to control the distress, withdrawal of such an inhibitor would reinstate it. Finally, I suggested that not only innate inhibitors but later acquired organized behavior may have the same function of anxiety and distress inhibition.

I have noted that one particular set of cognitive and environmental conditions that turns arousal to the emotion I call anxiety is a general state of helplessness, or the unavailability of task- or situation-relevant plans or actions. In a state of arousal the organism who has no relevant behavior available and continues to seek situationally or cognitively

[4]The following section is reprinted in part from Mandler (1972b).

appropriate behavior is "helpless" and also may be considered, in terms of the common language, as being in a state of anxiety. Thus helplessness is not defined by an objective situation, but by the organism and its repertory of actions.

I am more concerned with discussion helplessness and disorganization than anxiety *per se*. If they do, as I believe, have a large degree of overlap in usage, I shall move toward an understanding of anxiety. If they do not have any common experiential or situational referents, I shall at least have made an attempt to understand phenomenal and situational helplessness.

It should be restated that the conditions that control distress and the conditions that produce it are not necessarily correlated—they may be independent. In that sense, I reject a view of anxiety that speaks of anxiety reduction or escape from fear or similar symmetric propositions. Variables that control the onset of a process or behavior need not be the same that control its offset (cf. Deutsch, 1960).

The interruption of plans or behavior is only *one* of the conditions that leads frequently to states of helplessness. When interruption leads to arousal and no appropriate behavior is available, either to substitute for the original plan or to find alternate ways to the original goal, then we have what I think is one typical state of anxiety. Interruption is thus probably sufficient for arousal and emotion to occur; it is certainly not necessary. Furthermore, it will lead to helplessness if and only if no adequate continuation behavior or substitute is available. Interruption is particularly relevant to helplessness because it may lead independently to disorganization or the absence of appropriate organized behavior. It is tempting to speculate that disorganization and helplessness may, in fact, be the same phenomenal and emotional state.

This kind of theoretical point of view avoids any prior judgment about the adaptive value of a particular set of behaviors. Organized behavior need not be "relevant" or "valuable"; it will serve to inhibit or control anxiety as long as it is organized or a well-organized plan exists.

Next I turn to an illustration, a brief clinical description of the consequences of interruption on its purest form. This was made available to me by Dr. Gordon D. Jensen of the University of California Medical School at Davis.

> D. is a nine-year-old boy referred to the Clinic because of failure in school and distractable behavior. Psychometric testing revealed an I.Q. of about 120, a normal neurological examination, a borderline EEG, and negative pediatric examination. The mother volunteered the following history and comments (the quotations are hers). When he was a

baby he would bang his head when he got "interrupted." "When he gets interrupted you can expect an explosion." He becomes "frustrated terribly when he is doing something and you ask him to do something [else]." He then stamps his feet, cries and protests with behavior resembling a temper tantrum. "Our family is not on much of a schedule, maybe he would be better off if he knows what's coming." "He can't seem to stand the exuberance and fun behavior of the family at home." When the noise or activity going on at home reaches a certain point he may go out and ride his bicycle to get away from it. Whenever the teacher talks to him in any angry voice or there is a "tense atmosphere," he withdraws; "he tunes you out" and acts as if he did not hear and did not understand anything that is being said to him. At these times he apparently cannot understand even simple directions. Those are the essential and basic facts of this history.

This boy is a distractable, nervous, but bright and attentive-appearing boy who relates readily, and initially interrupts me and his mother during the interview. He responded quickly to my setting limits. During my subsequent interview with him alone he was attentive, coherent, much better organized and readily understood all of my questions.

To comment on this boy I think most psychiatrists would diagnose him as borderline childhood schizophrenia; the catastrophic reaction (complete disorganization and withdrawal under stress) is apparent. However, I do not feel that this is a very satisfactory diagnostic classification. Instead, I conceptualize his most serious problems as a disorganization of thinking provoked by stress, but, more particularly, a *deficient ability* to maintain or carry out a cognitive plan when experiencing interruption or environmental disorganization.

I have also demonstrated another extreme case of helplessness in a series of animal experiments (Mandler and Watson, 1966; Mandler, 1972b). These studies showed that severe behavioral disturbances can be produced in animals when they are given extinction trials, but are not hungry (i.e., when they are satiated). Given a well-organized response sequence (maze running), the absence of both a goal object (food) and the drive state (hunger) places the organism in a situation in which neither completion nor substitute behaviors (food searching) are available. The result is behavioral disorganization and distress. These experiments also demonstrate that distress and helplessness are not necessarily dependent on the avoidance or escape from traumatic or noxious events.

These extreme cases of helplessness and reactions to them lead us to consider another extreme case of helplessness: hopelessness. Helplessness is, in a sense, an immediate reaction to the situation and is somewhat stimulus-bound. The person does not know what to do in this particular situation. However, we can assume that if this builds up over a variety of situations we might get to a generalized feeling of not knowing what to do in any situation, which is parallel to hopelessness. Hopelessness may also arise with repeated failures (noncompletions) of a single identifiable plan. However, this occurs apparently only if that plan has a high degree of salience, as in occupational efforts. It remains unclear why these kinds of situations lead into true depression, characterized typically by the effect of hopelessness, in some individuals and not in others. The concept of hopelessness and the generalized notion of not being able to complete a sequence or find an acceptable alternate or substitute for it must be related to the notion of self-esteem. If self-esteem is low, then the likelihood of finding such a substitute, the likelihood of finding a way out of the helpless situation will be judged to be very low. If it is judged to be very low, then there may be much less searching for acceptable alternate organized plans or behaviors. Or, possibly, in cases of low self-esteem, the slightest interruption of an organized sequence is interpreted as a final one, a reaction not unusual in persons either low in self-esteem or who are depressed. There usually occurs a special sensitivity to any signal of failure (interruption). Thus the depressive state can easily be subsumed as a further extension of the notion of anxiety and helplessness. At the same time, it should be acknowledged that this discussion covers only a part of the various symptoms and etiologies subsumed under the lable of depression (cf. Beck, 1967, both for an extensive coverage and a cognitive model consistent with much of the present discussion).

Contact should also be made with the well-known psychoanalytic notions of the relationship between guilt and depression. I discussed previously the question of anxiety and guilt in the context of the interruption sequence, and noted that the guilty person ruminates on his guilt. Generalized helplessness or hopelessness and depression would arise exactly out of such continuous attempts at undoing.

Let me go one step further in my investigation of hopelessness and look at the long-range consequences of a continuous state of not being able to undo the wrong we have done (real or imagined), and being faced with a state of low self-esteem that generates behavioral plans that are incapable of being completed or overestimates slight interruptions as final ones. Eventually, we become immobilized in a truly fundamental state of helplessness, unable to move, but continuously subjected to an extremely painful state of anxiety or distress that is unrelieved by any kind of organized behavior. The hopeless, depressed person then is left with one final, organized act, and that is the one of self-destruction, an act that seems to make rational sense, because it is designed to put an end to the state of continuing helplessness that nothing seems to be capable of relieving.

The intensity of true depressive reaction must be related to equally intensive cognitive and actions structures that are being interrupted. Hamburg, Hamburg, and Barchas (1975) have ascribed just such intense affects to both anger and depression. As a framework to the study of emotional expression in primates, they note that the blockage of tasks that are important for species survival leads to anger and, if the blockage is prolonged, to depression. The prolongation is *necessary* in order to generalize from helplessness to hopelessness.

The notion of helplessness has also been introduced in a similar context, although derived from animal experimentation, by Seligman and his associates (cf. Seligman and Maier, 1967; Maier, Seligman, and Solomon, 1969). The comparison between their use of helplessness and ours is—among others—an instructive study in the dangers of adopting attractive common language terms to serve precise communication. I adopted the term helplessness in 1964 specifically as an analog to the analysis of anxiety and subsequently developed it to the detail presented in this chapter. This development led to the use of hopelessness to describe helplessness transsituationally, and related to the symptoms and experience of depression (Mandler, 1972b).

Seligman and his coworkers use the term "learned helplessness" to refer to the acquisition of a cognitive state that follows the perception that the termination of a noxious state is independent of the organism's behavior. Under these circumstances, the probability of responding is perceived as independent of escape and thus produces little incentive for initiating any response. As matter of fact, it is assumed that this sequence of events reduces the "probability of doing anything active" (Maier, et al., 1969). From this position, Seligman (1972) appropriately generalized that learned helplessness was at the basis of human depression. We are thus left with our present use of helplessness for situational anxiety, and hopelessness for generalized depression, which Seligman, in turn, calls learned helplessness—beware of the common language.

More important, there is a difference between the two approaches. I am particularly concerned with the availability of relevant actions. Whenever a search of appropriate action systems indicates that, because of past experience or the generalized evaluation of personal competence, no actions are available that will achieve desirable ends, then helplessness or hopelessness will result. These means and ends need not be associated with the avoidance of aversive events; they may just as well relate to the unattainability of desirable states. Seligman is more specifically concerned with one of the antecedents of such unavailability; learned helplessness.

Chapter IX

Implications and Extensions

The Cognitive-Interpretive System and Its Early Development

If the cognitive-interpretive system is our primary means of lending meaning to our world, then the early aspects of its development must be important for its future functioning. We assume that, without further intervention, the nodes, pathways, pointers, and other connections within the system are maintained from childhood on and become the central skeletal framework on which the adult system is developed. The notion that the meaning of the adult world is a function of early infantile development is, of course, at the heart of psychoanalytic theory. In terms of our framework we assume that emotion and affect are a combination of autonomic arousal and interpretations or characterizations of the environment. Freud, under our interpretation, assumed that there were three major systems that produced arousal (or cathexis) and that could, depending on the course of the child's history, receive varying kinds of mental interpretations. These were the oral or alimentary system, the anal or elimination system, and the genital or sexual system. There is good reason to believe that these systems are not the only ones that develop specific arousal-characterization conjunctions of importance for later life. Two others might be the management of pain and of sleep or sleep deprivation. The general point that needs to be made is that arousal associated with oral, anal, genital, pain, or sleep management will make various aspects of these activities pleasureful or unpleasant depending on the attendant interpretation of the environment. We may assume with Freud that any event that, coupled with arousal, produces relief from distress or achievement of pleasant states will become effective as a positive characterization of the environment. Thus any event that signals relief from subjective or psychological hunger, or any signal that produces release from either prior or subsequent unpleasantness associated with urination or defecation, or any signal that is associated with pleasurable sexual excitement, or any event that signals relief from pain, or any signal that is associated with the termination of sleep deprivation—any of these may become, for the child, positive characterizations of the environment, available for the emotional or affective interpretation of arousal. The initial programs available tend to point toward the achievement of such states; we deal with an organism that is primarily directed toward the pleasure principle.

In other words, the general system may follow an executive program that says: when in a state of arousal and given that a state of positive affect is desirable, attempt to find states of environment that give rise to positive interpretations. The cognitive system "learns" initially which events and which interpretations lead to positive outcomes. Mental operations leading to actions that have desirable end states will be more likely to occur than those that have other effects. We could, of course, call these means-end relationships to be "wishful impulses." The notion of "wish" interpreted in our system is the seeking out of an event and an interpretation of it that will lead to "pleasant" consequences.

Freud wrote at length and instructed us importantly on the fact that some of these events and some of their interpretations and transformations that are perfectly acceptable during childhood may, during adulthood, not lead to the same pleasurable unconflicted outcomes. It is at this point that Freud introduced the notion of repression. I have dealt previously with the general notion of repression. Related also is the class of affects known as anxiety, which may signal the unpleasant consequences of previously pleasant trains of thought and action. The anticipation that a particular plan of action may not be completed serves as a releasing stimulus both for autonomic discharge and for the unpleasant affect of helplessness.

The relation between anxiety (and helplessness) and repression that is advocated here is quite similar to Freud's second theory of anxiety (cf. Chapter 8). Any meaning analysis or contemplated action that conflicts with some other analysis or potential action is likely to produce the inability to act; the choice between two possible but incompatible actions may produce inaction and helplessness. One solution to this dilemma is the repressive one, to block access to one of the analyses that generates the actual or potential action. If the choice is avoided (i.e., one of the meaning analyses is inaccessible) then conflict and anxiety are avoided. In that sense anxiety leads to repression. Repression can be undone when the individual learns that a new interpretation of one or the other situation and action does not lead to conflict—anxiety does not occur and repression may be lifted.

One interpretation of Freud's view of dreams is to suggest that the accessibility of these "repressed" structures is changed during dreams. Cognitive events, in the sleeping individual, cannot, by definition, lead to the feared action. Thus it is possible that repression only operates when the action becomes potentially possible. What repression does is to prevent the emergence of such a potentially dangerous interpretation of the world from the cognitive-interpretive system. In dreams, such "emergence" may be possible because no action is possible and real-world conflict can be avoided. What may still be the case is that the cognitive system, in self-monitoring consequences of its interpretation, may produce the prediction of cognitive conflict and, therefore, interruption. In that case, of course, even in the case of dreams, the affect of "anxiety" will appear. One of the ways in which this can be avoided is by use of dream symbols and symbolic actions, which are nodes related to but not identical with the repressed interpretation.

I am now moving toward the difference between early and late systems of cognition and meaning analysis or, in Freud's terms, between primary and secondary process. Secondary process is concerned with much of the reality which surrounds the adult, the complex transformations and plans necessary to achieve satisfaction of his needs, and the events that will produce positive rather than negative emotional consequences. Freud gave the appearance of primary process the character of irrational thought and behavior. It is irrational in the sense that it does not follow the rational reality imposed on it. However, the implication of psychoanalytic theory that the only way to undo the destructive effects of repressed thought processes is by a restructuring of cognitions through reinterpretation and replanning is not inevitable; the forming of new pathways with new nodes is not always necessary. There is no reason why behavior therapy, for example, may not lift the noncompletion command by demonstrating that completion of a particular sequence does not necessarily lead to disastrous consequences. Typically, this is done by small incremental steps, the first of which may not be anxiety arousing (i.e., conflictful) at all, and thus slowly removing the repression. Such a procedure may lead to the removal of phobias without inquiring about the aspects of the system that produced them. Nor is it necessary that such removal of the symptom need bring on a new one, unless the repression that produced that symptom also operates on parts of the cognitive system that affect other aspects of action systems. If it does not, behavior therapy should be just as effective as psychoanalytic therapy, and may even be more so.

Another way of talking about early experience and its importance for later development, or to make the distinction between primary and secondary process, is to look at infancy as the time when certain innate action systems are first activated and are given their characterization in terms of attendant environmental events. At the first occurrence of certain terminal response systems, including, of course, consummatory responses such as drinking and eating, the functional releasing stimuli for those action systems are registered and encoded. The occasions for eating (and, in parallel, the occasions for going hungry) or the occasions for elimination are loosely defined by the evolutionary and genetic background of the organism. What specific stimuli or interpretations will be encoded with the release of the consummatory or terminal responses depends on the very early experiences of the organism. Thus the initial functional stimuli for the release of innate consummatory responses (and possibly also for visceral discharge) are determined early in the life of the organism. This initial characterization and encoding is parallel to Freud's notion of primary process. It can be shown that the absence of adequate external stimulation, as in the case of early environmental deprivation, inhibits adequate coding and may lead to a lack of the proper development of functional releasing stimuli and to an inadequate characterization of the environment. The result is an inhibited, retarded, and sometimes absent arousal or action system—and an unemotional, flat style of response.

More generally, early experiences establish the central interpretive basis for subsequent encounters with the environment and its effect on innate arousal or action mechanisms. These initial interpretations of environmental releasers are in a sense "automatic," since they are often identical with, and at least similar to, automatically released innate action patterns. This is most visible in lower animals, but presumably occurs to some extent in humans. What can hide it is the very rapid development, even in the infant, of complex information processing and rudimentary planning, such that the consequences of particular inputs can be evaluated and alternative actions taken in light of the "reality" of the environment. This use of the reality principle through complex cognitive transformations gives rise to Freud's secondary process.

The last example again stresses both the importance and impotence of our instinctual biological makeup. On the one hand we are reminded of our evolutionary heritage; on the other, we note the ubiquitous role of our socio-cultural-economic status that directs our cognitions and may channel, exacerbate, or deny the expression of instinctual patterns. What is seen as frightening and aggressive, loving and sexual, warm and reassuring may be influenced by the similar evolutionary products, but will be vastly different depending on our cognitive-cultural history. Our perception of society and environs changes with its structure, culture, and economics. Social and historical understanding is more likely to lead to human understanding than ethological analogies, just as the analysis of individual cognitions will lead to a better individual comprehension than the appeal to immutable early childhood experiences.

Changing Mental Structures

One of the consequences of a distinction between "conscious" and "unconscious" processing is a possible difference in the kind of changes that may be brought about in the cognitive and action systems. Before such a change can take place, we require hypotheses about the structure of our thoughts and actions, and the testing and retesting of such hypotheses. This process of testing and examination of possible hypotheses takes place primarily in consciousness. It is only when a hypothesis or "theory" about a particular mental structure is "correct," in the sense that it makes adequate predictions about the outcomes of those structures, that it might be possible to manipulate those structures. In other words, to effect changes in human action, we must generate some plausible explanations of its cognitive and environmental antecedents. In effecting behavioral changes, consciousness plays an important part, even though some structures may be changed "unconsciously," primarily by external manipulation by others (whether they be psychotherapists, friends, or prison wardens). In any case *hypotheses* about cognitive structures occur in consciousness and, once the consequences of cognitive structures are evaluated in consciousness, it becomes possible to consider possible new structures and new consequences.

One of the new directions in psychology over the past decade or two is the notion that acquisition and loss, or learning and forgetting, are not symmetric processes. The notion of symmetry has a long and well-embedded history in psychology. It used to be thought that the events that instigate a particular drive state and the events that reduce it are symmetrical, or that the conditions that produce the learning of some behavior and its forgetting or unlearning are isomorphic and complementary. Theory and research, in the motivational area (e.g., Deutsch, 1960), as well as in learning and psychotherapy (Costello, 1970), suggest that turning a particular process on and turning it off may rely on two completely different and unrelated mechanisms.

Central to the symmetry notion has been the relation between acquisition and extinction of behavior, which has been ascribed to reinforcement and its absence, respectively. At the same time, it has been obvious that while a response that is not reinforced may be inaccessible in the future, that does not necessarily entail that it has been lost or unlearned. This particular issue is complex, but it is introduced as an illustration of the complexities that we face when dealing with the acquisition, change, or loss of mental structures.

A particular mental schema structures a set of environmental events so that they ensue in certain behavioral outcomes. When, in the course of everyday life or as a result of deliberate intervention, these structures are changed so that the same event now leads to a new outcome, several possibilities exist as to how this may come about. First, the old structure may be changed to a new structure, such that the new structure leads to a new outcome. When that happens, the old structure may still be available and, in fact, both old and new outputs may occur. Thus we may learn that a particular park may be appreciated for its lovely flowers and need not be entirely evaluated in terms of poignant memories of unrequited love. The second possibility is that a new action outcome is assimilated into the old structure—in which case the old outcome would not be available any more. For example, a student may come to address his old professor by his first name. The cognition of respect and love would be essentially unchanged, but it would assimilate "Peter" instead of "Professor Pan" as one of its behavioral outcomes. Finally, a new structure with a new outcome may be developed—and the old structure is changed or deleted so as not to be accessible any more. A patient might learn to reevaluate his interactions with women. Instead of the perception of threat and consequent avoidance, he now perceives acceptance and warmth and behaves accordingly.

Since the differences between the old and the new outcomes may be differences between emotional reactions on the one hand and nonemotional ones on the other, the process of such change is of particular interest to our current goals. I am concerned with processes whereby old structures change into new ones and the question of the fate of the old structure under those circumstances. I shall note that in some cases of behavior therapy, the replacement of old with new outcomes while maintaining the old structure is of interest, although in many cases of behavior therapy that structure may change.

Neisser (1962), following Piaget's notions of assimilation and accommodation, described three kinds of structural changes: *absorption,* where new structures are developed that contain effectively all of the old structures; *displacement,* where the old and new structure continue to "exist side by side"; and *integration,* where new structures—at a more comprehensive level—still contain parts of the old. In the following pages I shall deal illustratively with some of these processes.

The change of a mental structure is dependent on the history and evaluation of the old structure and the development and value of the new structure, just as if they were theories of the individual's behavior. It is fairly clear that the acquisition of new structures that do not interfere significantly with existing ones is a different problem from that of *replacing* existing ones with new ones. For example, if a child learns a particular structure for the manipulation of algebraic symbols (i.e., he learns algebra), there is very little in the way of existing structures that needs to be replaced. In such a case it appears that the individual may often be given a verbal program for those structures that, given the appropriate translations of the verbal symbols, may be applied to the material manipulated, and a slow development of a new structure takes place, unimpeded by old structures. One interesting aspect of the acquisition of new structures is the difference between telling somebody what a structure ought to be and letting him manipulate the objects or symbols that are to be structured; the distinction between classical instructional and discovery methods (Bruner, 1961).

Therapeutic Change

If the establishment of a new structure is like the establishment of a new theory in science—hypotheses to be applied to a given body of data—the parallel also extends to the current existence of old structures, current theories that must be replaced by new ones. The suggestion is that this replacement occurs as it does *historically* in the development of science, not the way it necessarily occurs for the individual scientist. It consists of a partly deductive, partly inductive process, in which new hypotheses about the structure of the individual's behavior and experience are generated and tested. The process involves asking questions about the "whys" and "hows" of one's actions. Given an existing old structure that handles the data base, although it may have unwanted outcomes, as in the case of neurotic behavior, the replacement is relatively slow. New cognitive evaluations are evaluated and tested with possible actions and their consequences. New behavior may be attempted in order to check its satisfactory fit to the new structure. This is what is generally known as "working through" or "experiencing" in the therapeutic situation. The individual develops new hypotheses about the structures that mediate his behavior; he tries out these hypotheses against his experience and may use some of these structures to generate new behaviors in whole or in part. In the process, the structure of the new "theory" about inputs and desired outputs is slowly developed, tested, and established. This may be done in daily life, and probably is done in many cases without the benefit of clergy, therapists, or friends. It may also be the case that the information necessary to produce the new structure is available, but the conceptual work has not been done. This is one of those cases where a therapist may tell a patient: "Consider what you have done, look at what you're doing, examine the relationship between these various things that have happened, discover that outcomes have always been of a particular kind; does it not make sense that the following hypothesis adequately accounts for your experiences and your behavior?" In that case a new theory or structure may be created relatively quickly. A similar case may occur when an individual, given a new hypothesis, generates the data from his experience, from his memory of himself, and finds that many things that have happened in the past fit with the new hypothesis, which may then be tested and established.

In none of these cases does it appear to be necessary that the old structure be changed at all. It is just replaced by a new one. The "residual" old structures may become the basis for some types of fantasy experience (Rosenbaum, 1972).

The creation of new structures replacing old ones describes much of what occurs in behavior therapy. On the other hand, classic dynamic theorists have always maintained that the old structures are "still there" and, even though the old behavior may not occur, these old structures may "show up" in other unwanted behavior (see, for example, Weitzman, 1971).

Under what conditions *are* the old structures deleted, absorbed, or integrated? Another aspect of insight therapy consists of an examination of what the old structure is—what is my old "theory"? In that case it is necessary to examine one's thought and action and to determine what theories, or structures, adequately explain the current link between inputs and outputs. It may be that insight therapy, and the extensive processes of psychoanalysis, require an investigation of the current experience *and* an examination of hypotheses that will fit it. These hypotheses, or old structures, may be changed by changing parts of the old structures into new ones. In the cases where old structures are changed to new ones, they are "brought into consciousness"; by continuously developing and testing hypotheses, they become available to consciousness. The "making conscious" of old "unconscious" processes consists of the development of hypotheses and their test, just as the development of new structures goes through the same process.

It may also be assumed that unsuccessful cases of psychotherapy are those where structures or theories are developed that are appealing (i.e., sound useful) but are, in fact, nonworking. The use of bad theories that only explain an inadequate part of the data is not unknown in science, and scientists hold on to those just as jealously as the individual holds on to pseudoexplanations of his own behavior.

I have made repeated reference to the use of consciousness in examining and changing existing structures, and some discussion of the relation between action and consciousness is in order.

Action and Consciousness

First, it should be understood that action systems subsume the potential for all external observable actions and behaviors of the organism. Thus scratching one's ear, speaking a sentence, or being aggressive toward a colleague are all part of action systems. I now wish to examine the relationship between these actions and the private experience that accompanies them.

Any particular action has associated with it cognitive structure that translates environment or input into a particular action system. I further assume that the same cognitive structure may, but need not, be used for output to both action and conscious contents.

This conception might lead to theoretical developments on the question of insight into personal motivation. Clearly, if we want to know why we have done something, we need to know the input-output structure that leads to a particular action system. We may have available an "explanation" of our "motive"—a structure "about the action" that has an output to conscious experience. What is the relation to the structure that actually leads to action? The identity of these two structures is not a necessary one. Thus we might believe that a particular structure is "responsible" for a certain action when, in fact, some other "unconscious" structure leads to the action.

In general we say that a person has "insight" into his action when the identical structure has output to both action and to a conscious state. Other variations are interesting exercises in the varieties of human insight and delusion.

The question of insight into personal motivation is important in the context of psychotherapy because it is well known that to tell somebody what their "underlying" motives are is of no particular utility in modifying their behavior. When a psychotherapist infers what the input-output structure is that leads to a particular kind of action and then tells the patient, his "telling the patient" is not equivalent to the patient's inspection of the cognitive system; it is just another input. In some unusual circumstances this input may be checked against the input-output structure; it may be found to be similar, and insight may be accomplished. However, since the verbal formulations of the therapist are likely to be quite deviant from the input-output structure that mediates a particular action, that case is unlikely. It is necessary to encourage the patient to test and elaborate on what the structures might be that mediate certain actions. If these hypotheses are correct (i.e., if he is developing the appropriate hypotheses about that particular structure), then it is likely that he would be able to interfere with and change it. In other words, by "knowing and using" these structures, first insight might be developed, and change can then follow. Changes will occur to the extent to which the patient can use the experience and action system as his own private laboratory for generating and testing hypotheses. Once again, cognitive structures are changed and generated by action.

The Psychotherapy of Everyday Life

One of the traditions of contemporary psychology is that behavior can often best be understood by looking at the extremes, by investigating the causes and cures of abnormal cases. That point of view is reasonable and has been very useful, as in the case of Freud's investigations, but the complementary case has often been ignored and should also be considered. Specifically, what can we learn about abnormal behavior by looking at the frequent or normal case? To illustrate, let us consider some normal phobias that are amenable to intervention without any extensive therapeutic apparatus or intensive treatment of the patient.

Consider the traveler who has been told that he must not under any circumstances drink any water in Slobovia. He is given detailed and gory descriptions about the consequences of any transgression. His behavior is clearly phobic as we observe him in Slobovia. He avoids water like the plague, rinses the top of soft drink bottles with distilled water, refuses to eat fruits and vegetables that might have been rinsed in the local water, and even eyes beer with suspicion if it is of local production. We might assume that to cure the poor man of his phobia would involve either extensive psychotherapy to discover the unconscious motives that have imbued water with some special symbolic significance or extensive sessions with a behavior therapist during which he slowly approaches Slobovian water by first just thinking about it and, finally, after extensive work, being able to take a sip. Such are the consequences of thinking of normal behavior in terms of an abnormal model. In fact, many cases similar to our unfortunate traveler can usually be cured in one session, which is never considered to be therapeutic in the psychological sense, nor does it involve much expenditure of effort or funds. Any authoritative statement from somebody whose opinion he respects (e.g., his physician or a local resident whom he has known for many years), which asserts that Slobovian water is perfectly safe or that it is actually better than the water he has been drinking all his life immediately cures the phobia with hardly any remnant of the phobic behavior or any fear that the "underlying conflict" would reappear in some other context.

The lesson to be drawn from this example, and there are many others in everyday life, is simple: there are many programs and structures that are available in consciousness and addressable in ordinary language. Being available and being capable of unequivocal statement, they apparently are easily changed and either removed or suppressed. There is nothing new about the existence of such programs. A whole variety of different plans and structures are continuously being changed without any great difficulty; they include simple things such as how to drive to a particular location, or complicated ones such as understanding social relationships and who talks to whom and why. The insight provided by our example is that the same kind of programs apparently exist for abnormal and for superficially maladaptive behavior, and we should consider how structures that underlie "true" maladaptive behavior may be affected; some simple interventions may often be quite useful.

The difference between the "true" phobia and our example is, of course, that the real phobic cannot usually be treated with a simple instruction from an authoritative source. The question then is, why not? The psychoanalytic answer, and one quite appropriate within our point of view, is obvious: the structures that underlie phobic behaviors are not available in consciousness, cannot be spoken, and therefore are not amenable to change by simple instructions. The obvious answer is to make these programs as available to consciousness as is the program of our Slobovian traveler.

I have indicated two general ways in which structures that are not available in consciousness, and therefore not available to immediate testing, may be changed. One system invokes laborious methods of hypothesis testing and determining what the underlying structures are; the other involves building new structures and circumventing the unpalatable consequences of the existing structures. The latter is often described as the major goal of behavior therapy. It is useful at this point to spend some more time on an analysis of what happens when the methods of operant conditioning are used in the alleviation of unwanted symptoms.

The methods developed in the conditioning laboratory and used so effectively in the management of both lower animals and some human situations have one very specific characteristic. They are unequivocal in developing structures between inputs and outputs, they allow little variance in behavior, and they are invariant with respect to the specific means-ends relations of the particular situation. Operant conditioning techniques, in particular, have been especially useful in demonstrating these characteristics. Data from Skinner boxes are cleaner, more easily repeatable, and permit more insight into the behavior of a single animal. I argue that any conditioning technique, whether it be operant or Pavlovian or whatever, builds up structures between inputs and outputs. When the method that develops such structures is equivocal, it will take much longer for the organism to develop a stable structure that has a specified outcome. Just as I can tell somebody to put a pencil on the table and can be fairly sure that his behavior will be easily predictable, I can also achieve the same result by operant reinforcement techniques. It just takes much longer. However, in an organism that cannot use language, either because it is not human or not quite fully grown human, as in the case of the very young child, I have no better way of instructing him of what is required, what the proper means-end structure is, than to use operant conditioning techniques.

Thus we can view operant conditioning and shaping techniques as a way of instructing the organism about new and more desirable structures (designed, for example, to avoid unpleasant consequences). The operant methods and, by analogy, the methods used by behavior therapists and behavior modifiers, are a way of instructing organisms who either cannot talk or cannot speak about the programs that we wish to change. The former case applies to rats and infants, the latter case to the phobic patient. Thus we can speak a program to be used or we can teach it. Or, to turn B. F. Skinner's viewpoint around, operant conditioning may be used as a short cut when language is not available, just as language may be used as a shortcut for extensive response-reinforcement chains.

Personality, Pathology, and Individual Differences

In this section I shall examine a variety of different topics raised in previous chapters from one general point of view: how are differences among individuals generated, personality patterns initiated, and extreme (or abnormal) emotional states or action patterns produced?

Interruption: Pathology and Therapy

Most theories of maladjustment, psychopathology, and personality deal with anxiety in one way or another as a central concept. If anxiety, helplessness, and distress can be deduced from the interruption situation by coupling emotional arousal with the unavailability of relevant or substitute actions, a variety of speculations in the field of psychopathology and personality theory emerge.

The notion that reactions to interruption or frustration are central to personality development is not new in psychology (cf. Rosenzweig, 1944). The emphasis on the consequences of interruption, however, permits us to look afresh at some classical problems.

Among the important consequences of interruption—from the point of view of psychopathology—are those that do and those that do not provide substitutable behavior. Any highly organized sequence that is interrupted and that does not then lead to some substitute completion will result in the phenomenon of free-floating anxiety, in this case engendered by helplessness and the absence of an appropriate organized action. In this view, free-floating anxiety does not stem from the generalization of the anxiety response to a variety of stimuli from some initial traumatic association but, instead, anxiety is seen as conditional on the absence of appropriate environmental stimuli and associated actions.

Symptom formation might occur when some objectively inappropriate response systems are used in the completion of the interrupted sequence. Just as in psychoanalytic theory, and in keeping with the inhibition model of anxiety that Kessen and I have advocated (1961, cf. Chapter 8), the symptom protects the organism from the appearance of anxiety because it avoids the deleterious effects of interruption. But, instead of asking what satisfaction of what need has been frustrated, as the psychoanalytic theorists and Rosenzweig might inquire, I would suggest that we investigate the specific "goal path" that has been diverted, with both goal and path being given equal weight.

This argument suggests that therapeutic efforts should deal equally with acceptable substitute completion sequences (not necessarily including the original "goal"), with a change of path that might bypass the interruption, with removal of the environmental or intrapsychic blocking agent, and with actual achievement of the original goalpath. Such a conceptual approach suggests that both behavior therapy (e.g., Wolpe, 1958; Kanfer and Phillips, 1970) and depth therapy may contribute to the alleviation of symptom and anxiety, that these approaches are complementary rather than mutually exclusive.

Therapy, then, may successfully tackle the problem of maladaptive behavior from any one of a variety of vantage points, and the opposing claims of different schools of psychotherapy may express mainly preferences for attacking one or another facet of the problem. What may be important for the therapist to decide is the locus in the sequence where an attack offers the most likely signs of success. Depending on whether the goalpath should be retained, whether plans need replacing, or whether some other intervention seems most promising, different therapeutic techniques might be indicated. But first the therapist might usefully consider what it is that has been interrupted.

For illustrative purposes only, I would like to cite some quite different but relevant examples from the literature. In his work on so-called fixated behavior, Maier (1949) has found that the most successful method for breaking the "fixation" consisted of guiding the animals to the new response sequence, or forcing the performance of the consummatory response from which the new organized sequence could then be built up.

In an entirely different context, Lindemann (1944) has discussed the symptomatology of acute grief, the emotional behavior following the "sudden cessation of social interaction." In discussing the management of these reactions, he stresses the importance of "finding new patterns of rewarding interaction." And immediately relevant to our present formulation is his suggestion that it is not necessarily the affectionate nature of the interaction with the deceased but rather its intensity that determines the severity of the grief reaction. Parkes (1972) has provided an enlightened discussion of grief and bereavement within the concept of attachment theory (Bowlby, 1973), stressing the loss of significant companions. Grief is an important emotional consequence of interruption and, in an extensive review of the nature and significance of grief, Averill (1968) has concluded that grief "comprises a stereotyped set of psychological and physiological reactions of biological origin." He assumes that grief has an adaptive role to play in insuring the cohesiveness of the group in those species where a social group is necessary for the species' survival. I do not believe that it is necessary to ascribe a specific innate role to the emotion of grief. While Averill makes the very useful distinction between mourning, behavior determined by particular social and learned factors, and grief, which he considers to be of biological origin, it is my present contention that the extreme degrees of disruption and interruption occasioned by the loss of a loved member of one's group are adequate to explain the appearance of grief. In particular, it is highly likely that in groups that are socially cohesive and where cohesiveness has become a factor in the survival of the group, increasing numbers of plans and structures exist that incorporate particular individuals. Thus the more elaborate the cognitive structures are that need particular individuals for their execution, the more complex will be the interruptive and disruptive reactions to loss. How intense the effect of such a loss can be is seen in Parkes' (1972) description of the high levels of anxiety, sometimes approaching panic, that characterize grief. Averill's summary and review also suggest that the degree of the involvement and relationship with the lost individual determines the intensity of the grief, which would be consistent with my formulation. In any case, Averill's review is an important resource and reminder for the psychologist who wants to study a generally neglected but powerful emotional reaction.

A final word on frustration tolerance. What the organism does in the face of interruption may, of course, depend on previous experiences with interruption situations. Freud (1911) has eloquently argued that the ability to delay gratification (completion) marks the triumph of the reality principle, or rational man. Given an interrupted sequence of behavior, the ability to delay, the tendency not to employ the immediately available substitutes or completions simply makes it more likely that, as the situation changes, more appropriate substitution responses will become more probable. The ability to delay following an interruption provides a wider choice of possible substitute actions. Thus the problem of frustration tolerance becomes the problem of being able to "hold" in the face of mounting arousal and distress. Similar to a learned tendency to delay, there may be learned tendencies to remove the tension brought about by interruption. But here I am back in the mainstream of personality theory, and the readers can complete this sequence according to their own theoretical predilections.

Personality Differences

The problem of individual differences in emotional dispositions or emotional reactions is complex and, at the present time, there is no adequate description of personality dimensions that goes beyond the suggestive or that leads to reasonable predictive and explanatory systems. The fact that most personality evaluations and scales available today have relatively little descriptive and explanatory value (Mischel, 1968) suggests two possible conclusions. One is that the highly variable nature of early experiences and child-rearing practices (and the resulting cognitive interpretations of the environment) makes it unlikely that simple dimensions can be found that will account for a reasonable amount of the variance of differences in individual behavior. The second possibility is that there are no overriding innate, biological characteristics that characterize individuals over and above the large degree of variance introduced by cognitive interpretations, which are developed during their early and later experience.

In a sense, the emotional system we have ascribed is a system of individual differences. The general model with which we have been dealing is a system that says that emotional experiences are, to a very large extent, idiosyncratic and that, short of knowing the complete biological inheritance of individuals and their complete history, it is essentially impossible to predict their reactions to specific situations. This is not the counsel of despair but, instead, a general statement that scientific systems are not designed and do not intend to predict the behavior of objects or systems, which are unique combinations of innumerable variables. Scientific systems discuss the operations of variables, often in the abstract, but not the particular concatenation within an individual object or system.

Two possible strategies of finding significant individual variation are available to us. One of them is to describe some general sensitivities to environmental events that may characterize an individuals' emotional reaction and that may allow some prediction; the other is to discover whether, within a particular culture or society, there are preferred cognitive systems that will predict differences in emotional response. The former approach leads to the construction of personality scales (e.g., the multivariate analyses of Eysenck and others). The second is represented by the psychoanalytic approach, which suggests that there are major sources of cognitive interpretations that lead to the functional release of emotional reactions, and that these major sources are few in number and related to specific complexes of early childhood experiences.

In terms of our current conceptual model, both approaches are concerned with cognitive-mentalistic structures that describe habitual ways of reinterpreting environmental events in emotional contexts.

Personality Scales

As far as paper and pencil personality tests are concerned, I suggested, in Chapter 8, that answers to questions on a personality questionnaire indicate predilections toward interpreting a set of situations in a particular way. The scales provide one index (and only one out of a range of possible ways of measuring cognitive structures) of the way in which a set of stimuli are functionally interpreted. Thus individuals scoring high on a text-anxiety scale interpret test situations as threatening, interrupting. These situations are reinterpreted and become functional arousers for the autonomic nervous system; at the same time, the test situation is interpreted as noxious and unpleasant. If this says that pencil and paper tests only tell us what people "think" about situations, it is probably correct but should not be dismissed lightly. The way in which a person thinks about a situation tells us how it is evaluated and appraised; in short, it tells what structures are used to transform the situation into the kind of stimuli with which the action and arousal systems must eventually deal.

Eysenck (e.g., 1967) has interpreted two major dimensions of personality tests, which he calls introversion-extroversion (I-E) and neuroticism (N), in terms of conditionability (for the I-E dimension) and emotionality (for the N dimension). Gray (1970) has criticized this particular interpretation and substituted sensitivity to punishment and nonreward for the I-E dimension and sensitivity to reinforcing events in general for the N dimension. Assuming that a two-dimensional system does, in fact, account for much of the variance of paper and pencil personality tests, the question arises how our particular system might account for them.

As far as the I-E dimension is concerned, we can argue that it describes degree of arousal in response to arousal signals, or it may be related to the perception of arousal, or to the interpretation of signals as being relevant to arousal. Thus, in terms of our system, either the conditioning explanation or the punishment-frustration explanation of I-E would have to be more specific as to the locus of its effect. It is possible that individuals differ in the degree to which they interpret certain events in the environment as relevant for arousal, or they differ in the degree of arousal, or they differ in their perception of arousal. As far as the arousal system is concerned, it seems unlikely that differential levels of arousals account for the I-E dimension unless it can be shown that all kinds of arousal signals, whether they are aversive or not (including both fearful and joyful situations), elicit the same idiosyncratic degree of arousal for a given person. Gray shows that the difference in arousal along the I-E dimension only occurs for aversive signals. However, then we must argue that with a single arousal system, as we propose, the individual differences must be found in the interpretation of the environment and in the differential likelihood that individuals will see the world as threatening or not. Once they see it as threatening, the arousal system comes into effect. If the dimension is, in fact, indexed by a greater degree of conditionability, specifically to threatening stimuli, or by a greater sensitivity to punishment or frustration, then it seems unlikely that either the arousal system or, by the same argument, the perception-of-arousal system is involved but, instead, that we are dealing with a perceptual-cognitive phenomenon. If that is the case it might be possible to use the N dimension to account for differences in the arousal system. Clearly, whether we call that dimension "emotionality" or "sensitivity to reinforcers," individual differences in degree of arousal would produce differences both in degree of emotionality and in differential sensitivity to reinforcement. Thus both a positive and a negative reinforcement, interpreted appropriately, would produce arousal signals, the effect of which would be attenuated or amplified by the individual's arousal system and its tendency to be activated.

It should be kept in mind that degree of arousal is relative to the base level of arousal and will be perceived as arousal only if it is significantly different from the base level. This is at least one of the reasons why the perception-of-arousal system is necessary.

To summarize, we assume that Eysenck's introversion-extroversion dimension orders individuals according to their tendency to interpret events as threatening, punishing, or frustrating, while the neurotocism dimension orders people in terms of differential degrees of arousal.

Personality Types

The syndrome or type notion is more complex than a dimensional analysis. In the first instance, I shall explore further the use of semantic networks.

I am adopting a general schema of semantic organization that is consistent with most current notions of semantic networks. As noted in Chapter 2, I am assuming that a hierarchical organization of the semantic network best represents its major working characteristics. Increasingly higher levels show more and more abstract notions or higher level concepts. It is preferable to use nodes in the hierarchy without specific labels. One difficulty of using labels is that it harks back to behaviorist positions on concepts and abstract ideas, which are defined by verbal labels. While a particular node frequently expresses a particular abstract idea, the definition of the idea characterized by the node resides in the relations it has with both subsidiary and higher-order concepts within the network. Thus, for purposes of theory, it is best to leave the nodes unlabeled, although for practical purposes, it will be necessary to talk about and label specific concepts, abstract ideas, and images.

It is possible for any one of the nodes in a particular network to be related to an "emotional" structure. The idea, notion, concept, or image that the node represents may be part of a structure that terminates in a functional releaser of the arousal system. In the history of the individual any given node may have become part of such an "emotional" structure. Thus it is possible that a high-level node is a member of an emotional structure, but that none of the lower-level components that are subsumed under that node are directly part of such a structure. Similarly, of course, it is possible for lower-level concepts to be part of an emotional structure without involving any of the higher-level ones directly. In fact, emotional structures will involve some higher levels and some lower-level nodes in various semantic networks. It is assumed here that the system contains many different such networks and that members of one such network may also be members of another network. For example, the concept of "dog" may be part of a network that organizes our knowledge about animals, but it also may be part of the network, for particular individuals, that characterizes their childhood and the individuals and objects with which they played.

Next, the question of emotional syndromes involves the processing and the search patterns that take place when a hierarchy is entered. We have assumed that typically, although not always, entry at any one point into the network produces an information search that generally operates up or sideways, and rarely does it produce a search pattern that goes downward. Thus, when the node "dog" is entered, it is assumed that it will be classified immediately as a domesticated animal, an animal, and a living thing. On the other hand, it is rare that when we think of animals that we sample all the specific instances or that we think of all the specific instances of dogs when that node is entered. Thus the node "dog" generally activates the node "animal," but only in a particular case are the nodes "wolfhound" or "Scotch terrier" activated. None of this implies that these search patterns may not go in the other direction at times. For example, if somebody tells me that they own a dog that likes to hide under a couch, it is highly likely that I will restrict the concept of dog in this case by searches downward to find examples that fit under couches. But, in general, and frequently enough to be the basis of the argument to be developed below, automatic search patterns in the semantic network go in the more abstract rather than the less abstract direction.

It follows from this argument that whenever a particular node has been involved in an emotional structure, there is a given probability that whenever nodes *below* that particular item are entered, the emotional structure will be activated and will lead to emotional experience and action. For example, the love of dogs tends to generalize to all dogs since, when a particular dog is seen and evaluated, upward information seeking will arrive at the "dog" node. Conversely, however, it is possible to love Scotch terriers without loving dogs in general, and one may at the same time dislike or even hate Great Danes. In the therapeutic situation, which more frequently tries to deal with fears than with loves, it is important to know whether a particular phobia is an example of a more general case or whether it is specific to the instance. Thus we can be afraid of snakes without being afraid of animals, but presumably not vice versa. Behavior therapy deals with the restructuring of emotional interpretations of a specific and limited set of objects and is particularly useful in the case of phobias. The argument from the psychoanalytic school that dealing with the symptom of a particular phobia does not necessarily resolve the underlying conflict can now be seen in a different light.

It is quite possible for a particular phobia to be quite specific to a narrow range of objects (e.g., snakes) without implying a broader, more abstract "underlying" syndrome. On the other hand, such syndromes may exist at a higher, abstract level. Thus the argument between behavior therapists and analysts on the adequacy of one or the other method again may be resolved by assuming that both positions are correct in different cases, and that we have to evaluate what the specific phobia implies, whether it involves a higher level abstraction or not, before we can say which therapy might be more useful and which is likely to lead to an alleviation of the symptom. When there is no higher order "motive," quite clearly behavior therapy would be adequate. More important, however, altering the emotional structure for a particular low-level concept may, with adequate experiential processing, spread to other parts of the system. In the long run even

behavior therapy may deal with the restructuring of higher-level
abstract nodes; the cognitive system may undergo a change at a
higher-level structure as a result of a lower-level change. For example,
assume that there is an "unconscious" fear of all furlike objects, but
that it is expressed primarily in a fear of dogs, which is treated in
behavior therapy. As a result of an adequate change of the emotional
structure involving dogs, there is also a change in part of the emotional
structure involving furry animals and related objects. This may be
further extended, by working through in consciousness and by
repeated hypothesis development and testing, to involve other
instances of furry animals and objects.

I noted earlier that semantic networks are built up out of early
childhood experiences. It is central to the psychoanalytic theory of
personality constellations that specific emotional structures are
developed very early in life in respect to the major modes of mastering
the environment in the oral, anal, and genital areas. Semantic networks
are built up that give meaning to the environment in relation to these
early concepts, whether they are part of emotional structures or not. It
is assumed, for example, that a very high-level abstract "oral" node
becomes related not only to modes of taking in food, but also to
attitudes toward and ideas about supplies of love and support, uses of
the oral apparatus in speaking and communicating, and to a variety of
other minor ways of expressing oral concerns. Similar arguments are
made for anal retentive attitudes relating to other abstract nodes (e.g.,
to problems of money management). The semantic network model and
the notion that nodes at different levels may be part of emotional
structures support such a concept but, at the same time, suggest that
empirical support may be difficult to marshall. The more abstract and
higher in the hierarchy a concept that is related to an emotional
structure is, the more diffuse will be its expressions at the lowest levels
of specific everyday concepts and uses. Thus, in order to show that
one's attitude toward savings banks is related to a thirty-year-old node
at the "anal" abstract level requires extensive information seeking
within the semantic hierarchy; the search may often be sidetracked or
the structures changed in the course of experience. Clearly, the more
abstract the emotional structure, the more diffuse will be its
manifestations, the less consistent the behavior that it is supposed to
predict, and the fewer the hard data with which to support it. On the
other hand, the lower a particular emotional structure occurs, the easier
it is to demonstrate its applicability to very specific situations and very
specific behavior, the more likely its expression in a limited set of
behaviors, and the easier the marshalling of data in its support. As a
corollary, the more diffuse the evidence and the manifestations of a
higher-order abstract emotional structure, the less likely it is to be

immediately obvious in the day-to-day life of the individual, and the more difficult it will be to intervene, that is, to change the unwanted relationship between the abstract notion and emotional expression.

The semantic network model suggests the possibility of the broad abstract personality structures that psychoanalytic theory assumes but, at the same time, it implies that their function is going to be of relatively less importance than that of structures that are at a lower level of abstraction and of more immediate relevance to the life of the individual. Thus Mischel's (1968) conclusion that situational factors frequently override personality dispositions should not be surprising.

Finally, the restriction of these abstract structures to oral, anal, and genital events has seriously hampered the development of a useful psychoanalytic taxonomy of personality types. By limiting the number of types to three or four or five, we are forced into an unnecessarily restrictive classification. There should be no reason to exclude other abstract nodes, dealing with equally important events that may be at the same level of abstraction and importance as the ones suggested by Freud. Among these, as I have suggested earlier, are the management of pain, problems of cold and hunger, the management of sleep, the relation to violence and aggression, and many others. These abstract syndromes will vary in importance as a function of the individual's background, his social class, and his specific experiences. The systems developed by Freud for a middle-class, turn-of-the-century society and its syndromes may not be appropriate in the middle of the twentieth century for classes other than the ones with which he dealt.

In summary, I suggest that not only would lower-level concepts of personality structure produce better predictions, but also that a better analysis of the more abstract levels might increase the predictability of individual personality dispositions.

Psychopathy

Individual differences in the sensitivity or lability of the autonomic nervous system may be, as suggested earlier, of great relevance in emotional development and expression. In a provocative paper on the origins and functions of the psychopathic personality, Schachter and Latané (1964) have proposed that the psychopath or sociopath is constitutionally adrenalin-sensitive and at the same time has learned to ignore his autonomic reactions. They have shown that psychopaths are more responsive to adrenalin (i.e., they show stronger autonomic nervous system reactions to adrenalin injections), but they also show less emotion which, in light of Schachter's other work on emotional behavior, suggests that they ignore their autonomic reactions. I have suggested some possible mechanisms during the early learning of autonomic perception that are relevant both to the antecedents of psychopathic personality structures and to the development of emotion-sensitive, possibly neurotic, personality structures.

If—...—the psychopath grows up in an environment that either ignores, punishes, or indiscriminately reinforces emotional responses that occur with autonomic stimulation, he will learn not to discriminate his autonomic stimuli. We assume that he has learned to ignore normal levels of arousal. However, there will be some occasions when the psychopath's physiological stimuli are so intense that they cannot be ignored, and emotional responses will in fact occur. It also appears that even the psychopath likes to 'feel' every now and then. Now, if he can only distinguish high levels of stimulation then, by definition, his threshold for emotional responsiveness is very high; low levels or autonomic stimulation which drive the emotional behavior of the normal are not effective for the psychopath. If—as I believe—the normal has to learn to keep his autonomic level relatively low in order not to be in a constant state of emotional upheaval, then the psychopath need not learn to keep his autonomic level low. His autonomic stimuli can operate—in response to external stimulation or not—at a much higher level than they do in the normal, and without producing continuous upheaval. What I am suggesting is that while the normal learns to be adrenalin- or stimulation-insensitive in order to be able to remain calm, the psychopath handles the problem by just not noticing the stimulation. But then high levels of autonomic arousal will occur more frequently in the psychopath than in the normal. Thus, the "ignoring" mechanism can produce both high levels of autonomic response and low levels of emotion. The psychopath may in fact be more sensitive (autonomically) to emotional stimuli in the environment since he—or at least some psychopaths—in fact seeks levels of autonomic stimulation high enough to produce emotion (the "kick-seeker"). Similarly, the normal who has not learned to keep levels of autonomic stimulation at low levels becomes an anxiety neurotic, continuously exposed to autonomic levels above his threshold (Mandler, 1964b).

Valins (1970) has followed up this suggestion in offering the hypothesis that "although the psychopath experiences and perceives his bodily changes, he ignores them in the sense of not utilizing them as cues when evaluating emotional situations." In support Valins found that psychopathic subjects were unaffected by a procedure that misinformed them about the actual heart rate they were experiencing, while normal subjects would use this heart rate feedback as a cue for evaluating emotional stimuli. Similarly, a study by Stern and Kaplan (1967) showed that psychopathic subjects were unable to "produce" galvanic skin responses, which normal subjects could do. Thus the psychopath does tend to ignore autonomic feedback and also is less able to influence his autonomic nervous system reactions. On the other hand, no systematic data are available to indicate that the psychopath may seek autonomic stimulation that he cannot ignore, that is, stimulation at levels well above that produced in the normal individual.

The hypothesis, which is quite speculative and still seeks adequate support, states that the psychopath fails to respond to the moral imperative of his autonomic response and thus displays antisocial behavior. He also may seek the emotional stimulation that he lacks and thus enter into and produce situations that are more deviant from the ones usually sought out or generated by normals.

In another discussion of psychopathic processes Melges and Bowlby (1969) have related the problem of hopelessness to two kinds of psychopathological processes. Following Miller, Galanter, and Pribram's notions of plans and their importance in the structure of behavior and experience, and Bowlby's ideas about goal-corrected systems, they discussed at length the importance of hope and hopelessness as being relevant to an individual's estimate of the probability of achieving goals. Their discussions of such factors as the assignment of possible goal achievement to one's own skill or to change, the reliance on others to assist in the achievement of goals (trust as opposed to distrust), and long-term versus short-term expectations of goal achievement are entirely congenial to the present formulations. Melges and Bowlby also make contact with psychoanalytic theory by noting that the concept of "continuing goals is related to that of the super-ego, the concept of long term goals to that of the ego-ideal, and the concept of an integrated and balanced set of goals—short term, long term, and continuing—to that of a strong ego."

They then go on to discuss the psychopathology of depression and sociopathy. I previously had occasion to discuss the relationship between depression and hopelessness, and Melges and Bowlby's discussion is entirely consonant with mine. They point out in addition, however, that the depressed patient is usually an individual who has continuing and long-range goals and who has committed his own personal skills to the achievement of such goals. In other words, these individuals consider themselves responsible for their own fate and tend to blame themselves for their failures.

Interestingly, however, Melges and Bowlby consider sociopathy (or psychopathy) as the other side of the coin of depression. They suggest that the sociopath has "long since abandoned future concerns and turned to the present." He has few long-range goals, and he lacks also an integrated set of goals; in other words, his super-ego and ego development have suffered. As a result, the sociopath is only concerned with goals that are obtainable in the present and has given up the attempt at forming reasonable long-range interpersonal goals. The notion that sociopathy and depression are both related to hopelessness contrasts somewhat with our notions about psychopathy. We have assigned the major roles in the development of psychopathy to a defective arousal system; the sociopath is an individual who is continuously seeking new experiences that will be sufficiently arousing so that he can find deep emotional experiences and feelings. There is no need to make a choice decision between these two formulations, since both of them may well be operating. What is of interest is that notions of hopelessness might, under another point of view, also be assigned to the development of sociopathy.

Emotional Involvement

It is commonplace to say that a particular situation becomes emotionally important or relevant to the extent that one feels personally involved or feels that the situation is personally relevant. This is not an explanatory statement, but it asserts that there are mechanisms whereby innocuous situations become personally important or relevant. An explanation might be sought by considering a particular example and seeing how degree of personal involvement changes as various aspects of the situation change. Consider a range of situations in which the same event occurs, but which have significant differences and different emphases.

The general event of a child being run over by an automobile may come to our attention from reading a brief notice in an out-of-town newspaper, from a similar notice in the local paper referring to a nearby street corner, from that same notice referring to the child of a neighbor, from actually seeing it happen to a child we know, and, in the extreme case, from being the child involved in such an accident. The degree of emotional involvement clearly increases from an initial nonemotional, intellectual taking-in of the information to personal terror, fear, and grief. To "explain" this range of reaction in terms of a generalization gradient or in terms of similarity is mistaking description for explanation. Except for physical stimuli, which can be related to differential receptor excitation, terms such as generalization or similarity are evocative rather than explanatory in nature.

The degree of personal involvement can be measured by the degree to which the situation concerned permits the individual to include himself as a participant in the events or scene described or imagined.

Descriptions and experiences of complex events are assumed to be represented in the cognitive system as images, as representations that are manipulable within that system. There may exist a program that asks, To what extent can I put myself as an actor into that situation? Such an operation on or transformation of an image from involving other people to one involving the self is relatively simple, when one of the actors could potentially be the self. The example I have used requires that the image of the accident be made "relevant" to the individual by establishing a relationship between some of the actors in the image and the perceiver. The injections of the self into the image may take a variety of forms; consider two major ones. One of them makes the child involved a child of the perceiver; the other puts the perceiver in the role of the driver of the car. Which particular projection of the self we will engage in is a function of the structure of the cognitive system, that is, a function of the previous experiences and history of the individual. However, it seems to be fairly clear that putting the self into the image and carrying out the actions involved produces certain consequences that, in turn, may be functional, releasing stimuli for arousal. Thus the loss of a child (in terms of interruption theory) or having caused the death of a child (in terms of guilt and its consequences) may lead to outcomes that produce arousal and thus emotional response and involvement.

Another example, more useful because it demonstrates some of the other mechanisms involved in the use of central images, can be found in the area of human sexuality. An account of homosexual behavior may vary in its emotional consequences to the degree to which the situation described is one in which the self may reasonably be a participant. Such an evaluation will vary with a description of the scene involved, the circumstances under which it takes place ("Are these circumstances in which the self may in fact ever appear?"), and the reality aspects of the situation. Clearly, there may also be repressive consequences for some of the outcomes, once the self has been put into the image. The very notion of seeing oneself in a homosexual situation may, on the basis of past history, range from most pleasurable to highly frightening. In the latter case, a repressive mechanism or such classic mechanisms as denial ("I don't even see the situation as a homosexual one") may be operating. It is interesting to speculate that one of the reasons why bad pornography is frequently sexually nonarousing is that the descriptions of the situations are so ludicrous and unrealistic that people find it very difficult to imagine themselves as participants.

Finally, since there is good evidence that individuals vary in their use of visual imagery, how might these differences affect emotional functioning? Our own research (Hollenberg, 1970; Stewart, 1965;

Anderson, 1973) has suggested that individuals who prefer visual codes tend to be concrete; that is, they see situations as presented and do not generalize to the generic case as easily as those who use verbal codes. Therefore high-imagery individuals who tend to generate visual images of a particular scene are more likely to see it in its specific context rather than as an example of a more general (and less threatening?) situation. They are also more likely to be tied to the immediate emotional demands of that situation. Concreteness and emotionality may go hand in hand. McFarlane Smith (1964), in reviewing relations among differences in electrical activity of the brain, imagery, and personality types, suggests that visualizers may be hypersensitive, while verbalizers are calm and even tempered.

Panic

I have previously discussed the relation between attention, arousal, and performance in general (cf. Chapter 6). This section extends that discussion to extreme states of threat and panic. From a theoretical point of view, there are some interesting parallels between panic and guilt. In the latter the individual is involved with repeating—cognitively—a sequence of actions, the outcome of which is fixed (i.e., in the past) and unchangeable. What happens when an individual goes through a similar sequence with respect to overt actions? In that context the actions are attempted in order to solve a particular real-life problem, but they do not solve the problem, they do not reach some "goal"; "failure" is implicit either in the environment or in the individual's perception of the situation. The same inevitability of repeated interruption occurs as in the case of guilt. However, the problem situation keeps the individual in the field, within the situation that again and again leads to the initiation of the sequence that inevitably "fails." These are the ingredients of panic.

Paniclike behavior may be found in rather innocuous situations. We may find that it is suddenly not possible to open the door leading from a room—for some reason it is stuck. Again and again we may try to go through the same motions, pushing, pulling, exerting more force, or even more intelligence. We run through the gamut of possible reactions to interruption but, with each interruption, we potentiate further the autonomic arousal that follows interruption. The more intensive and demanding the signals that initiate the actions, the more likely the repetition, the greater the subjective perception of interruption, and the more intense the degree of arousal. At the extremes we find the kind of behavior usually described as panic.

Typically, panic is produced in many "normal" situations with little predictability. There are, however, sets of conditions where panic is more likely to occur. One of these occurs in diving, where some sudden malfunction of equipment, or the appearance of some objective threat, will initiate behavior to "solve the problem." If such attempts are not successful, they are likely to be followed by repetitions, more interruptions—all with a degree of intensity indicative of an extreme arousal-producing situation. Bachrach (1970) has discussed the psychological problem of panic in diving and describes it as "a strong, fearful perception by an individual that he is out of control, that he is not capable of coping with the situation in which he finds himself, leading to behaviors that not only do not solve the problem posed by the danger but actually may work directly against such solution."

Repeated interruption not only produces increased arousal, but it also seems to work against the likelihood that adaptive solutions will be found. We assume that high degrees of arousal make problem solving less efficient, a suggestion we have previously encountered in our discussion of the relation among arousal, action, and cognition. There is good evidence, dating to an important paper by Callaway and Dembo (1958), that increased arousal, particularly at very high levels, leads to a narrowed range of attention. Given the limited span of consciousness and processing ability of the human organism in the first place, any situation that demands attention will further decrease the probability of being able to scan the environment adequately to find new solutions, new conditions. Callaway and Dembo (1958) concluded that "both emotional states, such as anxiety, panic, and orgasm, and chemical states, such as amphetamine and carbon dioxide, produce a similar narrowing of attention. . . . [A] correlation between narrowed attention and central sympathomimetic activity is demonstrated." Thus, in the panic condition, there is an insistent signal to keep repeating some set of actions, its continued interruption drives the arousal higher and higher and, as the arousal level increases, there is increasing autonomic stimulation that demands and receives attention. As a result, the effective attentional range is reduced, and the likelihood that the individual will be able to retrieve or perceive some more effective mode of action is reduced. This in turn keeps the original ineffectual action dominant, and the vicious circle continues.

Baddeley (1972) has summarized some of the literature on performance in dangerous environments. He arrives at very similar conclusions that danger affects performance by narrowing the breadth of attention. He specifically indicates that extreme threat increases arousal which, in turn, focuses attention on the most important aspects of the current environment. Just as Easterbrook (1959) suggested, if such focusing centers on the current task, performance improves; if it does not, performance suffers. Baddeley concludes his survey by raising the question about the mechanism that might mediate the effect of arousal on attention. Hopefully, this discussion provides one possible such mechanism.

An apparent discrepancy between this discussion and the suggestion in Chapter 6 that the autonomic nervous system may generate increased scanning activity by the organism needs to be resolved. What is apparent for the present is that the kind of attention-enhancing mechanism discussed in Chapter 6 is true for relatively low levels of arousal, while the attention narrowing mechanism operates at high levels of arousal. The adaptive advantages of the latter process should be apparent, since some degree of attentional focusing might be useful when a single event is likely to threaten the organism.

I have alluded to the similarity between guilt and panic. The major differnce, of course, is that in the case of guilt it is often possible to change the situational demands, to "think of something else," or to find some of the solutions we indicated earlier. These solutions are not available in panic which, in addition, because of the intensity of the signals involved (such as threat of death), produces much more intense effects as a rule.

Sex—A Different Emotion?

Until now we have assumed that the arousal involved in emotional states is all of one piece—general autonomic, usually sympathetic, arousal, which is perceived as a global stimulus and integrated with cognitive signals. But there is one arousal system that is significantly different from the primarily sympathetic system that I have discussed up until now. In the brief discussion of the autonomic nervous system the distinction was made between sympathetic and parasympathetic arousal. I noted that these two systems tend to be complementary and acting in concert rather than being alternate ways of responding. It is also likely, in terms of their function, that these two systems have different evolutionary significances and histories.

If all the usual kinds of emotions, such as love, hate, fear, and euphoria, are determined by the coaction of sympathetic arousal and cognitive interpretations—how about sexual arousal? In the first instance sexual arousal seems to involve perception of visceral arousal, which is, at least intuitively and anecdotally, different from the perception of general emotional arousal in the other emotions cited.

Several authors (e.g., Wenger, Jones, and Jones, 1956) have noted the significant role played by the parasympathetic nervous system during sexual arousal. The initial phases of sexual activity and of arousal tend to be dominated by parasympathetic nervous system responses but, as sexual activity proceeds, sympathetic activity becomes more important until it overshadows parasympathetic activity completely at the time of orgasm. Most of the data on the subject are fairly new and come from the pioneering work of Masters and Johnson (1966). The available data on physiological measures of sexual arousal have been summarized by Zuckerman (1971). The data tend to support the importance of parasympathetic arousal in the immediate response to sexual stimulation. It appears that such visceral responses as tumescence, vasodilation, genital secretions, and rhythmic muscular movements constitute a cluster of responses that are uniquely characteristic of sexual arousal and sexual responses. In particular, the occurrence of tumescence and of vaginal lubrication, which are apparently parasympathetically innervated, are not only characteristics of sexual arousal but, and this is important from the present point of view, obviously and uniquely subject to differential internal perception and thus play psychologically functional roles. On the other hand, massive sympathetic arousal is typical of the later phases of sexual arousal and plays the same role, in the emotions produced and felt, as sympathetic arousal does for all the various emotional states considered by us so far.

The effect of drugs on sexual arousal is also a case in point. Drugs that tend to depress sympathetic nervous system activity interfere with the latter phases of sexual activity, for example ejaculation. On the other hand, drugs that inhibit parasympathetic activity may inhibit early features, such as erection.

As Zuckerman points out, the data on sexual arousal, outside of specific stimulation during and preceding sexual activity, are relatively inconclusive, but it could be argued that one of the distinctions that we need to make in the discussion of emotional states is, *in this case only,* determined by differential autonomic arousal. Sexual stimuli may thus be considered to differ from other stimuli in that they produce parasympathetic arousal, a specific perceptual syndrome consequent on such arousal, and structures that are specifically related to sexual and lustful emotion.

Some interesting conjectures arise concerning the interaction between these two emotional systems. One suggestion was offered by Zuckerman (1971): "The possibility that sympathetic dominance may inhibit arousal and facilitate ejaculation may explain why sexual anxiety may be expressed in an inability to attain or maintain an erection, *or* premature ejaculation. Assuming that anxiety creates a state of heightened autonomic arousal these effects would follow." Thus we may speculate that the sympathetically dominated emotions may actually interfere with the initial phase of sexual arousal. While sympathetic arousal does not seem to interfere with erection during the orgasmic phase, it does seem to inhibit erection during the early phases. Thus the interaction between sympathetic and parasympathetic systems is complex, but what is more important is that the interference of the sympathetic emotions with sexual arousal need not be restricted to anxiety, as Zuckerman and others have suggested.

If we are correct in assuming that the majority of all emotional states depend on autonomic arousal, which is primarily sympathetic, then any such state, given the appropriate environmental events, should in principle interfere with the early parasympathetic phases of sexual arousal.

It has been suggested and is consistent with the current point of view that romantic love falls into the general continuum of the sympathetically aroused emotions (Walster and Berscheid, 1971). This leads to the interesting prediction that an excess of romantic love during the early stages of sexual arousal may effectively interfere with adequate erection and lubrication, both important concomitants of sexual behavior and experience. An excess of romantic love may interfere with sexual performance. This conjunction is not as farfetched as it may sound. Anecdotal evidence abounds about cases of impotence and frigidity on the wedding night. The disjunction between love and lust is often carefully avoided in Western society (at least it is verbally denounced), but in individual experience it may, in fact, be an important factor. For example, the excessive demands made on women in our society to display romantic love may be one of the factors that leads to an increase in frigidity and lack of sexual arousal.

Even more interesting is a speculation about the structures that relate cognitive interpretations to one or the other of these arousal systems. Consider the condition in which a structure relates sympathetic arousal to sexual objects, or one that relates parasympathetic arousal and genital feelings to nonsexual objects. If we are to "love" and not lust after certain individuals, this might inhibit sexual response. On the other hand, the sexual response in turn may be specifically related to the significant persons whom one does not, cannot, or should not love. The twentieth century might not be the best example for some of these concatenations, although they may exist in individuals just as they may have existed for large sections of the society in the nineteenth century. Then, the middle class in Western society was frequently taught that love emotions are to be expressed toward members of the same class, while lust emotions were reserved for others. Whether it was the Victorian gentleman who reserved his lust for women outside his connubial relationship, or whether the Victorian lady was only able to express her lustful emotions with gamekeepers, the examples illustrate our general argument. Sexual structures that reserve the lust emotion to very specific cognitive objects, whether they be prostitutes or husbands, conversely produce inhibition of lust and sexuality toward others. At the same time, the emotion of love is necessarily restricted to a different set of individuals. When the occasions and persons that produce love and those that produce lust are different, difficulties in both sexual arousal and interpersonal relations will result.

Another consequence of this dissociation can be seen in the effects of drugs such as tranquilizers and alcohol, which will vary depending on the particular emotion (love or lust) that is evoked. Alcohol can act as a depressant for either parasympathetic or sympathetic arousal and thus may have rather differential effects. If it suppresses anxiety, it encourages lustful sexual behavior; if it suppresses sexual arousal, it obviously does not. Which of the two systems will be more sensitive to the intervention of drugs will depend on the biological and psychological history of the individual.

Our argument about love and lust applies equally to other emotions that may be aroused in sexual contexts. It is not my purpose to explore the wide range of sexual deviations from the norm that could be fitted into the current framework. I am primarily thinking about the kinds of events and people that may arouse sympathetic responses within the sexual sphere, or the kind of nonsexual objects that may have become part of the structure of sexual, parasympathetic arousal. Perversities come in at least two flavors.

Consider the example of sexual masochism. Melzack and Casey (1968, 1970) and Melzack and Wall (1965) have put the experience of pain within the general framework of emotional experience. They point out that the salient features of emotion (inputs from sensory systems, arousal, and cognitive processes) determine the experience of pain just as they determine the experience of other emotions. To a very large extent, the motivational-affective dimension of pain is influenced by cognitive activity. The noxious experience of pain is derived in part from early experiences as to the meaning of so-called "painful" stimuli as, for example, in the evaluation of source of the painful stimuli or the seriousness of the injury that they produce. It is therefore not surprising that under some circumstances the sensory aspects of "painful" stimuli may be redirected or restructured by sensory-motivational-cognitive systems that imbue these events with positive effects. The basic phenomenon of masochism is not that all so-called painful stimuli become pleasurable, but that "painful" stimuli, under certain conditions are interpreted as pleasurable. It is not unlikely that early experiences with painful stimuli that occurred in relation to a loving parent may, under certain conditions, produce interpretation of a painful stimulus as pleasurable. Two consequences may then follow. First, the events and cognitions that are present at the time of such pleasurable interpretations of pain may also be occasions for other kinds of emotional experiences. For example, the

cognitive interpretation of the individual who inflicts the pleasurable
pain may also be an interpretation that leads to sexual excitement.
Under those circumstances there will be a conjunction between
pleasurable pain and sexual arousal—to the point that the painful
event becomes interpreted in terms of sexual arousal, possibly
accompanied by a unique mixture of sympathetic and parasympathetic
arousals. The second consequence refers to the difficulty of modifying
this complex syndrome. The individual knows that under other
circumstances the painful stimuli do, in fact, give rise to noxious and
aversive experiences and "prefers" the positive interpretation whenever
possible. At the same time the conjunction between the painful
stimulus and the pleasurable sexual experience further reinforces the
utility of the masochistic structure. Thus the masochistic individual
will most reluctantly change the interpretive structures because
abandonment may lead to noxious experiences, but it also involves the
loss of pleasant sexual experiences. A structure that avoids noxious
experiences and leads to pleasurable experiences at the same time
should be more difficult to change than a structure that does only one
or the other.

Some Tender Feelings—Aesthetics and Creativity

One of the possible difficulties with an arousal-cognitive
interpretation theory of emotion is that it seems to fail to account for
positive emotional feeling tones that occur in aesthetic appreciation.
The degree of emotional involvement on hearing a particular piece of
music, seeing an outstanding piece of art, or appreciating a new and
masterful recipe seems to have very little to do with arousal. While it
is highly likely that there is a degree of arousal during such aesthetic
appreciation, it becomes difficult to specify the functional stimulus for
such arousal. It is unlikely that the particular configurations used by
Beethoven, Rembrandt, or Rodin have innate releasing qualities. Much
as some philosophers of aesthetics have argued for an immediate
appreciation of the beautiful in music and art, it is unlikely from a
biological or psychological point of view that such preformed
structures, in fact, exist in the human organism.

It is more likely that the arousal function of a piece of art can be
derived from an interaction between it and the viewing, listening, and
tasting individual. The probable source for the arousal can be found in
certain structures that have been built up in relation to works of art.
These structures may vary in the degree to which they anticipate the
artistic event, that is, the degree of which the actual event does or does
not conform to the particular structure and therefore interrupts or
disrupts it. Best known for attempts in this direction are Helson,

McClelland, and Atkinson in developing the notion of the adaptation level and deviations from it. For example, McClelland (1951) suggests that the confirmation of expectations with a low probability lead to negative affect, the confirmation of expectations with medium probabilities lead to positive affect, and the confirmation of expectations with high probability lead to boredom. Berlyne (1960) believes that the degree of competition between incompatible response tendencies or expectations determines the degree of emotional tension. He also noted the possibility of using information theory to describe the degree of competition among these expectations. These are just some examples of a variety of theories that eventually come to grips with the informational content of a stimulus complex and its relation to affective reactions. Werbik (1971) has described and criticized these theories and suggested his own interpretation of the relationship between the information content of a work of art and its emotional effect. His main thesis is that degree of activation (arousal) varies with the discrepancy between stimulation and central anticipation. The intensity of an anticipation is a monotonically increasing function of the objective conditional probability of a particular stimulus in the appropriate context. His discussion of musical perception and the relationship between the informational content of a stimulus sequence and the degree of activation released by the perception of a sequence is consistent with the present position that when an event conforms with certain central mental structures, no disruption or interruption will occur and therefore no arousal will take place.

It can be assumed, together with a variety of aesthetic theorists, that the complexity of a work of art generates further and finer differentiations of its content. The greater the informational content, the greater the possibility of new interpretations and new differentiations. Thus we would expect that the aesthetically meaningful experience (i.e., meaningful in the emotional sense) will be related to continuous attempts at analysis. These analyses will, by definition, be discrepant with previously developed structures that involve that work of art. It is this continuing analysis and new appreciation and reappreciation of a work of art that produces the discrepancy, thus the arousal, and finally the affective reaction. Werbik and others have shown that amount of artistic training is related to the affective response to a work of art. The popular song that permits few new interpretations quickly loses its affective content, just as the less complex and less "interesting" work of art quickly loses its emotional impact. Since different structures involving works of music or art will be used by different individuals, we can expect that different people will find different pieces of artistic creations more or less emotionally satisfying and arousing.

The cognitive constituents that produce positive emotions in appreciating a work of art are the achievement of a new interpretation, a new view of the aesthetic object, and the development of new mental structures. On the other hand, there must be cases where the arousal that goes with a particular work of art would also produce negative emotional reactions. This is most frequently seen in the response to the radically new or revolutionary art form. Presumably, in these cases, there are no structures available that can handle, interpret, or analyze the work of art that is presented. When an attempt is made to analyze a stimulus complex and that attempt is unsuccessful because no structures are available, the conditions for anxiety and helplessness that I have discussed elsewhere will have been met. Thus the new art form, whether it is Beethoven's in his time or Picasso's in his, is frequently responded to as unpleasant and negative. With education and experience, structures are developed that can integrate this material, and the emotional reaction changes from negative to positive.

The appreciation of art may be related to problems of creativity and originality and their origins in early development. It can be argued from what I have said about the appreciation of a work of art and the accompanying emotional experience that the creative and original individual must not only be able to create new forms and structures in the world, but must also have certain emotional characteristics. First, such an individual should be able to tolerate the emotions engendered when the new structure, the new work of art, the new theory are produced; and second, as a corollary, such emotional situations should be attractive. The perception of the new structure, the interruption of the old, and their emotional consequences must be positive, desirable cognitive interpretations.

On the basis of anecdotal evidence, I have entertained a hypothesis about creativity that has two aspects, neither of which is necessarily new. First, the creative work, whether it is in art or in science, requires an act of destruction of the existing forms and structures. The artist who breaks new paths in the forms of musical or visual expression or the scientist who proposes a new theory both know that by that very act they are destroying or at least undermining existing structures, structures that have been accepted by their colleagues and by society at large. Thus the creative individual must be able to tolerate and even seek out the destructive consequences of the creation. In a sense, that destruction must not be "aggressive" in the normal sense of intending to hurt someone but, instead, must be seen as neutral, vis-à-vis the other artist and scientist, and destructive only of ideas in the service of creating new structures. If it were seen as destructive of people, it will (and should) frequently (although clearly not always) have negative aversive characteristics and may inhibit the creative effort.

Second, and this is the more speculative part of the thesis, it appears that creative individuals very frequently have a cross-sex parent who has been thwarted or frustrated in some artistic or intellectual endeavor. Under certain circumstances this frustration may be seen in the same-sex parent, but not typically so. In a sense the cross-sex parent and the child are characteristic of Rank's (e.g., 1932) distinction between two kinds of nonconformist: the parent as the thwarted nonconformist and the child as the creative one.

If we assume that there is a relatively high degree of emotional contact between a child and the cross-sex parent, by appealing, for example, to the latent or manifest romantic and sexual attraction between the two (cf. Mandler, 1963), then the positive emotional ties between the child and the cross-sex parent will color their relationships. I am suggesting that the parent "lives out" his or her thwarted ambitions by driving, encouraging, and motivating the child toward continuously new and different achievements. No particular stage of development is adequate; a higher level and a better one must be reached. Thus just as the child reaches a stable structure in relationship to intellectual, artistic, or scientific endeavors, the parent interferes directly by producing a new structure that is to supplement it, a new level of achievement that is to be attained. In the context in which positive emotional ties between parent and child are already present, the disruption of existing structures is added, and the achievement of new structures becomes a positively viewed and positively valued objective. The change of old structure becomes a positive "destructive" goal rather than a negative aggressive one directed against others, and this creative change is viewed as positive and desirable. Arousal (whether "sexual" or not) is provided by the parent and by the disruption of old patterns; positive evaluation is derived both from the parent and the achievement of new structures. Some of the empirical literature about creative persons (e.g., by MacKinnon, 1962; and Barron, 1968) supports the general notions of increased nonconformity, ability to accept destructiveness, and the kind of parent-child relationships suggested here.

In summary then, the creative act, being both destructive and productive of new structures, is learned during early life as a desirable and acceptable way of interacting with the environment. In contrast, the uncreative individual may shy away from the destruction of existing structures because it is seen as aggressive, or the arousal produced in the denial or disruption of old structures cannot be tolerated because such arousal is accompanied by negative rather than positive cognitive appraisals.

It is appropriate in this context to return to some of the things said and implied in the section on aggression in Chapter 6. If the context of early childhood interactions colors the emerging emotional tone of creativity, how much more does the prevailing character of society affect that interaction? It is the character of the society that determines the cognitive evaluations of feelings and actions in the last analysis. Regardless of the parent-child interaction, the values of society are a prior condition. To be able to tolerate the destruction of the old and to see it as creative instead of aggressive depends in the first instance on the social values that inform both creativity and aggression. Thus a society that directs creative acts toward competition and personal achievement, that equates competition and aggression, and that rewards creativity but also competitive, aggressive achievements will tend to undermine the free creative act that—in the ideal cases noted above—can see the change of the old in the positive light of personal and social achievement rather than as an additional sign of interpersonal aggressive competition.

I would like to end on that note. When all has been said about mental processes, we can return to the importance of the social conditions under which they operate, the realization that life and society determine consciousness, not vice versa.

Bibliography

Adrian, E. D. Consciousness. In J. C. Eccles (Ed.), *Brain and conscious experience.* New York: Springer , 1966.

Amsel, A. The role of frustrative nonreward in noncontinuous reward situations. *Psychological Bulletin,* 1958, **53,** 102–119.

Amsel, A. Frustrative nonreward in partial reinforcement and discrimination learning. *Psychological Review,* 1962, **69,** 306–328.

Amsel, A., and **Roussel, J.S.** Motivational properties of frustration: I. Effect on a running response of the addition of frustration to the motivational complex. *Journal of Experimental Psychology,* 1952, **43,** 363–368.

Anderson, R. E. Individual differences in the use of imaginal processing. Unpublished doctoral dissertation, University of California, San Diego, 1973.

Arnold, M. B. An ecitatory theory of emotion. In M. L. Reymert (Ed.), *Feelings and emotion: The Mooseheart symposium.* New York: McGraw Hill, 1950.

Arnold, M. B. *Emotion and personality.* New York: Columbia University Press, 1960.

Arnold, M. B. Human emotion and action. In T. Mischel (Ed.), *Human action.* New York: Academic Press, 1969.

Arnold, M. B. (Ed.) *Feelings and emotions: The Loyola Symposium.* New York: Academic Press, 1970a.

Arnold, M. B. Perennial problems in the field of emotion. In M. B. Arnold (Ed.), *Feelings and emotion.* New York: Academic Press, 1970b.

Auersperg, A. P. Vom Werden der Angst. *Nervenarzt,* 1958, **29,** 193–201.

Averill, J. R. Grief: Its nature and significance. *Psychological Bulletin,* 1968, **70,** 721–748.

Averill, J. R. Autonomic response patterns during sadness and mirth. *Psychophysiology,* 1969, **5,** 399–414.

Averill, J. R. Personal control over aversive stimuli and its relationship to stress. *Psychological Bulletin,* 1973, **80,** 286–303.

Ax, A. F. The physiological differentiation of fear and anger in humans. *Psychosomatic Medicine,* 1953, **15,** 433–442.

Ax, A. F. Neurophysiology discovers the mind. *Contemporary Psychology,* 1971, **16,** 365–367.

Bachrach, A. J. Diving behavior. In *Human performance and scuba diving.* Chicago: Athletic Institute, 1970.

Bacon, S. J. Arousal and the range of cue utilization. *Journal of Experimental Psychology,* 1974, **102,** 81–87.

Baddeley, A. D. Selective attention and performance in dangerous environments. *British Journal of Psychology,* 1972, **63,** 537–546.

Bain, A. *The emotions and the will.* (4th ed.) London: Longmans, 1899. First edition, 1859.

Bandura, A. Social learning theory of aggression. In J. F. Knutson (Ed.), *The control of aggression.* Chicago: Aldine, 1973.

Barber, T. X. Toward a theory of pain: Relief of chronic pain by prefrontal leucotomy, opiates, placebos, and hypnosis. *Psychological Bulletin,* 1959, **56,** 430–460.

Barefoot, J. C., and **Straub, R. B.** Opportunity for information search and the effect of false heart-rate feedback. *Journal of Personality and Social Psychology,* 1971, **17,** 154–157.

Barron, F. *Creativity and personal freedom.* Princeton, N.J.: Van Nostrand, 1968.

Bateson, G., Jackson, D. D., Haley, J., and **Weakland, J.** Toward a theory of schizophrenia. *Behavioral Science,* 1956, **1,** 251–264.

Beck, A. T. *Depression.* New York: Hoeber, 1967.

Beck, A. T. Cognition, anxiety, and psychophysiological disorders. In C. D. Spielberger (Ed.), *Anxiety: Current trends in theory and research.* Vol. II. New York: Academic Press, 1972.

Bem, D. J. Self-perception: An alternative interpretation of cognitive dissonance phenomena. *Psychological Review,* 1967, **74,** 183–200.

Berkowitz, L. Aggressive cues in aggressive behavior and hostility catharsis. *Psychological Review,* 1964, **71,** 104–122.

Berlyne, D. E. *Conflict, arousal and curiosity.* New York: McGraw Hill, 1960.

Berlyne, D. E. *Structure and direction in thinking.* New York: Wiley, 1965.

Berlyne, D. E., Craw, M. A., Salapatek, P. H., and **Lewis, J. L.** Novelty, complexity, incongruity, extrinsic motivation and the G.S.R. *Journal of Experimental Psychology,* 1963, **66,** 560–567.

Bindra, D. B. Emotion and behavior theory: Current research in historical perspective. In P. Black (Ed.), *Physiological correlates of emotion.* New York: Academic Press, 1970.

Birch, D., Ison, J. R., and **Sperling, S. E.** Reversal learning under single stimulus presentation. *Journal of Experimental Psychology,* 1960, **60,** 36–40.

Black, A. H. Heartrate changes during avoidance learning in dogs. *Canadian Journal of Psychology,* 1959, **13,** 229–242.

Black, P. (Ed.) *Physiological correlates of emotion.* New York: Academic Press, 1970.

Bolles, R. C. Species-specific defense reactions and avoidance learning. *Psychological Review,* 1970, **77,** 32–48.

Bonn, J. A., Turner, P., and **Hicks, D. C.** Beta-adrenergic receptor blockade with practolol in treatment of anxiety. *Lancet,* 1972, **1,** 814–815.

Bowers, K. S. Pain, anxiety, and perceived control. *Journal of Consulting and Clinical Psychology,* 1968, **32,** 596–602.

Bowlby, J. *Attachment and loss.* Vol. I. *Attachment.* London: Hogarth Press and Institute of Psychoanalysis, 1969.

Bowlby, J. Reasonable fear and natural fear. *International Journal of Psychiatry,* 1970, **9,** 79–88.

Bowlby, J. *Attachment and loss.* Vol. II. *Separation.* London: Hogarth Press and Institute of Psychoanalysis, 1973.

Brady, J. V. Emotion and sensitivity of psychoendocrine systems. In D. C. Glass (Ed.), *Neurophysiology and emotion.* New York: Rockefeller University Press and Russell Sage Foundation, 1967.

Brady, J. V. Toward a behavioral biology of emotion. In L. Levi (Ed.), *Emotions: Their parameters and measurement.* New York: Raven Press, 1975.

Brown, J. S., and **Farber, I. E.** Emotions conceptualized as intervening variables—with suggestions toward a theory of frustration. *Psychological Bulletin,* 1951, **48,** 465–495.

Bruell, J. H. Heritability of emotional behavior. In P. Black (Ed.,) *Physiological correlates of emotion.* New York: Academic Press, 1970.

Bruner, J. S. Human problem solving. *Harvard Educational Review,* 1961, **31.**

Brunswick, D. The effects of emotional stimuli on the gastro-intestinal zone. *Journal of Comparative Physiology,* 1924, **4,** 19–79, 225–287.

Bühler, K. *The mental development of the child.* New York: Harcourt, Brace, 1930.

Butterfield, E. C. The interruption of tasks: Methodological, factual, and theoretical issues. *Psychological Bulletin,* 1954, **62,** 309–322.

Bykov, K. M. *The cerebral cortex and the internal organs.* New York: Chemical, 1957.

Callaway, E. III, and **Dembo, D.** Narrowed attention: A psychological phenomenon that accompanies a certain physiological change. *AMA Archives of Neurology and Psychiatry,* 1958, **79,** 74–90.

Cannon, W. B. The James-Lange theory of emotions: A critical examination and an alternative theory. *American Journal of Psychology,* 1927, **39,** 106–124.

Cannon, W. B. *Bodily changes in pain, hunger, fear and rage* (2nd ed.) New York: Appleton-Century-Crofts, 1929.

Cannon, W. B. The Linacre lecture on the autonomic nervous system: An interpretation. *Lancet,* 1930, **218,** 1109–1115.

Chevalier-Skolnikoff, S. Facial expression of emotion in nonhuman primates. In P. Ekman (Ed.), *Darwin and facial expression.* New York: Academic Press, 1973.

Chomsky, N. Review of B. F. Skinner's *Verbal behavior. Language,* 1959, **35,** 26–58.

Claparède, E. *La genèse de l'hypothèse.* Geneva: Kundig, 1934.

Cofer, C. N., and **Appley, H.** *Motivation: Theory and research.* New York: Wiley, 1964.

Collins, A. M., and **Quillian, M. R.** How to make a language user. In E. Tulving and W. Donaldson (Eds.), *Organization of memory.* New York: Academic Press, 1972.

Costello, C. G. Dissimilarities between conditioned avoidance responses and phobias. *Psychological Review,* 1970, **77,** 250–254.

Craik, F. I. M., and **Lockhart, R. S.** Levels of processing: A framework for memory research. *Journal of Verbal Learning and Verbal Behavior,* 1972, **11,** 671–684.

Craik, F. I. M., and **Watkins, M. J.** The role of rehearsal in short-term memory. *Journal of Verbal Learning and Verbal Behavior,* 1973, **12,** 599–607.

Crespi, L. P. Quantitative variation of incentive and performance in the white rat. *American Journal of Psychology,* 1942, **55,** 467–517.

Darwin, C. *The expressions of the emotions in man and animals.* London: John Murray, 1872.

Davitz, J. R. *The language of emotion.* New York: Academic Press, 1969.

Deets, A. C., Harlow, H. F., and **Harlow, M. K.** Development of aggression in primates. Paper presented at AAAS meetings, December 1971.

Deutsch, J. A. *The structural basis of behavior.* Chicago: University of Chicago Press, 1960.

Deutsch, M. Field theory in social psychology. In G. Lindzey (Ed.), *Handbook of Social Psychology.* Vol. 1. Cambridge: Addison-Wesley, 1954.

Dollard, J., and **Miller, N. E.** *Personality and psychotherapy.* New York: McGraw-Hill, 1950.

Duffy, E. *Activation and behavior.* New York: Wiley, 1962.

Dumas, G. La mimique des aveugles. *Bulletin de l'Académie de Médicine,* 1932, **107,** 607–610.

Easterbrook, J. A. The effect of emotion on cue utilization and the organization of behavior. *Psychological Review,* 1959, **66,** 183–201.

Ekman, P. Cross-cultural studies of facial expression. In P. Ekman (Ed.), *Darwin and facial expression.* New York: Academic Press, 1973.

Elliott, R. Effects of uncertainty about the nature and advent of a noxious stimulus (shock) upon heartrate. *Journal of Personality and Social Psychology,* 1966, **3,** 353–356.

Eysenck, H. J. *The biological basis of personality.* Springfield, Ill.: Charles C Thomas, 1967.

Fanconi, G., and **Ferrazzini, F.** Kongenitale Analgie: Kongenitale generalisierte Schmerzindifferenz. *Helvetica Paediatrica Acta,* 1957, **12,** 79–115.

Fehr, F. S., and **Stern, J. A.** Peripheral physiological variables and emotion. *Psychological Bulletin,* 1970, **74,** 411–424.

Festinger, L., Burnham, C. A., Ono, H., and **Bamber, D.** Efference and the conscious experience of perception. *Journal of Experimental Psychology Monograph,* 1967, **74,** (4).

Ford, C. S., and **Beach, F. A.** *Patterns of sexual behavior.* New York: Harper, 1952.

Frankenhaeuser, M. Some aspects of research in physiological psychology. In L. Lennard (Ed.), *Emotional stress.* New York: American Elsevier, 1967.

Frankenhaeuser, M. Experimental approaches to the study of human behavior as related to neuroendocrine functions. *In L. Levi (Ed.), Society, stress, and disease. Vol. I. London: Oxford University Press, 1971a.*

Frankenhaeuser, M. Behavior and circulating catecholamines. *Brain Research,* 1971, **31,** 241–262 (b).

Frankenhaeuser, M. Experimental approaches to the study of catecholamines and emotion. In L. Levi (Ed.), *Emotions: Their parameters and measurement.* New York: Raven Press, 1975.

Frankenhaeuser, M., Nordheden, B:, Myrsten, A.-L., and **Post, B.** Psychophysiological reactions to understimulation and overstimulation. *Acta Psychologica,* 1971, **35,** 298–308.

Frankenhaeuser, M., and **Pátkai, P.** Interindividual differences in catecholamine excretion during stress. *Scandinavian Journal of Psychology,* 1965, **6,** 117–123.

Frankenhaeuser, M., and **Rissler, A.** Effects of punishment on catecholamine release and efficiency of performance. *Psychopharmacology,* 1970, **17,** 378–390.

Freeman, G. L. The relationship between performance level and bodily activity level. *Journal of Experimental Psychology,* 1940, **26,** 602–608.

Freud, S. Formulations regarding the two principles in mental functioning. In *Collected Papers.* Vol. 4. London: Hogarth, 1925. First German publication, 1911.

Freud, S. The unconscious. In S. Freud, *Collected Papers.* Vol. IV. London: Hogarth, 1925a.

Freud, S. Instincts and their vicissitudes. In S. Freud, *Collected Papers.* Vol. IV. London: Hogarth, 1925b. First published in *Internationale Zeitschrift für Psychoanalyse.* Vol. 3. 1915.

Freud, S. *New introductory lectures on psychoanalysis.* New York: Norton, 1933.

Freud, S. *The problem of anxiety.* New York: Norton, 1936. First German publication, 1926. British translation published in 1936 as *Inhibitions, symptoms and anxiety.*

Freud, S. *The interpretation of dreams.* New York: Modern Library, 1938. First German publication in 1900.

Freud, S. *A general introduction to psychoanalysis.* Garden City, N.Y.: Doubleday, 1952. First German publication 1916–1917.

Fromm, E. *The anatomy of human destructiveness.* New York: Holt, Rinehart and Winston, 1973.

Fry, P. S., and **Ogston, D. G.** Emotion as a function of the labeling of interruption produced arousal. *Psychonomic Science,* 1971, **24,** 153–154.

Funkenstein, D. H. Nor-epinephrine-like and epinephrine-like substances in relation to human behavior. *Journal of Mental Diseases,* 1956, **124,** 58–68.

Gallistel, C. R. Motivation as central organizing process: The psychophysical approach to its functional and neurophysiological analysis. In *Nebraska symposium on motivation: 1974.* Lincoln, Neb.: University of Nebraska Press, 1974.

Garner, W. R. *Uncertainty and structure as psychological concepts.* New York: Wiley, 1962.

Garner, W. R. *The processing of information and structure.* Hillsdale: N.J.: Lawrence Erlbaum Associates, 1974.

Glass, D. C., Singer, J. E., Leonard, H. S., Krantz, D., Cohen, S., and **Cummings, H.** Perceived control of aversive stimulation and the reduction of stress responses. *Journal of Personality,* 1973, **41,** 577–595.

Goldstein, D., Fink, D., and **Mettee, D. R.** cognition of arousal and actual arousal as determinants of emotion. *Journal of Personality and Social Psychology,* 1972, **21,** 41–51.

Goldstein, K. *The organism: A holistic approach to biology.* New York: American Book Company, 1939.

Goldstein, M. L. Physiological theories of emotion: A critical historical review from the standpoint of behavior theory. *Psychological Bulletin,* 1968, **69,** 23–40.

Graham, F. K., and **Clifton, R. K.** Heart rate change as a component of the orienting response. *Psychological Bulletin,* 1966, **65,** 305–320.

Gray, J. A. The psychophysiological basis of introversion-extraversion. *Behavior Research and Therapy,* 1970, **8,** 249–266.

Gray, J. A. The mind-brain identity theory as a scientific hypothesis. *Philosophical Quarterly,* 1971, **21,** 247–252(a).

Gray, J. A. *The psychology of fear and stress.* London: World University Library, 1971b.

Gray, J. A. Causal theories of personality and how to test them. In J. R. Royce (Ed.), *Multivariate analysis and psychological theory.* New York: Academic Press, 1973.

Hamburg, D., Hamburg, B., and **Barchas, J.** Anger and depression: Current psychobiological approaches. In L. Levi (Ed.), *Emotions: Their Parameters and measurement.* New York: Raven Press, 1975.

Harlow, H. F. The nature of love. *American Psychologist,* 1958, **13,** 673–685.

Hastings, S. E., and **Obrist, P. A.** Heart rate during conditioning in humans: Effect of varying the interstimulus (CS-UCS) interval. *Journal of Experimental Psychology,* 1967, **74,** 431–442.

Hebb, D. O. On the nature of fear. *Psychological Review,* 1946, **53,** 259–276.

Hebb, D. O. *The organization of behavior.* New York: Wiley, 1949.

Heider, F. *The psychology of interpersonal relations.* New York: Wiley, 1958.

Hess, E. H. Attitude and pupil size. *Scientific American,* 1965, **212,** 46–54.

Higgins, J. D. Set and uncertainty as factors influencing anticipatory cardiovascular responding in humans. *Journal of Comparative and Physiological Psychology,* 1971, **74,** 272–283.

Hinde, R. A. Changes in responsiveness to a constant stimulus. *British Journal of Animal Behavior,* 1954, **2,** 41–55.

Hinde, R. A. Ethological models and the concept of "drive." *British Journal of the Philosophy of Science,* 1956, **6,** 321–331.

Hohmann, G. W. Some effects of spinal cord lesions on experienced emotional feelings. *Psychophysiology,* 1966, **3,** 143–156.

Hollenberg, C. K. Function of visual imagery in the learning and concept formation of children. *Child Development,* 1970, **41,** 1003–1015.

Horney, K. *Our inner conflicts: A constructive theory of neurosis.* New York: Norton, 1945.

Hull, C. L. The rat's speed of locomotion gradient and its relation to the goal gradient. *Journal of Comparative Psychology,* 1934, **17,** 392–422.

Hunt, J. McV., Cole, M. W., and Reis, E. S. Situational cues distinguishing anger, fear, and sorrow. *American Journal of Psychology,* 1958, **71,** 136–151.

Izard, C. E. *The face of emotion.* New York: Appleton-Century-Crofts, 1971.

James, W. What is an emotion? *Mind,* 1884, **9,** 188–205.

James, W. *Principles of psychology.* New York: Holt, 1890.

Janis, I. L. *Psychological stress.* New York: Wiley, 1958.

Johansson, G., and Frankenhaeuser, M. temporal factors in sympatho-adrenomedullary activity following acute behavioral activation. *Journal of Biological Psychology,* 1973, **1,** 67–77.

Kagan, J. *Change and continuity in infancy.* New York: Wiley, 1971.

Kahn, M. The physiology of catharsis. *Journal of Personality and Social Psychology,* 1966, **3,** 278–286.

Kanfer, F. H. and Phillips, J. S. *Learning foundations of behavior therapy.* New York: Wiley, 1970.

Kantor, J. R. An attempt toward a naturalistic description of emotion. *Psychological Review,* 1921, **28,** 19–42 and 120–140.

Katz, J. J., and Fodor, J. A. The structure of a semantic theory. *Language,* 1963, **39,** 170–210.

Kelley, H. Attribution theory in social psychology. In D. Levine (Ed.), *Nebraska symposium on motivation: 1967.* Lincoln, Neb.: University of Nebraska Press, 1967.

Kessen, W. *The child.* New York: Wiley, 1965.

Kessen, W. Early cognitive development: Hot or cold? In T. Mischel (Ed.), *Cognitive development and epistemology.* New York: Academic Press, 1971.

Kessen, W., and Mandler, G. Anxiety, pain, and the inhibition of distress. *Psychological Review,* 1961, **68,** 396–404.

Kierkegaard, S. A. *The concept of dread.* (2nd ed.) Princeton, N.J.: Princeton University Press, 1957. First published in 1844.

Kimmel, H. D. Instrumental conditioning of autonomically mediated responses in human beings. *American Psychologist,* 1974, **29,** 325–335.

Kintsch, W. Notes on the structure of semantic memory. In E. Tulving and W. Donaldson (Eds.), *Organization of memory.* New York: Academic Press, 1972.

Kubie, L. S. A physiological approach to the concept of anxiety. *Psychosomatic Medicine,* 1941, **3,** 263–276.

La Barre, W. The cultural basis of emotions and gestures. *Journal of Personality,* 1947, **16,** 49–68.

La Berge, D. Acquisition of automatic processing in perceptual and associative learning. In P.M.A. Rabbitt and S. Dornic (Eds.), *Attention and performance V.* London: Academic Press, 1974.

Lacey, B. C., and **Lacey, J. I.** Studies of heart rate and other bodily processes in sensorimotor behavior. In P. A. Obrist, A. Black, J. Brener, and L. DiCara (Eds.), *Cardiovascular psychophysiology: Current mechanisms, biofeedback and methodology.* Chicago: Aldine-Atherton, 1974.

Lacey, J.I. Psychophysiological approaches to the evaluation of psychotherapeutic process and outcome. In E. A. Rubenstein and M. B. Parloff (Eds.), *Research in psychotherapy.* Washington, D.C.: American Psychological Association, 1959.

Lacey, J. I. Somatic response patterning and stress: Some revisions of activation theory. In M. H. Appley and R. Trumbull (Eds.), *Psychological stress: Issues in research.* New York: Appleton-Century-Crofts, 1967.

Lacey, J. I., Kagan, J., Lacey, B. C., and **Moss, H. A.** The visceral level: Situational determinants and behavioral correlates of autonomic response patterns. In P. H. Knapp (Ed.), *Expression of the emotions in man.* New York: International University Press, 1963.

Laird, J. D. Self-attribution of emotion: The effects of expressive behavior on the quality of emotional experience. *Journal of Personality and Social Psychology,* 1974, **29,** 475–486.

Landis, C., and **Hunt, W. A.** *The startle pattern.* New York: Farrar, 1939.

Lange, C. *Om Sindsbevægelser.* Kjφbenhavn, 1885.

Lange, C. *Ueber Gemüthsbewegungen.* Leipzig: Theodor Thomas, 1887.

Lazarus, R. S. A laboratory approach to the dynamics of psychological stress. *American Psychologist,* 1964, **19,** 400–411.

Lazarus, R. S. Emotions and adaptation: Conceptual and empirical relations. In W. J. Arnold, (Ed.), *Nebraska symposium on motivation: 1968.* Lincoln, Neb.: University of Nebraska Press, 1968.

Lazarus, R. S., and **Alfert, E.** Short-circuiting of threat by experimentally altering cognitive appraisal. *Journal of Abnormal and Social Psychology,* 1964, **69,** 195–205.

Lazarus, R. S., Averill, J. R., and **Opton, E. M. Jr.** Toward a cognitive theory of emotion. In M. B. Arnold (Ed.), *Feeling and emotion.* New York: Academic Press, 1970.

Lazarus, R. S., Speisman, J. C., Mordkoff, A. M., and **Davison, L. A.** A laboratory study of psychological stress produced by a motion picture film. *Psychological Monographs,* 1962, **76,** (34) (Whole No. 553).

Levi, L. The urinary output of adrenaline and noradrenaline during pleasant and unpleasant emotional states. *Psychosomatic Medicine,* 1965, **27,** 80–85.

Levi, L. Stress and distress in response to psychosocial stimuli. Laboratory and real life studies in sympathoadrenomedullary and related reactions. *Acta Medica Scandinavia,* Supplement 528, 1972.

Levi, L. *Emotions: Their parameters and measurement.* New York: Raven Press, 1975.

Levi-Montalcini, R., and **Angeletti, P. W.** Biological properties of a nerve growth promoting protein and its antiserum. In S. S. Kety and J. Elkes (Eds.), *Regional neurochemistry.* New York: Pergamon, 1961.

Lewin, K. *A dynamic theory of personality.* New York: McGraw-Hill, 1935.

Lewin, K. Formalization and progress in psychology. *University of Iowa Studies in Child Welfare,* 1940, **16** (3), 9–42.

Libby, W. L. Jr., Lacey, B. C., and **Lacey, J. I.** Pupillary and cardiac activity during visual attention. *Psychophysiology,* 1973, **10,** 270–294.

Liebert, R. M., and **Morris, L. W.** Cognitive and emotional components of test anxiety: A distinction and some initial data. *Psychological Reports,* 1967, **20,** 975–978.

Lindemann, E. Symptomatology and management of acute grief. *American Journal of Psychiatry,* 1944, **101,** 141–148.

Lissner, K. Die Entspannung von Bedürfnissen durch Ersatzhandlungen. *Psychologische Forschung,* 1933, **18,** 27–89.

Lorenz, K. *On aggression.* London: Methuen, 1963.

Luce, R. D. *Individual choice behavior: A theoretical analysis.* New York: Wiley, 1959.

Luria, A. K. Towards the problem of the historical nature of psychological processes. *International Journal of Psychology,* 1971, **6,** 259–272.

MacKinnon, D. W. The nature and nurture of creative talent. *American Psychologist,* 1962, **17,** 484–495.

Macnamara, J. Cognitive basis of language learning in infants. *Psychological Review,* 1972, **79,** 1–13.

Maier, N. R. F. *Frustration: The study of behavior without a goal.* New York: McGraw-Hill, 1949.

Maier, S. F., Seligman, M. E. P., and **Solomon, R. L.** Pavlovian fear conditioning and learned helplessness. In B. A. Campbell and R. M. Church (Eds.), *Punishment and aversive behavior.* New York: Appleton-Century-Crofts, 1969.

Mandler, G. Stimulus variables and subject variables: A caution. *Psychological Review,* 1959, **66,** 145–149.

Mandler, G. From association to structure. *Psychological Review,* 1962, **69,** 415–427(a).

Mandler, G. Emotion. In R. W. Brown *et al.* (Eds.) *New directions in psychology.* New York: Holt, 1962b.

Mandler, G. Parent and child in the development of the Oedipus complex. *Journal of Nervous and Mental Diseases,* 1963, **136,** 227–235.

Mandler, G. The interruption of behavior. In D. Levine (Ed.), *Nebraska symposium on motivation: 1964.* Lincoln, Neb.: University of Nebraska Press, 1964a.

Mandler, G. Comments on Dr. Schachter's and Dr. Latané's paper. In D. Levine (Ed.), *Nebraska symposium on motivation: 1964.* Lincoln, Neb.: University of Nebraska Press, 1964b.

Mandler, G. Organization and memory. In K. W. Spence and J. T. Spence (Eds.), *The psychology of learning and motivation: Advances in research and theory.* New York: Academic Press, 1967a.

Mandler, G. Verbal learning. In G. Mandler, P. Mussen, N. Kogan, and M. A. Wallach, *New directions in psychology: III.* New York: Holt, Rinehart and Winston, 1967b.

Mandler, G. The conditions for emotional behavior. In D. C. Glass (Ed.), *Neurophysiology and emotion.* New York: Rockefeller University Press, 1067c.

Mandler, G. Anxiety. In D. L. Sills (Ed.), *International encyclopedia of the social sciences.* New York: Crowell-Collier 1968.

Mandler, G. Acceptance of things past and present: A look at the mind and the brain. In R. B. McLeod (Ed.) *William James: unfinished business.* Washington, D.C.: American Psychological Association, 1969.

Mandler, G. Organization and recognition. In E. Tulving and W. Donaldson (Eds.), *Organization of memory.* New York: Academic Press, 1972a.

Mandler, G. Helplessness: Theory and research in anxiety. In C. D. Spielberger (Ed.), *Anxiety: Current trends in theory and research.* Vol. II. New York: Academic Press, 1972b.

Mandler, G. Memory storage and retrieval: Some limits on the reach of attention and consciousness. In P. M. A. Rabbitt and S. Dornic (Eds.), *Attention and performance V.* London: Academic Press, 1974.

Mandler, G. The search for emotion. In L. Levi (Ed.), *Emotions: Their parameters and measurement.* New York: Raven Press, 1975a.

Mandler, G. Consciousness: Respectable, useful, and probably necessary. In R. Solso (Ed.), *Information processing and cognition: The Loyola symposium.* Hillsdale, N.J.: Lawrence Erlbaum Associates, 1975b.

Mandler, G. and Dean, P. Seriation: The development of serial order in free recall. *Journal of Experimental Psychology,* 1969, **81,** 207–215.

Mandler, G., and Kahn, M. Discrimination of changes in heart rate: Two unsuccessful attempts. *Journal for the Experimental Analysis of Behavior,* 1960, **3,** 21–25.

Mandler, G., and **Kessen, W.** *The language of psychology.* New York: Wiley, 1959.

Mandler, G., and **Kessen, W.** The appearance of free will. In S. C. Brown (Ed.), *Philosophy of psychology.* London: Macmillan, 1974.

Mandler, G., and **Kremen, I.** Autonomic feedback: A correlational study. *Journal of Personality,* 1958, **26,** 388–399. (Erratum, 1960, 28, 545.)

Mandler, G., and **Kuhlman, C. K.** Proactive and retroactive effects of overlearning. *Journal of Experimental Psychology,* 1961, **61,** 76–81.

Mandler, G., **Mandler, J. M., Kremen, I.,** and **Sholiton, R. D.** The response to threat: Relations among verbal and physiological indices. *Psychological Monographs,* 1961, **75,** (9) (Whole No. 513).

Mandler, G., **Mandler, J. M.,** and **Uviller, E. T.** Autonomic feedback: The perception of autonomic activity. *Journal of Abnormal and Social Psychology,* 1958, **56,** 367–373.

Mandler, G., and **Sarason, S. B.** A study of anxiety and learning. *Journal of Abnormal and Social Psychology,* 1952, **47,** 166–173.

Mandler, G., and **Watson, D. L.** Anxiety and the interruption of behavior. In C. D. Spielberger (Ed.), *Anxiety and behavior.* New York: Academic Press, 1966.

Mandler, G., and **Worden, P. E.** Semantic processing without permanent storage. *Journal of Experimental Psychology,* 1973, **100,** 277–283.

Mandler, J. M., and **Goldberg, J.** Effects of partially and continuously reinforced pretraining on choice and latency measures in the rat. *Journal of Comparative and Physiological Psychology,* 1973, **84,** 118–127.

Mandler, J. M. and **Mandler, G.** Good guys vs. bad guys: The subject-object dichotomy. *Journal of Humanistic Psychology,* 1974, **14,** 63–87.

Marañon, G. Contribution à l'étude de l'action emotive de l'adrénaline. *Revue française d'Endocrinologie,* 1924, **2,** 301–325.

Marx, M. H. Some relations between frustration and drive. In M. R. Jones (Ed.), *Nebraska Symposium on Motivation: 1956.* Lincoln, Neb.: University of Nebraska Press, 1956.

Masters, W. H., and **Johnson, V. E.** *Human sexual response.* New York: Little, Brown, 1966.

May, R. *The meaning of anxiety.* New York: Ronald Press, 1950.

May, R., Angel, E., and Ellenberger, H. F. (Eds.). *Existence: A new dimension in psychiatry and psychology.* New York: Basic Books, 1958.

McClelland, D. C. *Personality.* New York: Sloane, 1951.

McFarlane-Smith, I. *Spatial ability.* London: University of London Press, 1964.

Mednick, S. A. A learning theory approach to research in schizophrenia. *Psychological Bulletin,* 1958, **55,** 316–327.

Melges, F. T., and Bowlby, J. Types of hopelessness in psychopathological process. *Archives of General Psychiatry,* 1969, **20,** 690–699.

Melzack, R. *The puzzle of pain.* New York: Basic Books, 1973.

Melzack, R., and Casey, K. L. Sensory, motivational, and central control of pain: A new conceptual model. In D. L. Kenshalo (Ed.), *The skin sense.* Springfield, Ill.: Charles Thomas, 1968.

Melzack, R., and Casey, K. L. The affective dimension of pain. In M. B. Arnold (Ed.), *Feelings and emotions.* New York: Academic Press, 1970.

Melzack, R., and Scott, T. H. The effects of early experience on the response to pain. *Journal of Comparative Psychology,* 1957, **50,** 155–161.

Melzack, R., and Wall, P. D. Pain mechanisms: A new theory. *Science,* 1965, **150,** 971–979.

Millenson, J. R. *Principles of behavioral analysis.* New York: Collier-Macmillan, 1967.

Miller, G. A. The magic number seven, plus or minus two: Some limits on our capacity for processing information. *Psychological Review,* 1956, **63,** 81–97.

Miller, G. A. *Psychology: The Science of mental life.* New York: Harper and Row, 1962.

Miller, G. A., Galanter, E. H., and Pribram, K. *Plans and the structure of behavior.* New York: holt, 1960.

Miller, N. E. Learnable drives and rewards. In S. S. Stevens (Ed.), *Handbook of experimental psychology.* New York: Wiley, 1951.

Miller, N. E. Some reflections on the law of effect produce a new alternative to drive reduction. In M. R. Jones (Ed.), *Nebraska symposium on motivation: 1963.* Lincoln, Neb.: University of Nebraska Press, 1963.

Miller, N. E. Learning of visceral and glandular responses. *Science,* 1969, **163,** 434–445.

Mischel, W. *Personality and assessment.* New York: Wiley, 1968.

Mischel, W., and Metzner, R. Preference for delayed reward as a function of age, intelligence, and length of delay interval. *Journal of Abnormal and Social Psychology,* 1962, **64,** 425–431.

Mowrer, O. H. Stimulus-response analysis of anxiety and its role as a reinforcing agent. *Psychological Review,* 1939, **46,** 553–565.

Mowrer, O. H. *Learning theory and behavior.* New York: Wiley, 1960.

Murdock, B. B. Jr. The retention of individual items. *Journal of Experimental Psychology,* 1961, **62,** 618–625.

Natsoulas, T. Concerning introspective "knowledge." *Psychological Bulletin,* 1970, **73,** 89–111.

Neisser, U. Cultural and cognitive discontinuity. In T. E. Gladwin and W. Sturtevant (Eds.), *Anthropology and human behavior.* Washington, D.C.: Anthropological Society of Washington, 1962.

Neisser, U. *Cognitive psychology.* New York: Appleton-Century-Crofts, 1967.

Norman, D. A. Learning and remembering: A tutorial preview. In S. Kornblum (Ed.), *Attention and performance IV.* New York: Academic Press, 1973.

North, A. J., and Stimmel, D. T. Extinction of an instrumental response following a large number of reinforcements. *Psychological Reports,* 1960, **6,** 227–234.

Nowlis, V., and Nowlis, H. H. The description and analysis of mood. *Annals of the New York Academy of Science,* 1956, **65,** 345–355.

Ornstein, R. E. *On the experience of time.* Harmondsworth: Penguin, 1969.

Ornstein, R. E. *The psychology of consciousness.* San Francisco: Freeman, 1972.

Osgood, C. E., Suci, G. J., and Tannenbaum, P. H. *The measurement of meaning.* Urbana: University of Illinois Press, 1957.

Parkes, C. M. *Bereavement: Studies of grief in adult life.* New York: International Universities Press, 1972.

Pátkai, P. Catecholamine excretion in pleasant and unpleasant situations. *Acta Psychologica,* 1971, **35**, 352–363.

Peiper, A. *Die Eigenart der kindlichen Hirntätigkeit.* (2nd ed.) Leipzig: Thieme, 1956.

Pereboom, A. C. A goalless gradient. *Journal of Experimental Psychology, 1958, **55**, 31–33.*

Peters, R. S. Motivation, emotion, and the conceptual schemes of common sense. In T. Mischel (Ed.), *Human action.* New York: Academic Press, 1969.

Piaget, J. *The origin of intelligence in the child.* London: Routledge and Kegan Paul, 1953.

Piaget, J. Structuralism. New York: Basic Books, 1970a.

Piaget, J. Piaget's theory. In P. H. Mussen (Ed.), *Carmichael's manual of child psychology.* New York: Wiley, 1970b.

Piaget, J. *Insights and illusions of philosophy.* London: Routledge and Kegan Paul, 1971.

Piaget, J., and **Inhelder, B.** *The psychology of the child.* New York: Basic Books, 1969.

Pick, J. The evolution of homeostasis: The phylogenetic development of the regulation of bodily and mental activities by the autonomic nervous system. *Proceedings of the American Philosophical Society,* 1954, **98**, 298–303.

Pick, J. *The autonomic nervous system.* Philadelphia: Lippincott, 1970.

Plutchik, R. *The emotions: Facts, theories and a new model.* New York: Random House, 1962.

Plutchik, R. Emotions, evolution, and adaptive processes. In M. B. Arnold (Ed.), *Feelings and emotions.* New York: Academic Press, 1970.

Plutchik, R., and **Ax, A. F.** A critique of *Determinants of emotional state* by Schachter and Singer (1962). *Psychophysiology,* 1967, **4**, 79–82.

Posner, M. I. Short term memory systems in human information processing. *Acta Psychologica,* 1967, **27**, 267–284.

Posner, M. I., and **Boies, S. J.** Components of attention. *Psychological Review,* 1971, **78**, 391–408.

Posner, M. I., and **Keele, S. W.** Time and space as measures of mental operations. Paper presented at the Annual Meeting of the American Psychological Association, 1970.

Posner, M. I., and **Klein, R. M.** On the functions of consciousness. In S. Kornblum (Ed.), *Attention and performance IV.* New York: Academic Press, 1973.

Posner, M. I., and **Snyder, C. R. R.** Attention and cognitive control. In R. Solso (Ed.), *Information processing and cognition: The Loyola symposium.* Potomac,: Lawrence Erlbaum Associates, 1975.

Posner, M. I., and **Warren, R. E.** Traces, concepts and conscious constructions. In A. W. Melton and E. Martin (Eds.), *Coding processes in human memory.* Washington, D.C.: Winston, 1972.

Quillian, M. R. Semantic memory. In M. Minsky (Ed.), *Somantic information processing.* Cambridge, Mass.: M.I.T. Press, 1968.

Rank, O. *Art and artist: Creative urge and personality development.* New York: Knopf, 1932.

Rank, O. *The trauma of birth.* New York: Brunner, 1952. First German publication, 1924.

Rapaport, D. Emotions and memory. *Menninger Clinic Monograph Series,* No. 2, 1942. Reprinted by Science Editions. New York: Wiley, 1961.

Raven, B. H., and **Rietsema, J.** The effects of varied clarity of group goal and group path upon the individual and his relation to his group. *Human Relations,* 1957, **10,** 29–45.

Reymert, M. L. (Ed.) *Feelings and emotions: The Wittenberg symposium.* Worcester, Mass.: Clark University Press, 1928.

Reymert, M. L. (Ed.). *Feelings and emotions. The Mooseheart symposium.* New York: McGraw-Hill, 1950.

Rosenbaum, D. A. The theory of cognitive residues: A new view of fantasy. *Psychological Review,* 1972, **79,** 471–486.

Rosenzweig, S. An outline of frustration theory. In J. McV. Hunt (Ed.), *Personality and the behavior disorders.* New York: Ronald, 1944.

Rothballer, A. B. Aggression, defense and neurohumors. In C. D. Clemente and D. B. Lindsley (Eds.), *Aggression and defense: Neural mechanisms and social patterns.* (Brain function, Vol. 5). Los Angeles: University of California Press, 1967.

Rothbart, M. K. Laughter in young children. *Psychological Bulletin,* 1973, **80,** 247–256.

Rotter, J. B., Seeman, M. R., and **Liberant, S.** Internal versus external control of reinforcement: A major variable in behavior theory. In N. F. Washburne (Ed.), *Decisions, values and groups.* Vol. 2. London: Pergamon Press, 1962.

Rozin, P., and **Kalat, J. W.** Specific hungers and poison avoidance as adaptive specializations of learning. *Psychological Review,* 1971, **78,** 459–486.

Ruckmick, C. A. *The psychology of feeling and emotion.* New York: McGraw-Hill, 1936.

Rumelhart, D. E., Lindsay, P. H., and **Norman, D. A.** A process model for long-term memory. In E. Tulving and W. Donaldson (Eds.), *Organization of memory.* New York: Academic Press, 1972.

Ryle, G. *The concept of mind.* London: Hutchison, 1949.

Sartre, J.-P. *Being and nothingness: An essay on phenomenological ontology.* New York: Philosophical Library, 1956. First French publication, 1943.

Schachtel, E. G. *Metamorphoris.* New York: Basic Books, 1959.

Schachter, S. The psychology of affiliation: Experimental studies of the sources of gregariousness. *Stanford Studies in Psychology,* No. 1. Stanford University Press, 1959.

Schachter, S. The interaction of cognitive and physiological determinants of emotional state. In C. D. Spielberger (Ed.), *Anxiety and behavior.* New York: Academic Press, 1966.

Schachter, S. The assumption of identity and peripheralist-centralist controversies in motivation and emotion. In M. B. Arnold (Ed.), *Feelings and emotion.* New York: Academic Press, 1970.

Schachter, S. *Emotion, obesity, and crime.* New York: Academic Press, 1971.

Schachter, S., and **Latané, B.** Crime, cognition and the autonomic nervous system. In D. Levin (Ed.), *Nebraska symposium on motivation, 1964.* Lincoln, Neb.: University of Nebraska Press.

Schachter, S., and **Singer, J. E.** Cognitive, social and physiological determinants of emotional state. *Psychological Review,* 1962, **69,** 379–399.

Schachter, S., and **Wheeler, L.** Epinephrine, chlorpromazine, and amusement. *Journal of Abnormal and Social Psychology,* 1962, **65,** 121–128.

Schlosberg, H. The description of facial expression in terms of two dimensions. *Journal of Experimental Psychology,* 1952, **44,** 229–237.

Schneirla, T.R. An evolutionary and developmental theory of biphasic processes underlying approach and withdrawal. In M. R. Jones (Ed.), *Nebraska symposium on motivation: 1959.* Lincoln, Neb.: University of Nebraska Press, 1959.

Schoenfeld, N. An experimental approach to anxiety, escape and avoidance behavior. In P. H. Hoch and J. Zubin (Eds.), *Anxiety.* New York: Grune, 1950.

Scott, J. P. *Animal behavior.* **Chicago: University of Chicago Press, 1958.**

Scott, W. A. Social psychological correlates of mental illness and mental health. *Psychological Bulletin,* 1958, **55,** 65–87.

Selg, H. (Ed.) *Zur Aggression verdammt? Psychologische Ansätze einer Friedensforschung.* Stuttgart: W. Kohlhammer, 1971.

Seligman, M. E. P., and **Maier, S. F.** Failure to escape traumatic shock. *Journal of Experimental Psychology,* 1967, **74,** 1–9.

Seligman, M. E. P. depression and learned helplessness. Paper presented at the American Psychological Association meetings, Hawaii, 1972.

Selye, H. *The stress of life.* New York: McGraw-Hill, 1956.

Shallice, T. Dual functions of consciousness. *Psychological Review,* 1972, **79,** 383–393.

Sher, M. A. Pupillary dilation before and after interruption of familiar and unfamiliar sequences. *Journal of Personality and Social Psychology,* 1971, **20,** 281–286.

Skinner, B. F. *The behavior of organisms.* New York: Appleton-Century-Crofts, 1938.

Skinner, B. F. *Verbal behavior.* New York: Appleton-Century-Crofts, 1957.

Smart, J. J. C. Sensations and brain processes. In C. V. Borst (Ed.), *The mind-brain identity theory.* London: Macmillan, 1970.

Sokolov, E. N. *Perception and the conditioned reflex.* New York: Macmillan, 1963.

Solomon, R. L., and Brush, E. S. Experimentally derived conceptions of anxiety and aversion. In M. R. Jones (Ed.), *Nebraska symposium on motivation: 1956.* Lincoln, Neb.: University of Nebraska Press, 1956.

Solomon, R. L., and Wynne, L. C. Traumatic avoidance learning: The principle of anxiety conservation and partial irreversibility. *Psychological Review,* 1954, 61, 353–385.

Spence, K. W. A theory of emotionally based drive (D) and its relation to performance in simple learning situations. *American Psychologist,* 1958, 13, 131–141.

Sperling, G. Successive approximations to a model for short-term memory. *Acta Psychologica,* 1967, 27, 285–292.

Spielberger, C. D. Conceptual and methodological issues in anxiety research. In C. D. Spielberger (Ed.), *Anxiety: Current trends in theory and research.* Vol. II. New York: Academic Press, 1972.

Sroufe, L. A., Waters, E., and Matas, L. Contextual determinants of infant affective responses. In M. Lewis and G. Rosenblum (eds.), *Origins of fear.* New York: Wiley, 1974.

Sroufe, L. A., and Wunsch, J. P. The development of laughter in the first year of life. *Child Development,* 1972, 43, 1326–1344.

Staddon, J. E. R., and Simmelhag, V. L. The "superstition" experiment: A reexamination of its implications for the principles of adaptive behavior. *Psychological Review,* 1971, 78, 3–43.

Stern, R. M., and Kaplan, B. E. Galvanic skin response: Voluntary control and externalization. *Journal of Psychosomatic Research,* 1967, 10, 349–353.

Stewart, J. C. An experimental investigation of imagery. Unpublished doctoral dissertation, University of Toronto, 1965.

Strongman, K. T. *The psychology of emotion.* London: Wiley, 1973.

Sutherland, N. S., and Mackintosh, N. J. *Mechanism of animal discrimination learning.* New York: Academic Press, 1971.

Taylor, J. A. A personality scale of manifest anxiety. *Journal of Abnormal and Social Psychology,* 1953, 48, 285–290.

Taylor, J. A. Drive theory and manifest anxiety. *Psychological Bulletin,* 1956, 53,, 303–320.

Thayer, R. E. Measurement of activation through self-report. *Psychological Reports,* 1967, 20, 663–678.

Thayer, R. E. Activation states as assessed by verbal report and four psychophysiological variables. *Psychophysiology,* 1970, **7**, 86–94.

Theios, J., and **Brelsford, J.** Overlearning-extinction effect as an incentive phenomenon. *Journal of Experimental Psychology,* 1964, **67**, 463–467.

Tinbergen, N. *The study of instinct.* Oxford: Oxford University Press, 1951.

Tomkins, S. S. *Affect, imagery, consciousness.* Vols. I and II. New York: Springer, 1962, 1963.

Treisman, A. Strategies and models of selective attention. *Psychological Review,* 1969, **76**, 282–299.

Tversky, A. Elimination by aspects: A theory of choice. *Psychological Review,* 1972, **79**, 281–299.

Valins, S. Cognitive effects of false heart-rate feedback. *Journal of Personality and Social Psychology,* 1966, **4**, 400–408.

Valins, S. The perception and labeling of bodily changes as determinants of emotional behavior. In P. Black (Ed.), *Physiological correlates of emotion.* New York: Academic Press, 1970.

Valins, S., and **Ray, A. A.** Effects of cognitive desensitization on avoidance behavior. *Journal of Personality and Social Psychology,* 1967, **7**, 345–350.

Von Holst, E. V. Die relative Koordination als Phänomen und als Methode zentralnervöser Funktionsanalyse. *Ergebnisse der Physiologie,* 1939, **42**, 228–306.

Vygotsky, L. S. *Thought and language.* Cambridge, Mass.: M.I.T. Press, 1962.

Wagner, A. R. Conditioned frustration as a learned drive. *Journal of Experimental Psychology,* 1963, **66**, 142–148.

Walster, E., and **Berscheid, E.** Adrenaline makes the heart grow fonder. *Psychology Today,* 1971, **5**, 47–50.

Watson, J. B. *Psychology from the stand-point of a behaviorist.* Philadelphia: Lippincott, 1919.

Weakland, J. H. The "double-bind" hypothesis of schizophrenia and three-party interaction. In D. Jackson (Ed.), *The etiology of schizophrenia.* New York: Basic Books, 1960.

Weiss, P. Self-differentiation of the basic patterns of coordination. *Comparative Psychology Monographs,* 1941, **17**(4).

Weitzman, B. A reply to Wolpe. *Psychological Review,* 1971, **78,** 352–353.

Wenger, M. A. Emotion as visceral action: An extension of Lange's theory. In M. L. Reymert (Ed.), *Feelings and emotions: The Mooseheart symposium.* New York: McGraw-Hill, 1950.

Wenger, M. A. Jones, F. N., and **Jones, M. H.** *Psysiological psychology.* New York: Holt, 1956.

Wenzel, B. M. Immunosympathectomy and behavior. In G. Steiner and E. Schönbaum (Eds.), *Immunosympathectomy.* Amsterdam: Elsevier, 1972.

Werbik, H. *Informationsgehalt und emotionale Wirkung von Musik.* Mainz: B. Schott's Söhne, 1971.

West, L. J., and **Farber, I. E.** The role of pain in emotional development. Unpublished report, University of Oklahoma Medical School, 1961.

White, R. W. Motivation reconsidered: The concept of competence. *Psychological Review,* 1959, **66,** 297–333.

Wilkins, W. Perceptual distortion to account for arousal. *Journal of Abnormal Psychology,* 1971, **78,** 252–257.

Wine, J. Test anxiety and direction of attention. *Psychological Bulletin,* 1971, **76,** 92–104.

Wolf, S., and **Wolff, H. G.** *Human gastric function.* New York: Oxford University Press, 1943.

Wolpe, J. *Psychotherapy by reciprocal inhibition.* Stanford: Stanford University Press, 1958.

Woodward, A. E. Jr., Bjork, R. A., and **Jongeward, R. H. Jr.** Recall and recognition as a function of primary rehearsal. *Journal of Verbal Learning and Verbal Behavior,* 1973, **12,** 608–617.

Wynne, L. C., and **Solomon, R. L.** Traumatic avoidance learning: Acquisition and extinction in dogs deprived of normal peripheral autonomic function. *Genetic Psychology Monographs,* 1955, **52.** 241–284.

Zander, A., and **Quinn, R.** The social environment and mental health. *Journal of Social Issues,* 1962, **18,** 48–66.

Zuckerman, M. Physiological measures of sexual arousal in the human. *Psychological Bulletin,* 1971, **75,** 297–329.

INDEX OF SUBJECTS

INDEX OF NAMES

DATE DUE

JUN 08 2002	
MAR 09 2009	
FEB 09 2010	

GAYLORD   PRINTED IN U.S.A.